William Cowper

A Revaluation

NEIL CURRY

Greenwich Exchange
London

Greenwich Exchange, London

First published in Great Britain in 2015
All rights reserved

William Cowper: A Revaluation
© Neil Curry, 2015

Printed and bound by imprintdigital.net
Typesetting and layout by Jude Keen Limited, London
Tel: 020 8355 4541
Cover design by December Publications
Tel: 028 90 286559

Greenwich Exchange Website: www.greenex.co.uk

Cataloguing in Publication Data is available
from the British Library

ISBN: 978-1-906075-86-6

Acknowledgements

For their assistance and encouragement I would like to offer my warmest thanks to Richard Andrews, Dr Ian Davidson, Nicola Durbridge, Dr Bill Hutchings, Professor Vincent Newey, Tony Seward, the Trustees and staff of the Cowper and Newton Museum in Olney, the staff of the John Rylands Library of the University of Manchester and the staff of the Ulverston Library.

Note on the Text

All quotations from Cowper's verse are from *The Poems of William Cowper*, edited by John D. Baird and Charles Ryskamp (Oxford University Press, 1980-5). Quotations from the letters are from *The Letters and Prose Writings of William Cowper*, edited by James King and Charles Ryskamp (Oxford University Press, 1979-86). In view of the number of editions there have been of selected letters by William Cowper, it seems more convenient to give the date immediately after each letter rather than by reference to the King/Ryskamp edition.

Contents

1

His Mother's Son

A life of joy and peace

Not only was William Cowper the most popular poet of his day, he is also recognised as having been one of the most brilliant letter-writers of the century. Quite clearly he loved getting letters too, and we can feel and share his excitement when, at the beginning of Book IV of his poem *The Task*, he describes hearing the sound of the post-boy's horn as he comes riding over the bridge into Olney, heading for the Swan Inn on the High Street:

> Hark! 'tis the twanging horn! o'er yonder bridge
> That with its wearisome but needful length
> Bestrides the wintry flood, in which the moon
> Sees her unwrinkled face reflected bright,
> He comes, the herald of a noisy world,
> With spatter'd boots, strapp'd waist, and frozen locks,
> News from all nations lumb'ring at his back.
> True to his charge the close-pack'd load behind,
> Yet careless what he brings, his one concern
> Is to conduct it to the destin'd inn,
> And having dropp'd th'expected bag, pass on.
>
> (1-11)

"Careless what he brings", the post-boy is soon whistling off on his way again, but as Cowper then speculates what he may have brought for the town, we cannot help being reminded of Auden's 'Night Mail'. The same enthusiasm and vitality are there:

> Houses in ashes, and the fall of stocks,
> Births, deaths, and marriages, epistles wet
> With tears, that trickled down the writer's cheeks.
>
> (16-18)

The detail, coupled with the conversational ease of the blank verse are Cowper at his best. And conversational ease was what he liked best in letters, as he explained to his cousin, Harriot, Lady Hesketh, "When I read your letters, I hear you talk, and I love talking letters dearly, especially from you" (24th April 1786).

But among the hundreds, quite possibly thousands of letters he received, one of the most memorable came from another cousin, Mrs Anne Bodham, when in February 1790 she sent him a picture of his mother. Very little is known about Cowper's mother. Née Ann Donne and born in 1703, she came from a well-respected Norfolk family which claimed descent from Henry III by four different lines, including those of Mary Boleyn, the sister of Anne, and of the noble families of Carey, Howard and Mowbray. The family also claimed descent from John Donne, but while Donne had two sons he had no grandsons, and there cannot have been any lineal connection. Nevertheless Cowper chose to believe, understandably, that there was (letter to Mrs Bodham, 27th February 1790).

Ann Donne was already 25 when she married the Rev. John Cowper, nine years her senior, and moved into the rectory at Berkhamsted in Hertfordshire. She was, to judge from a miniature of her, painted when she was 20, a slight, fragile-looking young woman. In the nine years of her marriage, however, she was to endure six pregnancies, and to suffer a mortality rate high even for the eighteenth century. Her first child, a son, died when only five weeks old. Nine months later, twins – a boy and a girl – were dead within two days. Then William was born on 15th November 1731. A daughter born in 1733 survived to the age of two, but during that time another boy had died after just two weeks. Finally, William's brother, John, was born, but, sadly, Ann herself died within a week of his birth on 13th November 1737.

Cowper was clearly moved when he received the picture of his mother fifty-three years after her death, but just how *much* he was really moved and how genuine some of his recollections of her are, must, I think, be open to question. His letter of thanks to Mrs Bodham (27th February 1790) opens by punning on her name in such a self-consciously literary manner:

> My Dearest Rose,
> Whom I thought wither'd and fallen from the stalk, but who
> I find are still alive.

And considering that he had had no contact with this side of his family for some 27 years, the effusiveness which followed must have come as a surprise even to her:

> I loved you dearly when you were a child and love
> you not a jot the less for having ceased to be so.
> Every creature that bears any affinity to my own
> mother is dear to me, and you, the daughter of her
> brother, are but one remove distant from her; I love
> you therefore and love you much, both for her sake
> and your own. (27th February 1790)

He even goes on to claim:

> There is in me, I believe, more of the Donne than of
> the Cowper, and though I love all of both names and
> have a thousand reasons to love those of my own name,
> yet I feel the bond of nature draw me vehemently to
> your side.

The sincerity of this assertion is certainly questionable. It would seem that family love and loyalty depended on which side he was writing to, as in 1786, when corresponding with his cousin Harriot, it is quite a different story:

> … when you say you are a *Cowper* (and the better it is
> for the Cowpers that such you are, and I give them joy
> of you, with all my heart) you must not forget that I
> boast myself a Cowper too, and have my humours,
> and fancies, and purposes, and determinations, as well
> as any of my name, and hold them as fast as they can.
> (24th April 1786)

All in all, his letter to Mrs Bodham is disturbingly self-centred and concludes by singing his own praises. He claims to be able to trace in his "natural temper" something both of his mother and (though how this could possibly be, he does not say) of "my late uncle your father":

> Somewhat of his irritability, and a little, I would
> hope, both of his and her – I know not what to
> call it without seeming to praise myself which
> is not my intention, but speaking to *you* I will
> e'en speak out and say – Good nature.

"To *you*", he says, as though she were a close confidante of long standing, which she was certainly not. Biographers have chosen to ignore or to play down these aspects of the letter and have concentrated instead on his mention that he has hung the picture where it will be the last thing he sees every night and the first every morning. Charmingly sentimental though that sounds, it is a 'tradition' which could not have been in existence any longer than 48 hours.

One immediate and positive consequence of the picture's arrival is recorded in a brusque and businesslike manner at the end of a letter to his cousin, Lady Hesketh, dated 8th March 1790. "A new poem is born on the receipt of my mother's picture: thou shalt have it."

The new poem, which seems to have taken little more than a week to write, is one of his finest pieces, 'On the Receipt of my Mother's Picture out of Norfolk'. It is a very moving poem. Hazlitt, who was critical of certain features of Cowper's work, found it to be of "extraordinary pathos", and this is particularly true of the central section of the poem where Cowper recalls his mother's many kindnesses:

> Where once we dwelt, our name is heard no more;
> Children not thine have trod my nurs'ry floor;
> And where the gard'ner Robin, day by day,
> Drew me to school along the public way,
> Delighted with my bauble coach, and wrapp'd
> In scarlet mantle warm and velvet cap,
> 'Tis now become a hist'ry little known
> That once we call'd the Past'ral house our own.
> Short-lived possession! But the record fair,
> That Mem'ry keeps of all thy kindness there
> Still outlives many a storm that has effaced
> A thousand other themes less deeply traced.
> Thy nightly visits to my chamber made,
> That thou might'st know me safe and warmly lay'd;
> Thy morning bounties e'er I left my home,
> The biscuit, or confectionary plum;
> The fragrant waters on my cheeks bestow'd
> By thy own hand, 'till fresh they shone and glow'd;
>
> (46-63)

It is a bright and vivid picture he paints; there is so much going on in it, so much movement and the detail is so precise, the naming of the gardener adding to the feeling of authenticity. Cowper had written many thousands of lines of verse by this time and was a master of his craft, managing to avoid the sentimental while offering a richly sensuous texture: there are warmth and colour in the portrayal of the boy "wrapp'd / In scarlet mantle warm"; there is the taste of the "confectionary plum"; the scent of the "fragrant waters" and the touch of his mother's hand on his cheeks. All this serves to make palpable her "constant flow of love".

Not many of us, I think, can remember being six years old, and it is surprising – one might say doubtful – that Cowper could recall such details after so many years, but the lines have mostly been accepted at face value and have been linked with a letter he wrote to his long-time friend Joseph Hill in 1784 (6th November) in which he says of his mother, "I can truly say, that not a week passes, (perhaps with equal veracity say a day) in which I do not think of her" (6th November 1784). But when this letter is read in its entirety, it takes on a very different flavour. Hill had written to tell him of the death of his own mother at the age of eighty-seven, and Cowper's reply begins, "To condole with you on the death of a Mother aged 87 would be absurd." His reason for thinking so is that Hill ought rather to be congratulated "on the almost singular felicity of having enjoyed the company of so amiable, and so dear a relation so long". It is hard to imagine a more insensitive response to Hill's loss. *Absurd*? What is absurd is Cowper's claim to have thought of his dead mother every day for the past fifty-three years. *Veracity*? It is an exaggeration beyond all reason. The gist of Cowper's letter is: *You think your situation is sad, well what about mine?* He could not put it more bluntly:

> You may remember with pleasure, while you live, a blessing
> vouchsafed to you for so long; and I while I live, must regret
> a comfort of which I was deprived so early.

There is no further reference to Hill's situation. He goes on to tell him that in Olney they have lost "a lively and sensible neighbour in Lady Austen", but it doesn't matter to him, "while I can have the companion (Mrs Unwin) I have had these twenty years". He then concludes with the news that he has a new book of poems coming out soon, and a few days later he is thanking Hill for "a very good barrel of oysters" (4th December 1784). Again, it is all very self-centred.

Accepting Cowper's poem as literal truth has led many analysts, both professional and amateur, to speculate about its author's mental and emotional state, and with conflicting results. According to one commentator,

"His mother's death left an emotional toll on William that overshadowed the remaining years of his life."[1] Another felt: " … that the event could evoke only a sentimental response many years later will indicate how superficial the relationship between mother and son was."[2] James King, Cowper's most authoritative biographer, was prepared to go so far as to assert that "Cowper's life was irrevocably altered by his mother's death when he was six," and that "he clung relentlessly to his mother."[3] Yet it is hard to see how this latter statement can hold good in view of an essay Cowper published in *The Connoisseur* in March 1756 when he was 24. It begins:

> You have already given us several instances of those ambiguous creatures among the men, who are both male and female: permit me to add to them an account of those lady-like gentlemen, whom we may distinguish by the title of *their mother's own sons.*

He says he knows one "no more weaned from his mother, than if he had not yet quitted the nursery". And he continues:

> The delicate BILLY SUCKLING is the contempt of the men, the jest of the women, and the darling of his mamma … he is absolutely excluded from every order in society; for whatever his deserts may be, no assembly of antiquated virgins can ever acknowledge him for a sister, nature having as deplorably disqualified him for that rank in the community, as he has disqualified himself for every other.[4]

It would be interesting to speculate just how different the various biographies of Cowper might have been if this poem on his mother's picture had never been written. Indeed it would not have been written but for a quite unexpected and fortuitous visit by Johnny Johnson, Mrs Bodham's young nephew from Norfolk. Up to that time, as has already been noted, Cowper had had no contact with that side of his family for 27 years. There are very few references to his mother anywhere in his writing, and even in his memoir, written in 1765, she merits only the most perfunctory of passing references: "At six years old I was taken from the nursery and from the care of a most indulgent mother." There is no mention whatsoever of her death. In the opening lines of Book VI of *The Task*, mothers receive only the briefest afterthought, following almost twenty lines devoted to his regret that fathers are not fully appreciated, and when writing to his aunt, Mrs Madan (15th October 1767), he told her:

> It pleased the Lord … to make my Childhood and Youth in
> their most affecting Colours pass in review before me, and
> these were followed by such a tender Recollection of my dear
> Father, and all his Kindness to me, the Amiableness and
> Sweetness of his Temper and Character, that I went out into
> the Orchard and burst forth into Praise and Thanksgiving
> to God for having made me the Son of a Parent whose
> Remembrance was so sweet to me.

And yet, when writing to Samuel Rose (19th October 1787) he said, "When my Father died I was young, too young to have reflected much." And he was not six, but twenty-five when his father died.

Nothing is as straightforward as it seems, and using Cowper's poems as a quarry from which to excavate the building blocks of his life may, as this chapter is suggesting, lead a biographer into unsafe areas. Likewise it tends to undervalue the poems as poems. To leave aside speculation about the authenticity of Cowper's childhood memories in this poem allows us to recognise its importance as a poem, a poem about childhood and about memory.

It is not a ground-breaking work, but nothing Cowper wrote could ever be classed as that. It is part of the eighteenth-century genre of elegiac meditation. As far back as 1725 James Thomson, author of *The Seasons*, had written some rather high-flown 'Memorial Verses upon the Death of his Mother', but it is a genre which Cowper can be seen to have picked up and carried forward, and it exemplifies Wordsworth's well-known definition of poetry, a definition which nevertheless is worth restating:

> Poetry is the spontaneous overflow of powerful feelings; it
> takes its origin from emotion recollected in tranquillity: the
> emotion is contemplated till by a species of reaction the
> tranquillity gradually disappears, and an emotion, kindred to
> that which was before the subject of contemplation, is
> gradually produced.

Cowper's feelings when he first beheld the picture were certainly powerful, as he told Mrs Bodham:

> I received it the night before last, and viewed it with a
> trepidation of nerves and spirits somewhat akin to what I
> should have felt, had the dear Original presented herself to
> my embraces. (27th February 1790)

But the poem meditates on these emotions and ends in a celebration of reflection and contemplation.

In the opening section Cowper addresses the picture directly, wishing that it could speak to him. "O that those lips had language!" he says. His mother's smile is exactly as he remembers it, and here, even in these opening lines, he is already writing about himself and his own suffering, and thinking back to the solace she once gave him. He imagines her saying: "Grieve not, my child, chase all thy fears away!" The art which has brought this smile and these thoughts to him, and this momentary comfort, has, he says, defeated time:

> The meek intelligence of those dear eyes
> (Blest be the Art that can immortalize,
> The Art that baffles Time's tyrannic claim
> To quench it) here shines on me still the same.
>
> (7-10)

That art has the ability to do this is of course not a new idea and Cowper is clearly aware that this is not reality, that it is a dream world he is taken to, but a dream world which will allow him to return to his childhood and to his mother.

In the following lines he feels that the picture is bidding him to compose "an artless song" in her honour, and he declares that his Fancy "shall weave a charm" which he can dream is really her:

> And, while that face renews my filial grief,
> Fancy shall weave a charm for my relief,
> Shall steep me in Elysian reverie,
> A momentary dream, that Thou art She.
>
> (17-20)

This poem is by no means an "artless song" however, as is evident from the relaxed and conversational ease of its couplets – so very far removed from those of Alexander Pope – as well as the elegant yet disciplined syntax.

Addressing his mother directly now, and not the picture, he asks her if she knew of the tears he had shed at her death, and believes that her smile answers *Yes*. Moving into narrative mode allows him to recall and describe the day of her funeral. To assuage his grief, her servants told him that she would soon be coming back, but eventually he learned the truth. At this point one would expect an Evangelical to find some consolation and sign of salvation, but Cowper, even as a child, is forced to face up to tragedy and disappointment. He accepts that not even the most skilful art can change the bitterness of actuality:

> What ardently I wish'd, I long believed,
> And, disappointed still, was still deceived.
> By expectation ev'ry day beguiled,
> Dupe of to-morrow even from a child,
> Thus many a sad to-morrow came and went,
> Till all my stock of infant sorrow spent,
> I learn'd at last submission to my lot,
> But, though I less deplor'd thee, ne'er forgot.
>
> (38-45)

But in lines which Professor Newey has suggested contain more realism than reality[5] his Fancy paints that detailed and vivid sequence of memories of his mother's love and care for him: the "nightly visits" and the "confectionary plum". Recalling such events

> Adds joy to duty, makes me glad to pay
> Such honour to thee as my numbers may;
> Perhaps a frail memorial, but sincere,
> Not scorn'd in heav'n, though little noticed here.
>
> (70-3)

And then he asks: if it were in his power, would he wish Time to be reversed so that he could relive those days? But he decides that he would not wish his mother to leave heaven and be in "bonds" again.

What follows is a brilliant extended simile comparing her journey to heaven with that of a "gallant bark" safely weathering the storms of life and coming at last to anchor in a paradise of spice islands:

> Thou, as a gallant bark from Albion's coast
> (The storms all weather'd and the Ocean cross'd)
> Shoots into port at some well-haven'd isle,
> Where spices breathe, and brighter seasons smile,
> There sits quiescent on the floods, that show
> Her beauteous form reflected clear below,
> While airs impregnated with incense, play
> Around her, fanning light her streamers gay –
> So Thou, with sails how swift! hast reach'd the shore,
> 'Where tempests never beat nor billows roar.
>
> (88-97)

The last line, as Cowper's own note tells us, is a direct quotation from Samuel Garth's poem 'The Dispensary'. It is a deliberately literary effect, as was the echo of Gray's 'Elegy' with the words "frail memorial". This is no "artless song".

Turning to his own life, there is no thought of paradise. The image is that of a storm-tossed vessel, its sails all torn, lost and far from its intended course:

> Me howling blasts drive devious, tempest-toss'd,
> Sails ript, seams opening wide, and compass lost,
> And day by day some current's thwarting force
> Sets me more distant from a prosp'rous course.
>
> (102-5)

It is an image which Cowper had frequently used, and would use again in his final poem 'The Castaway', to express his own despair and the hopelessness of his situation. In a poem entitled 'To Mr Newton on his Return from Ramsgate', and written a decade before, he had concluded:

> Your sea of troubles you have pass'd
> And found the peacefull shore;
> I tempest-toss'd and wrecked at last,
> Come home to port no more.
>
> (13-16)

The conclusion of the poem on his mother's picture returns to the theme of time. It cannot be overcome; he has to accept that. But he has achieved what he had hoped for: contemplation has allowed him to relive those joys, and he ends by saying that Fancy will allow him to do so again as often as he wishes:

> Time has but half succeeded in his theft,
> Thyself removed, thy pow'r to soothe me left.
>
> (120-1)

He also admits, however, that all such joys are an illusion and that the "wings of fancy" offer only a brief escape from the harshness of reality. He admits, as Keats was to do in his 'Ode to a Nightingale' that "fancy cannot cheat so well / As she is fam'd to do, deceiving elf."

A contemplative poem about contemplation; about memory and the contemplation of memory; a poem about the joys of childhood, and the restorative powers of reflection – one cannot avoid thinking of Wordsworth, but that outdated term 'pre-Romantic' has no place here. Wordsworth and Coleridge both wrote of their admiration for Cowper and of their indebtedness to him; and this, I would contend, is a poem which bears a significance quite equal to that of 'Tintern Abbey' and deserves to be equally well known.

2

School Days

He will my shield and portion be

The *OED* has, astonishingly, 38 citations from Cowper's poem 'On the Receipt of my Mother's Picture out of Norfolk'. One is for 'bauble-coach'. It is not absolutely clear what a bauble-coach was, as this is the only recorded use of the term, but it sounds cute and seems to have been fun. And what a delightful image it gives us: Cowper as a little boy, with his velvet cap on his head and snugly wrapped in his scarlet mantle, being drawn along to school by Robin, the family gardener. It would have been a dame school he was on his way to, and cannot have been very far from the rectory, as Berkhamsted, though quite prosperous, was no more than a small market town of some 1,500 people at that time. Centuries earlier, during the reign of the Plantagenets, it had been of far greater importance, and the ruins of the once splendid Norman castle, where Chaucer had been the constable, and where Edward the Black Prince spent his honeymoon, were still there at the end of the High Street.

As with so many things, Cowper's attitude to Berkhamsted is, to say the least, ambiguous. Writing to William Rose, a young lawyer who would one day go on to defend William Blake in Chichester against the charge of sedition, he says: "There was neither Tree, nor Gate, nor stile, in all that country, to which I did not feel a relation, and the House itself I preferred to a palace" (19th October 1787). Yet 30 years earlier, when one would have thought the memory was a good deal fresher in his mind, he wrote to his friend John Duncombe:

> I believe no man ever quitted his Native place with less
> Regret than myself, and were it not for the sake of a Friend
> or two that I have left behind me ... I should never wish to
> see either the place or anything that belongs to it again. (16th
> June 1757)

There was a school for older boys in the town, but its buildings were in a deplorable state and the master and the usher were at loggerheads with each other in the courts; so, when the time came, William went to nearby Aldbury, to a school run by his father's friend the Rev. William Davies. He stayed there only briefly, and then moved on to a school in Markyate Street, a small town on the Hertfordshire border.

It seems harsh to have sent a boy of that age away to school, especially when he had just lost his mother. It is not that his father could not cope with him; the servants would, as was customary, have continued to care for him, as they did for his baby brother John. Nor was his father unfeeling. Cowper, as we have seen, recalled "all his Kindness to me, the Amiableness and Sweetness of his Temper and Character" (15th October 1767). Boarding school was then the accepted rite of passage for young boys of that age and class.

The school at Markyate Street was well-organised, and its headmaster, the Rev. William Pittman, had a reputation as a fine classical scholar, but he does not seem to have been aware of all that was going on under his roof. In his memoir, which he began in 1765 while living with the Unwins in Huntingdon, Cowper recorded how unhappy he had been there and how badly he was bullied:

> Here I had hardships of various kinds to conflict with, which I felt more sensibly in proportion to the tenderness with which I had been treated at home. But my chief affliction consisted in my being singled out from all the children in the school by a lad about fifteen years of age as a proper subject upon whom he might let loose the cruelty of his temper. I choose to conceal a particular recital of the many acts of barbarity with which he made it his business continually to persecute me. It will be sufficient to say that he had, by his savage treatment of me imprinted such a dread of his very figure upon my mind that I well remember being afraid to lift my eyes upon him higher than his knees; and that I knew him by his shoe buckles better than by any other part of his dress.[1]

That final image is so intensely visual – almost cinematic – that we may be convinced for a moment that we have actually seen it for ourselves. Mercifully, the bully was found out and expelled, and William taken away from the school.

Diagnosed as having some problem with his eyes, he was then sent to the home of an oculist, a Mrs Disney. In a letter to William Hayley (6th April

1792) he says she was "a female oculist of great renown at that time, in whose house I abode two years, but to no good purpose". In his memoir, however, he had written, "I continued a year in this family, where Christianity was neither known nor practised."[2] But this, we can be quite certain, is a typically Evangelical exaggeration. If it had been true, his father would never have sent him to such an establishment, no matter what the oculist's renown.

Whether he stayed there for one year or two, it must have been a lonely time for an eight-year-old and sensitive little boy, and it seems to have done him little good, as in his letters he was to complain of eye trouble throughout his life. He did once claim that the smallpox he contracted when he was thirteen had actually improved the situation, but medical opinion suggests that this is highly unlikely.

Then, when he was ten, he was, as he put it, "despatched to Westminster",[3] the school his father and grandfather had attended and where three of his cousins were already established as pupils when he himself arrived there in April 1742.

At this point a brief digression seems necessary. In every biography of Cowper there has been discussion and speculation about his possible hermaphroditism, or some other sexual deformity. But surely, if there were any truth in these suggestions, his father, amiable as we know him to have been, would *never* have sent him to an English boarding school, especially one where, in all probability, he had to share a bed during his early years. He would simply never have survived there, and he not only did survive, he was evidently very happy, becoming Head of House, a position never achieved, one can feel sure, in any age by a hermaphrodite.

Westminster School could claim that its origins went back as far as the latter half of the twelfth century, when a group of Benedictine monks founded a small charity school, but it was in 1560 that it was granted its Royal Charter by Elizabeth I. In Cowper's day the school was still located in the ancient monastic buildings, but the scholars' dormitory was relatively new having been designed by a former Westminster pupil, Sir Christopher Wren. The syllabus – if one can call it that – was still, as it would be for many years to come, the study of Latin and Greek, which meant translating and learning by heart large tracts of Homer and Virgil, Horace and Ovid, Aesop and Terence. The entire school of 350 boys was taught in the Great Hall, which was divided only by a curtain with the Upper Master on one side and the Under Master on the other. In addition there were six ushers which meant a ratio of one teacher to 50 pupils. It was, nevertheless, held to be on a par with Eton, though it was regarded as a Whig stronghold while Eton was determinedly Tory.

It was a school which had once been noted for its floggings. William B. Ober, in his remarkable book *Boswell's Clap*, quotes from Thomas Shadwell's play *The Virtuoso*, where a character by the name of Snarl begs for flagellation from his mistress, Mrs Figgup, saying, "I was so us'd to't at Westminster School that I could never leave it off since … Do not spare thy pains. I love castigation dearly."[4]

Cowper's headmaster, Dr John Nicholls, ran a very different regime. As one pupil observed, "He seemed determined so to exercise his authority, that our best motives for obeying him should spring from the affection, that we entertained for him."[5] He seems to have been an educationalist well ahead of his time. In *The Annals of Westminster* (1898) John Sargeaunt observed that there was no period in the history of the school "when less knowledge was imparted and few when more was acquired."[6] An ideal situation, one might say. The school had never before seen such a large assembly of peers, or so many men who would go on to win fame.[7] It was also celebrated for the number of poets it had nurtured: Jonson, Herbert, Cowley, Dryden and Prior. In his poem 'Table-Talk' Cowper recorded:

> At Westminster, where little poets strive
> To set a distich upon six and five,
> Where discipline helps op'ning buds of sense,
> And makes his pupils proud with silver-pence,
> I was a poet too.
>   (506-10)

But in a letter to William Unwin he also claimed: "When I was a Boy, I excell'd at cricket and Football" (28th May 1781). And in those days football was a very tough game with few rules and no yellow cards.

There was fun as well as games at Westminster. An elegant lady, so it is recorded,[8] once alighted from a sedan chair and asked to be shown around the school. As he escorted her about, Dr Nicholls was shocked by the laughter and rudeness of his pupils until he discovered that beneath the wig and the voluminous petticoats this elegant "lady" was one of his pupils.

One of the masters, Vincent Bourne, had a marked influence on Cowper. Writing to William Unwin he said:

> I love the Memory of Vinny Bourne … I love him too with
> a love of Partiality, because he was Usher of the fifth form at
> Westminster, when I passed through it. He was so good-
> natured, and so indolent, that I lost more than I got by him;

for he made me as idle as himself. He was such a sloven, as if he had trusted to his Genius as a cloak for everything that could disgust you in his person; and indeed in his writings he has almost made amends for all. (23rd May 1781)

Bourne himself seems to have had a lot to put up with. One of his pupils, the young Lord Richmond, "set fire to his greasy locks and then boxed his ears to put it out again" (23rd May 1781).

An accomplished classical scholar, Bourne also wrote Latin poems of his own, several of which Cowper translated, but translated in the eighteenth-century fashion of paraphrase rather than the crabbed literalness of metaphrase, frequently turning the staid elegiacs of the originals into the most charming of lyrics, as in these opening stanzas of one of Bourne's animal fables, 'The Snail':

> To grass, or leaf, or fruit, or wall
> The snail sticks close, nor fears to fall,
> As if he grew there, house and all,
> > Together.

> Within that house secure he hides
> When danger imminent betides
> Of storms, or other harm besides
> > Of weather.

> Give but his horns the slightest touch,
> His self-collecting pow'r is such,
> He shrinks into his house with much
> > Displeasure.

> Where'er he dwells, he dwells alone,
> Except himself has chattels none,
> Well satisfied to be his own
> > Whole treasure.

Cowper could not speak highly enough of Bourne. "I think him a better Latin poet than Tibullus, Propertius, Ausonius, or any of the writers in his way, except Ovid, and not at all inferior to him" (23rd May 1781). This comparison, especially with Ovid, is extravagant enough to be rather absurd, but it does show just how much he admired his eccentric and charismatic teacher.

Cowper was a success both socially and academically at Westminster. No timid introvert, he was Head of House, good at games and ranked third in the academic listings when he left. He made many lasting friendships there too, and so could look back on his schooldays with an unmixed delight. Indeed he assumed that everyone did:

> We love the play-place of our early days.
> The scene is touching, and the heart is stone
> That feels not at that sight, and feels at none.
> The wall on which we tried our graving skill,
> The very name we carved subsisting still,
> The bench on which we sat while deep-employ'd
> Though mangled, hack'd and hew'd, not yet destroy'd.
> The little ones unbutton'd, glowing hot,
> Playing our games, and on the very spot,
> As happy as we once, to kneel and draw
> The chalky ring, and knuckle down at taw,
> To pitch the ball into the grounded hat,
> Or drive it devious with a dex'trous pat,
> The pleasing spectacle at once excites
> Such recollection of our own delights,
> That viewing it, we seem almost t'obtain
> Our innocent sweet simple years again.
> This fond attachment to the well-known place
> Whence first we started into life's long race,
> Maintains its hold with such unfailing sway,
> We feel it ev'n in age, and at our latest day.
> ('Tirocinium', 297-317)

In John Sargeaunt's *Annals of Westminster School* (1898) there is an engraving of 'School' showing boys' names cut in large letters into the walls above the benches where they sat (p. 56), and another of boys playing marbles in the cloister; one boy is kneeling down next to the chalk ring while another is about to shoot the large marble at the smaller ones inside it (p. 215).

The poem in which these vivid recollections occur is 'Tirocinium' and they come as something of a surprise, as the poem as a whole is an attack on public schools and has as a subscript a 'Poem Recommending Private Tuition in Preference to an Education at School'.

The word *Tirocinium* was adopted into English in the seventeenth century and means 'a soldier's first service', hence 'a raw recruit' or being a pupil. Cowper's poem was published in November 1784, but in a letter to William Unwin dated 10th October of that year he said that he had "lately resumed" a poem on education which he had begun two years before. It was then 200 lines long, he told him, but less than a fortnight later it had been extended to 700, and within another week it had reached its final total of 922 lines, which means that he was writing on average some fifteen couplets a day.

As far back as 1776, so we learn from a letter written to Joseph Hill (6th July 1776), Cowper had been thinking of supplementing his income by taking three or four boys into his house to teach them Latin and Greek on "the Westminster Model of Instruction" and charging them 100 guineas each per term, but it remained no more than an idea, which is perhaps as well, as it is hard to know where they could have been lodged in Orchard Side at Olney, and it is doubtful whether Cowper would have proved to be a stimulating or effective teacher.

Then in September 1780, when William Unwin was wondering how best to educate his own two sons, Cowper wrote him three long letters warning of the evils of public schools and advising him to educate them himself at home. It is Cowper the Evangelical who is behind this view, as we can tell from his overriding concern that "In a Public School, or indeed in any school, his Morals are sure to be but little attended to, and his Religion not at all" (17th September 1780). Yet in his memoir he had said that Dr Nicholls had taken great pains to prepare his pupils for confirmation.[9]

The first 200 lines, the lines which he told Unwin he had begun in 1782, have little to commend them. Taking as their starting point the verses in Genesis which tell us that God gave man dominion over all other creatures, they follow a familiar path, asserting that what makes us different from such creatures is our soul, that "intellectual kingdom" (l. 12), that storehouse of memory and wisdom, reason and imagination. Being the crown of creation, man will, if he looks at creation properly, discover in it "Proofs of the wisdom of the all-seeing mind" (l. 94) and so realise that if he were simply to live and die his existence would be as worthless as that of beasts. Clearly there must be more to it; there must be "a world to come" (l. 102) It is therefore our duty – though exactly why is not explained – to lead

the minds of youth
Betimes into the mould of heav'nly truth,
That taught of God they may indeed be wise,
Nor ignorantly wand'ring miss the skies.
(105-8)

Parents, he says, begin the process splendidly with horn books with which they teach their children the Lord's Prayer, then introducing them to such godly books as *Pilgrim's Progress*, but as the child grows up and goes to school all this is forgotten.

It is a dull, long-winded, and all-too-familiar preamble with nothing new to catch our attention, but at line 201 the tone changes and we suddenly find ourselves being addressed by a voice which is assertive and bold, indeed one might say strident. The vocabulary is now quite unlike anything that has gone before:

> Would you your son should be a sot or dunce,
> Lascivious, headstrong, or all these at once,
> That in good time the stripling's finish'd taste
> For loose expence and fashionable waste,
> Should prove your ruin, and his own at last,
> Train him in public with a mob of boys,
> Childish in mischief only and in noise.
>
> (201-7)

The poem is didactic, but has shrugged off the decorum with which such ideas and attitudes might have been expressed earlier in the century. There is indeed a coarse actuality in the lines which follow when he gives examples of the out-of-school activities a boy is likely to follow:

> … pedantry is all that schools impart,
> But taverns teach the knowledge of the heart,
> There waiter Dick with Bacchanalian lays
> Shall win his heart and have his drunken praise,
> His counsellor and bosom-friend shall prove,
> And some street-pacing harlot his first love.
>
> (212-17)

They look up to their Head of House and follow his example:

> His wild excursions, window-breaking feats,
> Robb'ry of gardens, quarrels in the streets
>
> (227-8)

One of the fascinations of this poem is that although more than two centuries have passed since Cowper wrote it, many of his arguments are still being voiced today: the public schools may have produced great men in the past, but it's all very different now. Now they just "set the midnight riot in a blaze" (l. 287). Nevertheless, fathers still want their sons to go to the schools where they themselves got up to no good.

And public schools are all very well for the sons of the rich:

> The great indeed, by titles, riches, birth,
> Excused th'incumbrance of more solid worth,
> Are best disposed of, where with most success
> They may acquire that confident address,
> Those habits of profuse and lew'd expence,
> That scorn of all delights but those of sense,
> Which though in plain plebeians we condemn,
> With so much reason we expect from them.
>
> (347-54)

Lower-class parents hope that such schooling will help their sons to rise in the world, but if they do, Cowper says, it will not be because of the learning they acquire, but because of the contacts they make, the Old Boy network:

> A friend, whate'er he studies or neglects,
> Shall give him consequence, heal all defects,
> His intercourse with peers, and sons of peers –
> There dawns the splendour of his future years.
>
> (391-4)

And it could not be put more pithily when he states that "A parson knows enough who knows a duke" (l. 403).

Abuses in the Church always roused Cowper's ire, and here his couplets have an Augustan balance and bite to them which Pope himself would not have been displeased with:

> Behold your Bishop! well he plays his part,
> Christian in name, and Infidel in heart,
> Ghostly in office, earthly in his plan,
> A slave at court, elsewhere a lady's man,
> Dumb as a senator, and as a priest
> A piece of mere church-furniture at best;
> To live estranged from God his total scope,
> And his end sure, without one glimpse of hope.
>
> (420-7)

The contempt he expresses in that "piece of mere church-furniture" is particularly fine.

Attacks on schoolteachers are not uncommon. Here they are blamed for taking too much credit when their pupils do well, but insisting that when a boy fails "the fault was all his own" (l. 536). There has always been some truth in this, but the suggestion that "motives of mere lucre" (l. 518) are what sway most teachers would hardly be a valid argument today.

In one of his earlier letters to William Unwin, Cowper had painted a moving picture of a boy coming home for his holidays but, having been away so long, not knowing how to behave there:

> A Gentleman, or a Lady, are consequently such Novelties to him that he is perfectly at a Loss to know what sort of Behaviour he should preserve before them. He Plays with his Buttons or the Strings of his Hat; he blows his Nose, and hangs down his Head, is conscious of his own Deficiency to a Degree that makes him quite unhappy, and Tremble lest any one should speak to him, because That would quite overwhelm him. (5th October 1780)

It is a brilliant little vignette, but what is remarkable is that Cowper repeats it in essence so many years later:

> Arrived, he feels an unexpected change,
> He blushes, hangs his head, is shy and strange,
> No longer takes, as once, with fearless ease
> His fav'rite stance between his father's knees,
> But seeks the corner of some of some distant seat,
> And eyes the door, and watches a retreat.
> (567-72)

In both instances he has entered keenly into the awkwardness of the child's situation, and we cannot help wondering if this is how he himself felt when returning to a home where there was now the unfamiliar figure of a stepmother, and a stepmother whom his cousin Harriot once described as being "disagreeable enough in all conscience".[10] If so, it is doubly sad he should feel he needs to warn fathers that

thus estranged thou can'st obtain
By no kind arts his confidence again.
(585-6)

Fathers who cannot, for one reason or another, undertake their children's education at home are advised to employ a tutor, and as we read the advice Cowper gives them we can deduce how badly some domestic tutors must have been treated: obliged to eat alone or, if allowed to join the family, made the butt of sarcasm and jokes which their position obliged them to suffer in silence. As Cowper puts it,

Despised by thee, what more can he expect
From youthful folly than the same neglect?
(702-3)

At this point, and with a little over a hundred lines to go, the poem veers off in a different direction, but one which was a favourite of Cowper's: an attack on the abuse of power and the evils of city life. It was a long time since he had been living in a city, however, and the examples he gives are too generalised to carry any real weight. It seems as though he is perhaps not sure how to bring the poem to a close. He returns briefly to his theme, but with a piece of dubious reasoning: that fathers who care for their sons may in turn be cared for by them in their old age. One would not have thought that such blatant self-interest was something to be commended.

Finally, in answer to his own question whether he would like to have all public schools pulled down, he admits that that would be going too far, but concludes with something of an anti-climax:

I wish them, I confess,
Or better managed, or encouraged less.
(921-2)

Among the closing lines, it is interesting to see him turn again to an image he used so often, that of a shipwreck:

Thou would'st not, deaf to Nature's tend'rest plea,
Turn him adrift upon a rolling sea,
Nor say, *Go thither*, conscious that there lay
A brood of asps, or quicksands in his way,
Then only govern'd by the self-same rule
Of nat'ral piety; send him not to school.

(867-72)

It is hard to say what it was that raised such a passion in Cowper at this point in his life, for passion it was. Auden may have been right when he insisted that poetry made nothing happen, but Cowper clearly hoped that something would come of his strictures. In a letter to Newton shortly after the publication of 'Tirocinium' he wrote:

> … if it have the effect I wish it to have, it will prove much
> their enemy; for it gives no quarter to modern pedagogues,
> but finding them all alike guilty of supineness and neglect in
> the affair of Morals, condemns them, both School Masters
> and Heads of Colleges, without distinction.

This is an extravagant and quite irrational claim of course. The suggestion has been made that "the immediate stimulus" for the poem was a visit to Olney made in 1784 by the Rev. Henry Venn, who is said to have told Cowper that a surgeon had been appointed to Westminster School to attend to the boys who had contracted venereal disease.[11] This would most certainly have come as a great shock to Cowper, but there is no hint of any such thing anywhere in the poem. This is perhaps not surprising. How, at that time, could such a topic possibly be broached? But one very curious omission, in view of the famously vivid account in his own memoir, is that among all the ills and evils of which he accuses the public schools, there is no mention whatsoever of bullying.

3

Living and Loving in London

The Lord has promis'd good to me

When he left Westminster School in May 1749, Cowper did not, as the majority of his contemporaries did, go up to university. His life would have been very different had he done so. Instead he went home to Berkhamsted and stayed there for some nine months. The reason is by no means clear. Family life cannot have been totally happy: his stepmother, as we have already seen, was described by his cousin Harriot as "disagreeable enough in all conscience".[1] And there was really nothing for him to do there. It was not as though he needed to think about his future. That had already been decided. He came from a family of lawyers: his grandfather, Spencer Cowper, had been a judge, and his great-uncle, William, the first Earl Cowper, had twice been Lord Chancellor of England. It was settled. He had been admitted to the Society of the Middle Temple in 1748 while he was still at school. But it had been settled *for* him, and here we have an early instance of his reluctance or inability to take control of his own life. As he put it in his memoir, he was "sent to acquire the practice of the law with an attorney".[2] The attorney was a Mr Chapman who had offices in Greville Street, Holborn, where he stayed for three years before taking up chambers in the Middle Temple in 1753.

He went there, as he explained in an autobiographical letter to Mrs King, the wife of a fellow student at Westminster, to please his father:

> I was bred to the Law; a Profession to which I was never
> much inclined, and in which I engaged rather because I was
> desirous to gratify a most indulgent Father, than because
> I had any hopes of success in it myself. (3rd March 1788)

But Cowper, however unworldly, was not blind to the material benefits that might come from it. While still resident in the Temple, he told his friend John Duncombe:

> I am not fond of the law, but I am very fond of the Money
> that it produces, and have much too great a Value for my
> own Interest to be Remiss in my Application to it. (21st
> November 1758)

But looking back three decades later, he viewed the situation quite differently. Writing to Samuel Rose, a young admirer, he said:

> Had I employed my time as wisely as you, in a situation very
> similar to yours, I had never been a poet perhaps, but I might
> by this time have acquired a character of more importance in
> society, and a situation in which my friends would have been
> better pleased to see me. (23rd July 1789)

It is true that he had not exerted himself and was often fined for failing to meet the requirements and obligations of his situation, but he accomplished enough to be called to the bar in 1754, and in April 1757 he moved to the more fashionable Inner Temple, paying £250 for elegant chambers in Pump Court. From his window there he could look out onto the lime trees below and a view which was almost pastoral. Living in the Inner Court was, according to Boswell, "the most agreeable in the world for a single man".[3]

He was certainly enjoying life, as we can tell from letters he wrote to friends at this time, and his biographer Charles Ryskamp paints for us a very different picture from the timid introvert that earlier writers would have us think him:

> Cowper was all his life an elegant dresser … He fenced and
> had one of his eyes almost poked out; he went shooting. He
> danced all night, went to Marylebone Gardens, to the Italian
> operas, and to the theatre. He could and did drink a
> considerable amount. And so his early letters show him to
> be pretty much a young man of society.[4]

Had he been any different, he would never have become the close companion of Edward Thurlow while he was with Mr Chapman. Thurlow, who went on to become Attorney-General and Lord Chancellor, had been expelled from King's School, Canterbury and sent down from Cambridge for idleness and insubordination. He was a hard-drinking, blunt, not to say brutal man of unbridled ambition, yet he had a love of poetry and he would go along with Cowper to visit his uncle Ashley Cowper at 30 Southampton Row. "There was I," Cowper later wrote to his cousin Harriot, "the future Lord

Chancellor, constantly employed from Morning to Night in giggling and making giggle, instead of studying the Law" (17th April 1786).

William's uncle Ashley Cowper was of an altogether different personality from that of his father. He wrote verse, some of it rather risqué, and William was very fond of him. But, fond as he was of his uncle, it was the presence there of the three daughters, Elizabeth, Theadora and Harriot which was the main attraction of Southampton Row. Thurlow and Cowper were an unlikely duo. Thurlow must have cut a very dashing figure: tall, well-built, with a rugged, swarthy complexion and dark sparkling eyes. but it was Cowper, slight and far les exotic, the girls all fell for.

Even when she was in her seventies Harriot confessed to William Hayley: "There was no period in my life in which I should not have gloried in being known to the whole World, as the decided Choice of *Such a Heart as Cowper's*."[5] And in 1763 he had written to her, "Adieu, my dear Cousin! so much as I love you, I wonder how the deuce it has happened I was never in love with you" (9 August 1763). But it was her younger sister, Theadora, who had caught his heart and caused the giggles.

We get a clearer picture of all these giggles from a story Cowper published in *The Connoisseur* in 1756. Writing under the name of Mr Country he describes a visit to a friend who has three unmarried daughters – a very thin disguise for his cousins:

> Upon these occasions, my entry into the room is sometimes obstructed by a cord fastened across the bottom of the door-case, which as I am a little near-sighted, I seldom discover till it has brought me upon my knees before them. While I am employed in brushing the dust from my black rollers [stockings] or chafing my broken shins, my wig is suddenly conveyed away, and either stuffed behind the looking-glass, or tossed from one to the other so dexterously and with such velocity, that after many a fruitless attempt to recover it, I am obliged to sit down bare-headed, to the great diversion of the spectators.[6]

There is an interesting end to this piece when he adds:

> I shall be happy therefore, if by your means I may be permitted to inform the ladies, that as fusty an animal as they think me, it is not impossible but by a little gentler treatment than I have hitherto met with, I may be humanized into an husband.

William was 19 and Theodora was 16 when they first met in 1750. They seem to have behaved just as one would expect any young people to behave and it is good to see that the age of elegance could also be an age of horseplay.

William has left us a portrait of himself at this time in a poem called 'A Character' which begins:

> William was once a bashful Youth,
>   His Modesty was such,
> That one might say (to say the Truth)
>   He rather had too much.
>
> Some said that it was want of Sense,
>   And others want of Spirit;
> (So blest a thing is Impudence)
>   While others could not bear it;
>
> And some a different Notion had,
>   And at each other winking,
> Observ'd that tho' he little said
>   He paid it off with thinking;
>
> Howe'er it was, by Slow degrees
>   He mended and grew perter,
> In Company was more at ease,
>   And Dress'd a little Smarter;
>
> Nay now and then would look quite gay
>   As other people do,
> And often said or try'd to say
>   A witty thing or so.
>
> He eyed the Women and made free
>   To comment on their shapes,
> So that there was or seem'd to be
>   No fear of a relapse.
>
> The Women said, who thought him rough
>   Yet did not think him Foolish,
> The Creature may do well enough,
>   But wants a little Polish.

Of Theadora as she was then we know very little. Her sister Harriot tells us that she had the face and figure of an angel. We are also told that she was, like Cowper, modest, refined and shy, yet when challenged by her father as to what she would do if she married Cowper, she is said to have replied, "Wash all day, and ride on the great dog all night."[7] A very curious and curiously erotic reply for someone refined and shy.

Like all love affairs, their relationship had its ups and downs, and Cowper records them in a sequence of 17 love poems addressed to Delia, the name he chose, as was customary, to cover her real identity.

These poems, which have received almost no critical attention, were not published in Cowper's lifetime, and it was only in 1824 that James Croft inherited them from Theadora, who was his great-aunt. They had been written out for her by Cowper himself and Croft published them in 1825 under the title *Poems: The Early Productions of William Cowper*.

The poem with which the sequence begins cannot have been the actual first one, as it refers to a previous poem he had written, but which he would not let Delia see. This is by way of being a written apology. His muse, he says, feared that she was not up to the praise Delia truly deserved. In saying so he is of course praising her fulsomely:

> Did not my muse (what can she less)
> Perceive her own unworthiness,
> Could she by some well chosen theme,
> But hope to merit your esteem,
> She would not thus conceal her lays,
> Ambitious to deserve your praise.
> But should my Delia take offence,
> And frown on her impertinence,
> In silence, sorrowing and forlorn,
> Would the despairing trifler mourn;
> Curse her ill-tuned, unpleasing lute,
> Then sigh and sit for ever mute.

After apologising to her, in the next poem he is accusing her of being "Th'unkindest girl on earth". This time *she* is doing the refusing. He has asked for a lock of her hair, claiming that its possession will defy the "spoiler" time. It will not lose its gloss or colour, and so he will be preserving "everlasting youth":

Delia, th'unkindest girl on earth,
   When I besought the fair,
That favour of intrinsic worth,
   A ringlet of her hair,

Refused that instant to comply
   With my absurd request,
For reasons she could specify,
   Some twenty score at least.

Trust me, my dear, however odd
   It may appear to say,
I sought it merely to defraud
   Thy spoiler of his prey.

Yet when its sister locks shall fade,
   As quickly fade they must,
When all their beauties are decay'd,
   Their gloss, their colour, lost,

Ah then! if haply to my share
   Some slender pittance fall,
If I but gain one single hair,
   Nor age usurp them all;

When you behold it still as sleek,
   As lovely to the view,
As when it left thy snowy neck –
   That Eden where it grew –

Then shall my Delia's self declare,
   That I profess'd the truth,
And have preserved my little share
   In everlasting youth.

It is a common enough theme, and Cowper handles it quite skilfully. But there is more here than surface skill. The situation puts him in mind of Pope's *The Rape of the Lock*, even though he is a humble suitor and not Lord Petre, the villain and 'rapist' of that poem, and if we look carefully there are three echoes of Pope here. The first one looks rather insignificant, but is nevertheless present. In line 9 Cowper's "Trust me, my dear" calls up the famous speech of Camilla in Canto V of Pope's poem:

> And trust me, dear! good-humour can prevail,
> When airs, and flights, and screams, and scolding fail.
> (V.31-2)

But the second echo is more obvious. Cowper has written:

> Yet when its sister locks shall fade,
> As quickly fade they must

Here he is consciously echoing Pope's "The sister lock now sits uncouth, alone" (IV.171) and combining elements from four other lines by Pope:

> Curl'd or uncurl'd, since Locks will turn to grey;
> Since painted or not painted, all shall fade,
> (V.26-7)

and:

> When those fair suns shall set, as set they must,
> And all those tresses shall be laid in dust.
> (V.147-8)

Finally the lines

> Ah, then! if haply to my share,
> Some slender pittance fall

are a deliberate echo of the famous

> If to her share some female errors fall,
> Look on her face and you'll forget 'em all.
> (II. 17-18)

Now there is a real point to this. It is not simply source-hunting and echo-location. What it tells us is that this poem is *not* merely a hastily scribbled piece of light verse, done to amuse his girlfriend. It is light verse, but it was not hastily scribbled. It has been carefully considered and thought out. Carefully crafted too. And it is an intelligent piece of work. This young man is taking the writing of verse very seriously, even if the piece is light-hearted. He is already a real poet and, I would suggest, sees himself as one. The poem also adds something to the little we know of Theodora. Cowper must have expected her to recognise what he was doing. So this young girl (she was seventeen) must have read Pope and could be expected to pick up on the allusions. They didn't just giggle, these two young people.

So, there have been two quarrels, two fallings-out: he has refused to show her his poem and she has refused him a lock of her hair. Lovers' tiffs. But, as he says in the third poem in the sequence, a poem called 'This Evening, Delia, you and I', the great thing about lovers' tiffs is that they provide a splendid opportunity for making up again, and he concludes the poem with a delightful simile:

> For friendship, like a sever'd bone,
> Improves and gains a stronger tone
>   When aptly reunited.

It would be foolish to make extravagant claims for the poems in this sequence. There are some conventionalities one might wish were not there:

> Since for my sake each dear translucent drop
> Breaks forth, best witness of thy truth sincere,
> My lips should drink the precious moisture up,
> And e'er it falls, receive the trembling tear.

It was about this time that Theodora gave him a red carnelian seal ring portraying Omphale wearing the lion's skin of Hercules. Omphale was the queen of Lydia, and Hercules had become a slave in her palace. The message seems at first to be that Cowper would be Theodora's slave; but the future looked promising: Omphale freed Hercules and became his mistress, and he then spent his days in ease and indolence. One begins to warm to this young woman.

Some of the poems definitely refer to actual events in their love, and to actual quarrels. In the postscript to a whimsical letter to his friend Chase Price, dated 21st February 1754 Cowper writes:

> You may remember that there was some small Difference
> between me and the Person I hinted at in the Beginning of
> my Letter; the Enclosed was wrote [that curious piece of
> 18th-century grammar] upon that Subject since I saw you
> last. All is Comfortable & Happy between us at present and

I doubt not will continue so for ever. Indeed we had neither
of us any great reason to be Dissatisfied, & perhaps Quarrel'd
merely for the sake of Reconciliation – which you may be
sure made Ample Amends.

The poem he enclosed was the one entitled 'Written in a Quarrel'. It is rather
a stereotyped love poem, however, with little to commend it.

Sadly, the note of optimism in his letter was misplaced. Their happiness
was not to continue for ever. He soon begins to sense this. 'How blest the
youth whom fate ordains / A kind relief from all his pains' is how one poem
begins. He realises that he is not so blest. He fears 'Fortune's fickle pow'r'.
Then the expected blow arrives. The relationship had lasted several years,
but eventually Theadora's father put a stop to it. His reasons have attracted
speculation. In one respect it is hardly surprising. Cowper was obviously *not*
studying law and had neither prospects nor fortune. What would they live
on? It has also been suggested that he had serious doubts about Cowper's
mental health, and maybe of Theadora's too. Also, they were first cousins, but
had their kinship been a serious objection, he would have made his
opposition clear much earlier.

Whatever the reasoning, Cowper's response is contained in a poem called
'1755'. It has rather a pompous tone. It is all because of money, he says, and
his own obvious lack of it. "All-worshipp'd gold", he begins, and conjures up
images of him and Theadora together in Eden, where money would be
irrelevant. It is all very Miltonic with a lot of posturing. Though he may not
have money, he says at the close, he has Virtue, which, as the world goes, will
count for nothing against his lack of prospects.

In a poem beginning "Hope, like a short-lived ray" we see that he has not
totally given up hope, but realises the folly of it. What is interesting here is
that he uses an image of a drowning seaman. Years later he was to use this
image again in one of his most famous poems, 'The Castaway':

Oft have I thought the scene of troubles closed,
    And hoped once more to gaze upon your charms;
As oft some dire mischance has interposed,
    And snatch'd th'expected blessing from my arms.

The seaman thus, his shatter'd vessel lost,
    Still vainly strives to shun the threat'ning death;
And while he thinks to gain the friendly coast,
    And drops his feet, and feels the sands beneath,

Borne by the wave, steep-sloping from the shore,
    Back to th'inclement deep, again he beats
The surge aside, and seems to tread secure;
    And now the refluent wave his baffled toil defeats.
                                                    (9-20)

As so often seems to be the case, bad tidings come in threes. In 1756 Cowper's father died, and then his close friend Sir William Russell was drowned in the Thames:

Doom'd, as I am, in solitude to waste
The present moments, and regret the past;
Depriv'd of every joy, I valued most,
My Friend torn from me, and my Mistress lost;
Call not this gloom, I wear, this anxious mien,
The dull effect of humour, or of spleen!
Still, still, I mourn, with each returning day,
Him snatch'd by Fate, in early youth, away.
And Her – through tedious years of doubt, and pain,
Fix'd in her choice, and faithful – but in vain.

Indeed she was fixed in her choice and faithful, and again in 'Written after Leaving her at New Burns':

For on that day, relentless fate!
Delia and I must separate.
Yet e'er we look'd our last farewell,
From her dear lips this comfort fell;
'Fear not that time, where'er we rove,
Or absence, shall abate my love.'
                                        (32-7)

He knows that there will be other men interested in her and addresses one of them in a poem called 'Upon a Venerable Rival'. Apparently she is being courted by someone so venerable as to be thirty years old!

Full thirty frosts since thou wert young
    Have chill'd the wither'd grove,
Thou Wretch! And hast thou lived so long
    Nor yet forgot to love?

Then in what looks to be the closing poem in the sequence, and is simply called 'To Delia', he accepts the inevitability of their separation, but declares that as long as her future life is a happy one, he will be content. As for himself, apart from her, he can never be happy. He wants her to be happy, but not with anyone else. Not that happy! He of course will remain true to her for ever:

> Then can I ever leave my Delia's arms,
> A slave, devoted to inferior charms?
> Can e'er my soul her reason so disgrace?
> For what blest minister of heavenly race
> Would quit that heaven to find a happier place?
>
> (45-9)

Having little or nothing to do was always a hazard for Cowper as he well knew, once explaining to Harriot: "Dejection of Spirits, which, I suppose, may have prevented many a man from becoming an Author, made me one. I find constant employment necessary, and therefore take care to be constantly employed" (12th October 1785). The combination of having lost Theadora, and Southampton Row consequently now being closed to him, the death of his father and his friend, all led to a depression and then to a breakdown, which he described in his memoir:

> Day and night I was upon the rack, lying down in horrors, and rising in despair. I presently lost all relish for those studies, to which I had before been closely attached; the classics had no longer any charm for me: I had need of something more salutary than amusement, but I had no one to direct me where to find it.[8]

There is no mention of Delia here and her name never features in any of the hundreds of letters he was subsequently to write, not even in those to her sister.

It is clear that she never stopped loving him, and sadly the break-up seriously affected her already unstable mental health. In 1769, as we learn from a letter Cowper wrote to his friend Joseph Hill, she was admitted to Dr Cotton's private madhouse in St Albans, four years after Cowper himself had been allowed to leave there. But even in that letter he could not bring himself to name her; she is "a near Relation". Theadora outlived him by a quarter of a century, but never married. She kept every poem he had ever written to her and every scrap of paper relating to him. Late in life she wrote to Hayley:

"Among the evils attendant upon sorrow, it is not one of the least that by a long continuance of it, the mind loses the power of being susceptible of joy."[9] Yet she continued to send him gifts which came to him from 'Anonymous' and culminated in an annuity of £50 and a beautiful writing desk. He must surely have guessed who 'Anonymous' was, but he kept up the pretence, always referring to "him", once coyly asking Harriot:

> Who is there in the world that has, or even thinks he has, reason to love me to the degree that he does? … though I believe you, my Dear, to be in full possession of all this mystery, you shall never know me while you live, either directly or by hints of any sort, attempt to extort or to steal the secret from you." (17th April 1786)

To acknowledge that he knew who still loved him would perhaps have involved him in some awkward moments of conscience. When he was in need of money, especially Theadora's annuity, he was not above asking Harriot to hurry up with it. People had always helped him, and he began to expect it of them. It is not, it has to be said, an attractive side to his nature.

Cowper's depression, however, did not last long. What first alleviated his feelings, as he put it, was reading the poems of George Herbert:

> … gothic and uncouth as they were, I yet found in them a strain of piety, which I could not but admire … [but] At length, I was advised by a very near and dear relation, to lay him aside, for he thought such an author was more likely to nourish my melancholy than to remove it.[10]

Lay him aside he might have done, but he never forgot what he had read, and there are traces of Herbert to be found in the *Olney Hymns*.

Then a change of scene was recommended and some fresh air and exercise, and Cowper went to stay for some months in Southampton with Mr Hesketh, who was engaged to his cousin Harriot. There he walked one afternoon to Freemantle and appears to have experienced something of what Wordsworth was to discover in nature:

> The morning was clear and calm; the sun shone bright upon the sea; and the country on the borders of it was the most beautiful I have ever seen. We sat down upon an eminence at

the end of that arm of the sea which runs between Southampton and the New Forest. Here it was that on a sudden, as if another sun had been kindled that instant in the heavens on purpose to dispel sorrow and vexation of spirit, I felt the weight of all my misery taken off. My heart became light and joyous in a moment, and had I been alone, I could have wept with transport.[11]

To have recalled this event so vividly, and the emotions which it aroused, shows how powerfully it must have affected him, and yet he does not seem to have recognised the potential such feelings might have had for him as a poet. He seems to have failed to recognise that 'immanent divinity' in nature which a later generation of poets was soon to explore. It has been argued that Cowper was unable to reconcile joy in nature with the god worshipped by the Evangelicals of his day.[12] This god they held to be quite outside the natural world and so austerely opposed to all instinctive pleasure that he could only be truly worshipped by those who themselves recognised the worthlessness of nature as it existed both in and outside themselves. Unable to reconcile them, he came close to rejecting both. In the way in which he described it, that warmth of feeling he experienced at Freemantle was often regarded as a sign, or a prelude to the moment of conversion, to 'seeing the light'. Looking back at it from his later Evangelical point of view, Cowper claimed to "remember something like a glow of gratitude to the Father of mercies for this unexpected blessing, and that I ascribed it to his gracious acceptance of my prayers".[13] But Satan persuaded him otherwise, as he then put it, convincing him that it was all due to nothing but a change of scene and the amusing varieties of the place.

"Upon this hellish principle" he returned to London where he found a group of friends from his days at Westminster. Down from university now, they had gathered together to form what they called the Nonsense Club. Essentially, it was a dining club which met every Thursday, but what bound them together was their ambition to be recognised as writers. Cowper joined them.

Apart from one or two brief references in his letters, we know very little about the club, but if we may judge from those known to have been members, it seems to have been a very interesting and talented group. Bonnell Thornton, a prolific essayist, edited *The Connoisseur* which ran to 140 issues. George Colman, a joint editor of *The Connoisseur*, was a successful dramatist and became manager and then owner of the Haymarket Theatre. Robert Lloyd, the son of a popular master at Westminster, himself failed as a teacher there, then edited the influential *St James's Magazine,* but was a heavy drinker, went bankrupt and died in a debtors' jail. Among others, not members of the club but closely associated with it were Charles Churchill and Christopher Smart. Churchill, sometime priest and long-time libertine, was a satirist greatly esteemed by Cowper, while Smart was published in the *St James's Magazine* and performed his drag-act as *Mother Midnight* at Colman's Haymarket Theatre.

Cowper was much involved with the world of letters at this time, and among his contributions to *The Connoisseur* were a 'Dissertation on the Modern Ode', attacking the obscurity of Gray and Mason, playful pieces on people who spoiled polite conversation, and an essay on keeping secrets: the kind of topics, which, with their relaxed and ironic tone, were later to feature brilliantly in his letters from Olney. He was also writing verse. He published two sprightly versions of satires by Horace and churned out close to a thousand dogged couplets translating four books of Voltaire's *La Henriade*.

But while he was acquiring a growing reputation for his wit and learning, what he was not acquiring was money. His only income was £60 a year from his appointment as – somewhat ironically – Commissioner for Bankrupts. But, popular and always dapper in appearance, he was not short of friends. Samuel Greatheed records that "at jovial gatherings he was able to drink 4 or 5 bottles of claret without sensible effect,"[14] and he was known as something of a raconteur:

> With a low voice, and much apparent gravity and composure,
> he was accustomed repeatedly to surprise his hearers with
> observations, which not only proved him to be possessed of
> knowledge and taste, but evinced an extraordinary power of
> being ludicrous whenever he pleased.[15]

Not surprisingly, these changes in him seem to have brought about a change of mind in his uncle. He no longer opposed the marriage with Theodora, perhaps recognising that she had no mind to marry anyone else, and in order to provide the young couple with enough to live on, he proposed Cowper for the position of Clerkship of the Journals in the House of Lords, which would have given him a good salary for very little actual work. Suddenly a bright future lay ahead: a respected position, a substantial income, a life of elegance and ease in London, and a wife who adored him.

It is difficult to imagine, and of course it was not to be. But it was not a future which was snatched away from him, as it is so often portrayed; it was one he stepped aside to avoid.

4

The Black Dog

I once was lost

Cowper's rejection of Theadora was both inexplicable and cruel. They had met again at Margate in 1763, but, as Harriot recorded him saying two decades later:

> ... having been for many years separated, that their Union wou'd have *then* been practicable, as he then, with the Place offer'd him, cou'd have maintained a family. He said he saw My dear Father, who had always lov'd him *as a Son*, would have made no objections, and that, She herself was unchang'd – well, replied I, why did you *not* propose? To this question he replied what I can never forget ... "O yes I saw my Paradise before me – but I also saw the flaming Sword that must for ever keep me from it!"[1]

In Genesis a flaming sword kept Adam and Eve from returning to Eden, but we have no knowledge of what sin Cowper thought was barring him. It was, as we know, a blow from which Theadora never recovered. Even so, her father did not withdraw his generous offer of the position of Clerk of the Journals. Perhaps, having made the offer, he did not feel he could in honour do so, but, if he had had any inkling at all that Cowper was mentally unfit for the post, he would surely have opposed his appointment immediately. In view of all that followed it is important to recognise this.

It is also important to keep in mind that the only authority for what followed is Cowper's memoir, *Adelphi*, which he wrote while staying with the Unwins in Huntingdon in 1767, but which was not published until 1816, although it had become known to a small circle of his friends. This memoir is not an autobiography, in that it is not a straightforward record of the events of his early life. The events are secondary to their emotional and psychological causes and consequences. Cowper's own term for it was "a history of my heart".[2] If it is thought of as a 'conversion narrative', its purpose becomes clear. There is a long tradition of such narratives, and they should be seen as related to the oral testimonies which were delivered before judgemental elders of Independent churches by would-be new members. The purpose was to demonstrate that candidates had truly undergone a conversion, and this could best be done by confessing to a previous life of incorrigible sin in order to emphasise the change that had come over them since they first 'saw the light'. The story Cowper tells, we need to realise, is by no means unique, and Professor Hindmarsh has shown that "the sense that one was descending into madness and the urge to commit suicide were typical, if not universal, features of the Evangelical genre of spiritual autobiography."[3]

The unlikeliness of the opening sentence should be enough to prepare us for the true nature of what is to follow:

> I cannot recollect that till the month of December, in the thirty-second year of my life, I had ever any serious impressions of the religious kind, or at all bethought myself of the things of my salvation, except in two or three instances.[4]

And this from the son of an Anglican priest.

He hurries through his earliest years only pausing occasionally to tell us that at school he was "an adept in the infernal art of lying", that he then pursued a "rash and ruinous career of wickedness" and that in the Temple he indulged in "an uninterrupted course of sinful indulgences".[5] This kind of flag-waving can be ignored, but what is certain is that Cowper was given to fits of depression. His family had a history of depression. In a brief life story he wrote for Mrs King in 1791 he told her that "it pleased God that I should be born in a country where melancholy is the national characteristic and of a house more than commonly subject to it" (4th August 1791). One might say that after George Cheyne's book *The English Malady* (1773), it had indeed become a national characteristic, and the 'Black Dog', as it became known, plagued the lives of Johnson, Boswell, Gray and many others.

The events slowly closing in on Cowper were, in the first instance, narrated quite succinctly. His progress towards the position in the House of Lords was going smoothly until an opposition group began to voice objections to such automatic promotions and insisted that the candidate should be subjected to an examination at the bar of the House. It would have been a daunting experience for anyone, particularly as it seemed that much of the questioning would be hostile. It was not something Cowper could countenance:

> They whose spirits are formed like mine, to whom a public
> exhibition of themselves on any occasion is mortal poison,
> may have some idea of the horror of the situation; others can
> have none. My continual misery at length brought on a
> nervous fever. Quiet forsook me by day, and sleep by night.[6]

Cowper was confronted with a serious dilemma. He knew he could not face the examination, yet he could not withdraw from it without "ruining my benefactor's right of appointment, by bringing his discretion in the use of it into question".[7] How could he escape? In a very revealing paragraph he says: "I now began to look upon madness as the only chance remaining … My chief fear was that my senses would not fail me time enough to excuse my appearance in the House, which was the only purpose I wanted it to answer."[8]

At this point, straightforward narrative is succeeded by Evangelical rodomontade and it is difficult to know where the truth lies. A whole new direction is taken: "Now came the great temptation, the point to which Satan had all the while been drawing me, the dark and hellish purpose of self-murder."[9] In terms of a "conversion narrative", this is quite magnificent: a sin quite unlike any other and a sin from which he was to be saved by divine providence. But as the events unfold, they become more and more unbelievably melodramatic and border on the comic, and the tone is not helped by the frequent intrusion of such assertions as "Thus were the emissaries of the throne of darkness let loose upon me."[10]

His first option is poison, and he buys a phial of laudanum from an apothecary, a character who might have stepped straight out of Act V of *Romeo and Juliet*: "The man seemed to observe me narrowly," he says.[11] His next thought is to run away to France and find "a comfortable asylum in some monastery".[12] But the change of religion would have been seen as a sin as great as suicide. He rejects that idea, admitting that it was "absurd, even to a degree of ridicule".[13] Even more ridiculous is his next scheme. He takes a coach to Tower Wharf with the intention of drowning himself, but the tide is out and there is a porter sitting on some goods there "as if placed on purpose to prevent me".[14] But what was more likely to prevent him was that he was in fact a strong swimmer, and when he moved to Huntingdon he would swim three days a week in the River Ouse. He still had the laudanum, but "an invisible hand" keeps it from his lips and "divine intervention" persuades him to throw it out of the window.

He clearly did not intend to kill himself, and there is one very telling sentence in his account: " … having shut both the outer and the inner door,

[I] prepared myself for the last scene of the tragedy."[15] There is a theatricality to all these attempts on his life. He is play-acting. He then, he tells us, went to bed taking his penknife with him. Three times he tries to stab himself but the point is broken and "it would not penetrate." It is beginning to be hard not to laugh.

He hears the clock strike seven. It is the day of the examination and he has just enough time left to hang himself. He thought he had bolted the door but he hadn't. "I mention it because it looks as if the good Providence that watched over me kept every way open for my deliverance that nothing might seem to be left to hazard."[16] Or was it his own good providence ensuring that he was found in time? His three attempts to hang himself with his garter, which he thinks we need to know was "made of a broad scarlet binding with a sliding buckle being sewn together at the ends",[17] were all equally, and farcically, unsuccessful. He is of course found – by his laundress. A friend is sent for. He arrives and his words were, "My dear Mr Cowper, you terrify me; – to be sure you cannot hold the office at this rate – where is the deputation?" Cowper gave him the key of the drawer where it was deposited, "he took it away with him; and thus ended all my connections with the Parliament House."[18] A sentence which sounds like the end of the story.

But the story was not over. Whether Cowper did make all those attempts at suicide or only imagined them we cannot tell. Is it simply a coincidence that his several attempts tally so closely with the list in Juvenal's sixth Satire, where in Dryden's version the lines read:

> Art thou of every other death bereft?
> No knife, no ratsbane, no kind halter left?
>   (For every noose compared with hers is cheap)
>   Is there no city-bridge from which to leap?
>
> (42-5)

Even contemplating suicide was a mortal sin and he looked back upon it as a battle for his soul:

> The capital engine in all the artillery of Satan had not yet been employed against me; already overwhelmed with despair, I had not yet sunk to the bottom of the gulph. This was a fit season for the use of it. Accordingly I was set to inquire whether I had not been guilty of the unpardonable sin, and was presently persuaded that I had.[19]

Interestingly, James King in his biography of Cowper quotes a passage from Freud:

> ... the distinguishing features of melancholia are a profoundly powerful feeling of dejection ... and a lowering of the self-regarding feelings to a degree that finds utterance in self-reproaches and self-revilings and culminates in a delusional expectation of punishment.[20]

His brother and his cousin tried their best to convince him of Christ's mercy and his promise of salvation, but Cowper's description of his own mental state here shows an acute sense of self-awareness:

> At every stroke, my thoughts and expressions became more wild and incoherent. When they ceased, they left nothing but disorder and a confused imagination behind them; all that remained clear was the sense of sin and the expectation of punishment.[21]

Lord David Cecil, as so often, goes much too far in describing him as "a gibbering, raving maniac",[22] but Cowper was now obviously in need of professional care, and it was decided to send him to a private madhouse in St Albans run by a Dr Cotton.

The mere mention of an eighteenth-century madhouse instantly and inevitably calls to mind Hogarth's portrayal of the horrors of Bedlam, where the poor demented creatures were tormented by their jailers and jeered at by visiting gentry, but fortunately such brutality was not the rule. A notable instance, for which we have abundant evidence, was Dr Potter's establishment in Bethnal Green, where that brilliantly gifted poet Christopher Smart was shut away for almost seven years. We know from his long and eccentric poem *Jubilate Agno* that he had pen and ink and plenty of paper; that he had ready access to newspapers and books; that he had a garden where he grew pinks, and of course that he had Jeoffry, perhaps the most famous cat in English literature.

We also know that on 27th January 1763, three days before Smart managed to negotiate his release – or possibly escape – from Dr Potter's, a committee of the House of Commons had met to look into conditions in these privately run madhouses. Dr Battie of St Luke's and Mr Munro of Bedlam were called as expert witnesses. Statements were taken and the House did not like what it found. This must have caused something of a flutter among the people running such establishments, and no doubt conditions improved quickly, but while we have no such details as Smart left us, there is no reason to doubt that they were generally benign in Dr Cotton's house in St Albans. Nevertheless, when Cowper was taken in there on 7th December in that same year (1763), he seems not to have been so sure of this. He was clearly in a very distressed state of mind when he arrived, as he confessed in *Adelphi*:

> We arrived at the doctor's house. He had no sooner taken me by the hand than my spirits sunk, and all my jealousy returned. His dwelling house is at some distance from that where he keeps his patients; thither his own chaise would carry me. But perceiving now that I had trepanned myself into danger of close confinement, I refused to go into it, and made such resistance that three or four persons were employed to compel me, and as many to take me out again, when I arrived at the place of my destination.[23]

His trepidation is perhaps understandable. As he confessed in a letter to his friend John Newton, dated 19th July 1784, he had himself once been a visitor to Bedlam:

> In those days when Bedlam was open to the casual curiosity of Holiday ramblers, I have been a visitor there. Though a boy, I was not altogether insensible of the misery of the poor captives, nor destitute of feeling for them. But the Madness of some of them had such a humorous air, and displayed itself in so many whimsical freaks, that it was impossible not to be entertained, at the same time I was angry with myself for being so.

One has to admire his honesty.

But he need not have feared, for as well as being a highly qualified and skilled physician, Dr Cotton was one of the kindliest of men, as Cowper was later to acknowledge in a letter dated 4th July 1765 to Harriot Hesketh:

> I was not only treated by him with the greatest tenderness,
> while I was ill, and attended with the utmost diligence, but
> when my reason was restored to me, and I had so much need
> of a religious friend to converse with, to whom I could open
> my mind upon the subject without reserve, I could have
> hardly have found a fitter person for the purpose.

They also shared a common experience in that both their mothers had died when they were six years old,[24] and while Dr Cotton was a very reserved man, it is quite possible that they talked about this. They may also have talked about poetry. Dr Cotton had anonymously published a volume of poems for children, *Visions in Verse*, its popularity evident from its eleven editions.

Dr Cotton, one suspects, must have needed all his patience and diligence, skill and benevolence when dealing with Cowper in the first months that he was at St Albans, as there were times when he was so deranged that he had to be put in a straitjacket; even his shoe buckles being taken away, as he could not be trusted not to harm himself.[25]

Progress was slow. For the first seven months, he tells us in his memoir, "Conviction of sin, and expectation of instant judgement never left me." So convinced was he of such judgement that at times he even regretted that he had not sinned more.[26] In July 1764 his brother visited him at Dr Cotton's suggestion, but when he asked how he was, the reply, "As much better as despair can make me", cannot have been encouraging. However, John did not give up. He insisted that William's terror was all a delusion, and this did begin to have some effect. "If it be a delusion, then am I the happiest of beings," Cowper admitted, and "something like a ray of hope was shot into my heart."[27]

What follows in the memoir does not make for easy reading today: the religious emotionalism runs to such extremes. The night after his brother left, William had a dream: "I dreamed the sweetest boy I ever saw came dancing up to my bedside … The sight affected me with pleasure and served at least to harmonize my spirits upon waking so that I awoke for the first time with a sensation of delight on my mind."[28] Although he does not say so directly, we are surely meant to take this as a vision of the Christ Child.

He then recalls a previous occasion at Dr Cotton's when he came across a bible lying on a bench in the garden and opened it by chance at the narrative of Lazarus, a story of so much benevolence, mercy, so much goodness and sympathy with miserable mankind in our Saviour's conduct as melted my heart, and I almost shed tears after the relation. Little did I think that it was an exact type of the mercy which Jesus was upon the point of extending towards myself.[29]

Now, finding a bible near him once more, he opened it, again by chance, so he tells us, at Romans 3:25: "Whom God hath set forth to be a propitiation through faith in his blood, to declare his righteousness for the remission of sins that are past, through the forbearance of God."

It is the archetypal Evangelical conversion; that born-again moment which was held then to be essential for true salvation. We need not doubt what Cowper is telling us, but it has to be recognised as a traditional and necessary feature of all such spiritual autobiographies. He goes on to tell us that the full beam of the Sun of Righteousness shone upon him. He saw his pardon sealed in Christ's blood. This concentration on blood is another characteristic of the times. He could have died, he tells us, with gratitude and joy. His eyes fill with tears. His voice is choked and he can only "look up to heaven in silent fear, overwhelmed with love and wonder".[30] He is too happy to sleep and wants to spend every moment in prayer and thanksgiving. None of this was unusual. Smart had so taken to heart St Paul's injunction "Pray without ceasing" that he had gone knocking on people's doors insisting that they should pray with him. His family had him locked away, and it is hardly surprising that Dr Cotton was now alarmed by similar hysteria and took another twelve months before he thought him to have calmed down enough to go into the world again.

Oddly, when he did leave, he did not leave alone. He took with him as his personal valet one of Dr Cotton's servants, Sam Roberts, who had been attending to him. As he admitted, "It was with some difficulty the doctor was prevailed on to part with him."[31] But that was not all. He also took an eight-year-old boy by the name of Dick Coleman, the son of a drunken cobbler in St Albans. Cowper thought he was saving him from a life of degeneracy. He wrote to Joseph Hill on November 12th 1766:

> I was glad of an Opportunity to show some Mercy in a place where I had received so much, and hope God will give a Blessing to my Endeavours to preserve him. He is a fine Boy, of a good Temper and Understanding, and if the Notice that is taken of him by the Neighbours don't spoil him, he will probably turn out well.

With no resources of his own, Providence would, he felt sure, provide for them all, and Providence, in the shape of his immediate family and relations had no other option. Sam Roberts proved to be the most loyal of servants and was with Cowper until 1795, but Dick was a disappointment and seems to have inherited his father's love of drink.

*   *   *

Cowper's brother, John, a fellow of Corpus Christi, Cambridge, had found lodgings for him in Huntingdon, perhaps thinking that to have William too close to him was not a wise idea, and he was probably right. Huntingdon proved to be the retreat Cowper was looking for. He remembered "the pollution that is in the world" and his "heart ached at the thought of returning to it again".[32] William Cobbett, although writing some fifty years later, described Huntingdon as "a very clean and nice place, [with] many elegant houses", adding: "I think it would be very difficult to find a more delightful spot than this in the world."[33]

Because of its racecourse, the town attracted its fair share of the *beau monde* during the summer months – not that this was of any consequence to Cowper. As he explained to his friend Joseph Hill,

> Here is a Card-Assembly, and a Dancing-Assembly, and a Horse-Race, and a Club, and a Bowling-Green, so that I am well off, you perceive, in point of Diversions; especially as I shall go to 'em just as much as I should if I lived a Thousand Miles off. (3rd July 1765)

Cowper did not have what most of his contemporaries would have considered a sense of fun, but one of Huntingdon's attractions did appeal to him and that was the River Ouse, which was to play an important role in his life. Writing to Hill on his first arrival there he had declared:

> The River Ouze (I forget how they spell it) is the most agreeable Circumstance in this part of the World. It is a noble Stream to bath in, and I shall make that use of it three times a Week, having introduced myself to it for the first time this Morning. (24th June 1765)

But events did not work out quite as smoothly as he had hoped. He had never had to fend for himself, and had no idea about housekeeping, shopping or balancing his expenses. In only three months he had "contrived to spend the income of a twelvemonth", he later confessed to his cousin Harriot (6th November 1785). And surrounded by strangers, his spirits began to sink. He felt "like a traveller in the midst of an inhospitable desert, without a friend to comfort, or a guide to direct him".[34] Going to church for the first time since his recovery lifted his spirits, and then an event occurred which not only put an end to his loneliness but changed the whole course of his life. He met a young man called William Unwin. Cowper was 34 while Unwin was only 21 and still at university, but there was an instant rapport between them. He is "one of the most unreserved and amiable young men I ever conversed with," he told Harriot (14th September 1765). They had encountered each other coming out of church one Sunday, drank a dish of tea together in Cowper's lodgings, and the following Sunday he was invited to dine with the rest of the family in their gabled red-brick house in the High Street.

Cowper's first impression of William's father, the Rev. Morley Unwin, whom he referred to as the Old Gentleman, was that he was "a man of Learning and good Sense, and as simple as Parson Adams" (25th October 1765), but as he got to know him better he must have found him something of a disappointment. Far from displaying Evangelical zeal, he was an all too typical Anglican priest of his time. The parish books record several resolutions of censure against him for neglect of duty, and he once came near to being dismissed.[35]

Mrs Unwin, however, was of exactly the same frame of mind as Cowper, and he was instantly attracted to her. "His wife who is Young compared with her husband [she was 20 years younger than him and only seven years older than Cowper] has a very uncommon Understanding, has read much to excellent purpose, and is more polite than a Duchess," as he told Joseph Hill, (25th October 1765). The daughter, Susanna, he added, was "quite of a piece with the rest of the family".

Cowper's handling of his finances was getting worse. He told Joseph Hill that he was "in danger of bankruptcy" and as two pupils whom Morley Unwin was preparing for university, had recently moved out, he therefore "entered into an agreement with the Rev. Mr. Unwin to lodge and board with him", as he explained his new situation, so very formally, to Hill (5th November 1765). He moved in with the Unwins on 11th November 1765.

A year later he wrote to his cousin, Mrs Maria Cowper, famously describing their lifestyle:

Having told you how we *do not* spend our time, I will next say how we *do*. We Breakfast commonly between 8 and 9, 'till 11, we read either the Scripture, or the Sermons of some faithfull Preacher of those holy Mysteries; at 11 we attend divine Service which is performed here twice every day, and from 12 to 3 we separate and amuse ourselves as we please. During that Interval I either Read in my own Apartment, or Walk or Ride, or work in the Garden. We seldom sit an hour after Dinner, but if the Weather permits adjourn to the Garden, where with Mrs Unwin and her Son I have generally the Pleasure of Religious Conversation 'till Tea time; if it Rains or is too windy for Walking, we either Converse within Doors, or sing some Hymns of Martin's Collection, and with help of Mrs Unwin's Harpsichord make up a tolerable Concert, in which however our Hearts I hope are the best and most musical Performers. After Tea we sally forth to walk in good earnest. Mrs Unwin is a good Walker, and we have generally travel'd about 4 miles before we see Home again. When the Days are short we make this Excursion in the former part of the Day, between Church time and Dinner. At night we read and converse as before 'till Supper, and commonly finish the Evening either with Hymns or a Sermon, and last of all the Family are called in to Prayers. – I need not tell *you* that such a Life as this is consistent with the utmost cheerfullness, accordingly we are all happy, and dwell together in Unity as Brethren. (20th October 1766)

That final assertion that they were all happy and dwelling together in unity as brethren is open to question, however. There is no mention, we notice, of Mr Unwin, who seems to have had strong feelings about this religious alliance between Cowper and his wife. Samuel Greatheed told William Hayley, Cowper's first biographer that "When Mr. C. came to board in the family, a sudden and obvious revolution took place, apparently as much against the inclination of the old Gentleman, as that of France against Lewis 16th's."[36] There is no mention of the daughter Susanna either. When they first met, Cowper told his cousin:

> I was introduced to the Daughter alone; and sat with her near half an hour, before her Brother came in, who had appointed me to call upon him. Talking is necessary in a *tête-*

á-tête, to distinguish the persons in the drama from the chairs they are sitting on: accordingly she talked a great deal and extremely well; and, like the rest of the family, behaved with as much ease of address as if we had been old acquaintance. (18th October 1765)

But this was before he moved in with the family. We are told that "In her mother's company she says little." Subsequently she is rarely mentioned in Cowper's letters, but after her marriage, when she and her husband visited Cowper in Olney, he wrote to her brother none too kindly:

> Your poor Sister! – she has many good Qualities, and upon some Occasions gives Proof of a good Understanding; but as some People have no Ear for Music, so she has none for Humour. Well – if She cannot laugh at our Jokes, we can, however, at Her Mistakes, and in this way she makes us ample Amends for the Disappointment. (24th December 1780)

He seems not to realise that, as an eighteen-year-old girl, she probably did not approve of her mother's relationship with him, and, as she later told Hayley, she certainly did not approve of the £1,800 that she estimated her mother had wasted on caring for him.[37]

What the ultimate outcome of this state of affairs might have been – it persisted for over two years – we will never know, as on 29th June 1767 Morley Unwin was thrown from his horse and fractured his skull. He was a mile from home and too badly injured to be moved, so he was taken to a nearby labourer's cottage where he died four days later. Cowper's letters show no sign of grief, and only a week after the death he is telling his aunt that "By this means a Door is opened to us to seek an Abode under the Sound of the Gospel." He and Mrs Unwin have become "us" and have lost no time in making plans to get away from Huntingdon, "for my Soul within me is sick of the Spiritless unedifying Ministry at Huntingdon" (10th July 1767). Morley Unwin had been the man in charge of that ministry. Within another three days Cowper is explaining to his cousin: "The Effect of it on my Circumstances will only be a Change of the Place of my Abode, for I shall still, by God's leave, continue with Mrs. Unwin, whose Behaviour to me has always been that of a Mother to a Son" (13th July 1767). Whether Mrs Unwin saw their relationship in this light is another thing we do not know, but their neighbours did not. There was only seven years' difference in their ages, and the evening walks had already been causing gossip. Cowper complained to his aunt, Judith Madan, of "the black and shocking Aspersions which our neighbours here amuse themselves with casting upon our Names and Conduct" (10th August 1767). That he should have been so surprised only serves to prove his naivety, or his insensibility, in such matters.

The change of abode did not take long. William Unwin told his friend Dr Conyers of Mrs Unwin's bereavement. He in turn told the Rev. John Newton, the curate of Olney, and on 6th July Newton paid them a visit during which he offered to find them a more suitable place. As we have seen, Cowper was no longer enamoured of Huntingdon, and he looked on Newton's offer as opening "a Door for us out of an unEvangelical Pasture such as this is, into some better Ministry where we may hear the glad Tidings of Salvation and be nourished by the Sincere Milk of the Word" (13th July 1767).

A few days later he wrote to tell Judith Madan that "Mr. Newton seems to have conceived a great Desire to have us for Neighbours and I am sure we shall think ourselves highly favoured to be committed to the care of such a Pastor" (18th July 1767).

*   *   *

William Cowper and Zeal-of-the-Land Busy would seem to be light years apart, but the eighteenth-century Evangelical revival had at least some of its roots back in the religious excesses of the seventeenth century. It was, as it were, a reaction against the initial reaction, for, after the demise of Cromwellianism, the last thing the majority of the people of England wanted was any form of emotional extremism in their religious observances. But the alternative, rationalism, as it tightened its grip, led some into the cold-bloodedness of deism, a movement whose followers ceased to envisage God as a divine being, but rather as an intellectual abstraction they referred to as the First Cause, or the Prime Mover, while in the Established Church what had begun as a praiseworthy tolerance eventually dwindled into apathy. A position in the Church became for many a means of achieving social standing without having to do much to deserve, it and Cowper gives us a brilliant and entertaining portrait of just such clergymen in Book II of *The Task*:

> But loose in morals, and in manners vain,
> In conversation frivolous, in dress
> Extreme, at once rapacious and profuse,
> Frequent in park with lady at his side,
> Ambling and prattling scandal as he goes,

But rare at home, and never at his books
Or with his pen, save when he scrawls a card;
Constant at routs, familiar with a round
Of ladyships, a stranger to the poor;
Ambitious of preferment for its gold,
And well prepared by ignorance and sloth,
By infidelity and love o' the world
To make God's work a sinecure.
(II.378-90)

The spirit had gone out of it all, and the Evangelical movement strove to bring it back, but this was not to be a return to the attitudes of the seventeenth century. Unlike the Puritans before them, the Evangelicals of Cowper's day had no real interest in politics and very little in theology, but what they did share with those earlier times was an emphasis on inner conviction, a personal religion which did not simply conform to a regime of outwardly imposed rules and rituals. Their concern was with salvation. It was a Christ-centred religion, yet one which was more concerned with atonement than with incarnation.

What one's salvation depended on was, however, a matter which profoundly divided Cowper's generation. Calvinism was a powerful force, but its doctrine of predestination often had a touch of class distinction about it. Wesley, who preached to miners, factory workers and farmhands, saw it as a blasphemy and insisted that the "horrible decree of Predestination" represented God as worse than the devil.[38] The Duchess of Buckingham on the other hand clearly regarded herself and her friends as assuredly and exclusively among the saved and would have no truck with any notion to the contrary, famously leaving Lady Huntingdon, a staunch Methodist, in no doubt of her feelings on the matter:

> I thank Your Ladyship for the information concerning the *Methodist* preachers; their doctrines are most repulsive, strongly tinctured with Impertinence and Disrespect towards their Superiors, in perpetually endeavouring to level all Ranks, and do away with all Distinctions. It is monstrous to be told that you have a heart as *sinful* as the Common Wretches that crawl the earth. This is highly *offensive* and *insulting*; and I cannot but wonder that your Ladyship should relish any Sentiment so much at variance with High Rank and Good Breeding.[39]

Evangelicalism, as practised by Cowper and his companions, was a fundamentalist religion, centred firmly on the Bible, and like the Puritans before them, its adherents were criticised for indulging in excessive displays of piety. Cowper's description of an average day's pattern of worship is itself proof enough of this, and while they insisted that this brought for them true happiness, they were certainly opposed to most common forms of amusement and entertainment: no dancing, card-playing, theatre or music. But though Puritan in attitude, they were devout churchmen and did not hold with preaching in fields.

But for all their differences, the one thing which the various Evangelical groups shared was spiritual awareness: that moment of conversion when a believer felt born again. It was a feeling which Wesley experienced one afternoon in St Paul's Cathedral when he heard Psalm 130, *De Profundis*, sung as an anthem:

> I felt my heart strangely warmed. I felt I did trust in Christ,
> Christ alone, for salvation: and an assurance was given me.
> that he had taken away *my* sins, even *mine*, and saved *me*
> from the law if sin and death.[40]

This was the moment when God granted sinful man the undeserved and unlooked-for gift of his *Amazing Grace*.

5

John Newton

but now am found

William Cowper and John Newton: it is hard to imagine two men whose personalities and lifestyles were so disparate, and yet who became not only associates but close friends, for just as Cowper was leaving Westminster School where he had been studying Horace and Virgil and was about, however unwillingly, to embark on a career in the law, so John Newton was about to begin his career as a slave ship captain plying the infamous Atlantic triangle. The story of Newton's conversion gave him a lasting iconic status among Evangelical Christians, for, as the Rev. Josiah Bull put it in his book *John Newton: An Autobiography and Narrative*,[1] "The account of Mr Newton's early years is a story of adventure and of marvellous providential interventions which has few parallels." To understand Cowper's life in Olney – and that is not easy – we have to try to understand Newton, and that is not easy either.

Born into a seafaring family in the Thames-side borough of Wapping in July 1725, Newton received a caring and spiritual upbringing from his mother, and he claimed he could read any book put before him by the age of four.[2] But, curiously, just as in the case of Cowper and of Dr Cotton, she died when he was only six. When he was ten his formal education came to a stop, and the next year saw him on one of his father's ships sailing for the Mediterranean. In all, he made five such voyages under his father's captaincy and must have gained a very thorough grounding in seamanship.

In his teens he tried his hand at various jobs on shore, but could never settle, frequently falling out with his employers. Then, when he was 17, he was offered a position as the manager of a sugar plantation in Jamaica, a position which, if he had taken it, would have made his fortune, but a chance invitation to visit a cousin of his mother's living in Chatham sent him in quite a different direction, as there he fell in love with their thirteen-year-old daughter, Polly. It seems an unlikely story, but it was a love which lasted to his dying day. He dared not confess his love, not even to her; she was still a child and he was penniless, but the idea of going to Jamaica and not seeing her again for years was something he could not contemplate, and he deliberately stayed with the family until he had missed his sailing. Visiting them again two years later he unwisely went walking in Chatham. It was a naval base and England was on the brink of war with France. Able-bodied man were needed for the navy and Newton ran into a press gang.

His earlier service in the merchant navy brought him promotion to the rank of midshipman, but twice while the ship was at anchor he managed to get ashore to try to see Polly. The first time he was fortunate enough to get away with a reprimand, but the second escapade earned him a public flogging and reduction to the ranks. His vessel, *HMS Harwich*, then sailed for Madeira with an ordinary seaman on board who was now so sullen, resentful and rebellious that it is small wonder his captain was glad to exchange him for a sailor on a Guinea trading ship, the *Pegasus*. On board the *Pegasus* he met Andrew Clow, a slave-trader who operated off the coast of Sierra Leone, and Newton agreed to work for him, but when they landed, Clow's black mistress, known as Princess PI, took an instant dislike to him and when a bout of fever caused him to be left behind as Clow went up-river to buy slaves, she made Newton her own slave. She kept him in chains and so starved him that he was reduced to eating raw roots at night in the fields. Ironically, he only survived because of the care and kindness shown him by the black slaves around him.

One of the odder incidents he described in his later *Narrative* of these days is that he still had with him one book, a geometry textbook, and he kept himself from going mad by drawing Euclid's theorems in the sand with a stick. This story caught the eye of Dorothy Wordsworth, who copied it into one of the notebooks she was using in 1798, from where it found its way into Book VI of *The Prelude*:

> And I have read of one by shipwreck thrown
> With fellow Sufferers whom the waves had spar'd
> Upon a region uninhabited
> An island of the Deep, who having brought
> To land a single Volume and no more,
> A treatise of Geometry, was used
> Although of food and clothing destitute,
> And beyond common wretchedness depress'd,
> To part from company and take this book,
> Then first a self-taught pupil in those truths,
> To spots remote and corners of the Isle

By the sea side, and draw his diagrams
With a long stick upon the sand, and thus
Did oft beguile his sorrow, and almost
Forget his feeling;
    (VI.160-74)

When Clow returned from up-river he did not believe his companion's complaints, and Newton's existence was little better. At last, however, he managed to secure his release and joined another trader. Then, in this story of adventure, as Bull had put it, one of those "marvellous providential interpositions" occurred. Newton's letters home had reached his father, who sought the help of his friend Joseph Manesty, a Liverpool shipowner, one of whose vessels, the *Greyhound*, was about to sail for Sierra Leone. There being so few white men on that coast, finding Newton was not an impossible task. The *Greyhound*'s captain traced him and offered him a free passage home, and it was during this voyage that divine providence intervened and effected the most unlikely change,

Evangelical life stories, as we have already seen with Cowper's memoir, have at their centre that dramatic moment of conversion: the rebirth. John Newton's occurred during that voyage home. It was a long voyage, and once again he fell out with his captain. He drank excessively and his life, as he put it, "was a course of most horrid impiety and profaneness. I know not that I ever met so daring a blasphemer. Not content with common oaths and imprecations I daily invented new ones so that I was often seriously reproved by the captain."[3] There is probably some truth in this, but in narrative terms it only serves to make his conversion and change of lifestyle the more remarkable.

The *Greyhound* spent almost a year travelling south, trading in gold, ivory and beeswax before crossing the Atlantic to within sight of Brazil, then sailing up the east coast of North America to drop anchor briefly off Newfoundland. On 1st March 1748 the crew headed for England, but ten days later were caught in a North Atlantic gale of such ferocity that it threatened to sink them. After almost two years in equatorial waters the *Greyhound*'s timbers could not withstand such seas, and it was holed and flooded. One man had already been swept overboard to his death, and Newton joined the crew at the pumps. When all seemed hopeless, he heard himself say, "If this will not do, the Lord have mercy on us." The pumping worked, and so, it seemed to Newton, had his prayer:

> I thought I saw the hand of God in our favour. I began to
> pray. I could not utter the prayer of faith. I could not draw
> near to a reconciled God and call him Father – my prayer
> was like the cry of the ravens, which yet the Lord does not
> disdain to hear.[4]

What puzzles a reader today is that although, as he says, "I was no longer an infidel. I heartily renounced my former profaneness ... and was touched with a sense of God's undeserved mercy,"[5] it was not long before he accepted the captaincy of a slave ship of his own, the *Duke of Argyle*.

In a diary he began shortly before Christmas 1751, he resolved, "To spend the hours of the Sabbath entirely to the Lord". Such resolutions continue for three long paragraphs, and Bull adds that " ... leaving the coast of Africa, we find Mr Newton rejoicing in the leisure the sea afforded him for more regular and prolonged attention to religious exercises."[6] There is no mention whatsoever of the human cargo he was transporting from Africa, and the piety Bull celebrates is very much at variance with the ship's log which records that 20 slaves broke loose and fought with the crew. The ringleaders were put in iron collars and subjected to the thumbscrew for one hour. Newton's comment in the log continues, "They still look very gloomy and sullen ... but I hope (by the Divine Assistance) we are fully able to overawe them."[7] 'Gloomy' probably does not quite match their feelings.

It is so difficult for us to comprehend now. Apparently the thumbscrew was considered rather lenient, and on his second ship, the *African*, Newton was able to boast, perhaps justifiably, that on the fateful middle passage he had buried neither white nor black. Clearly there were many worse slave-traders than Newton, yet at the time he seems not to have appreciated the enormity of what he was doing, and his explanation, written in 1763 is hard to accept:

> The reader may perhaps wonder, as I now do myself, that,
> knowing the state of this vile traffic, to be as I have described
> and abounding with enormities I have not mentioned, I did
> not at the time start with horror at my own employment as an
> agent in promoting it. Custom, example, and interest had
> blinded my eyes. I did it ignorantly, for I am sure had I thought
> of the slave trade then as I have thought of it since, no
> consideration would have induced me to continue in it.[8]

It was in Liverpool that he met George Whitefield and John Wesley, and although he himself became well known as a lay preacher and for ministering to the poor, it was another seven years before he was successful in his application to be accepted as a priest in the Church of England. His years in the slave trade did not seem to go against him, but his class apparently did. His application to the archbishop of York was dismissed by a secretary with the words, "His Grace thinks it best for you to continue in that station which Providence has placed you in."[9] Ostensibly, another reason he was rejected was that he did not hold a degree from Oxford or Cambridge, but that had not held back others. As John Wesley put it,

> I had a good deal of conversation with Mr Newton. His case is very peculiar. Our church requires that clergymen should be men of learning, and to this end, have a university education. But how many have a university education and yet no learning at all! yet these men are ordained! Meantime, one of eminent learning, as well as unblameable behaviour, cannot be ordained because he was not at the university! What a mere farce is this! Who would believe that any Christian bishop would stoop to so poor an evasion.[10]

Newton's knowledge of Greek and Latin, which he had taught himself on board ship, was probably superior to that of most young graduates; it was his Evangelical fervour which was against him, his association with the Methodists. He was suspected of 'enthusiasm'. a damningly pejorative term in those days. The bishop of Bristol, Joseph Butler, once told John Wesley very plainly that "Enthusiasm … portending to extraordinary gifts and revelations of the Holy Ghost is a horrid thing, a very horrid thing."[11]

Newton admired the Methodists, but he did not want to be an itinerant preacher. He did admire certain individuals among them, but the practice itself was one he looked down on, as can be seen from an entry in his diary written in 1773: "I wish well to irregulars and itinerants, I am content that they should labour in that way who have not the talent to support the character of a parochial minister."[12] The tone is so typical of the man: he never doubted the rightness of his own ideas and never expected anyone else to. What he wanted was ordination into the Church of England and position as a parish priest. That he was able to achieve this ambition was, as he saw it, due to divine providence, but, more practically, it was due to his friendship with a young clergyman by the name of Thomas Haweis. Haweis had been curate of St Mary Magdalen in Oxford when Newton first met him in 1762, but was evicted not long after owing to his own 'enthusiasm'. Haweis had seen a series of letters Newton had written to a mutual friend of theirs in Yorkshire in which he described his life at sea, his slave-trading and his conversion. Haweis saw the Evangelical potential of this tale, and it was he who put the idea of publication into Newton's mind. In less than a month Newton had written the 35,000 words which became his *Authentic Narrative*. Haweis began circulating handwritten copies of these letters early in 1763, probably to test the market with a view to publication, but also to help the case for Newton's ordination. One recipient was the Earl of Dartmouth, a man of great wealth, power and patronage and one of the few noblemen of his time sympathetic to the Evangelical cause. Coincidentally, Lord Dartmouth had been at Westminster School at the same time as Cowper, and one of the livings in his gift, which was about to become vacant, was that of Olney in Buckinghamshire. His first thought was to offer it to Haweis, but in an act of selfless generosity Haweis asked for it to be given to Newton. Lord Dartmouth agreed and personally ensured Newton's acceptance into the Church. He was admitted to deacon's orders in the private chapel of the bishop of Lincoln at Buckden, near Huntingdon, on 29th April 1764 and finally ordained priest on 17th June.

Olney was markedly a working-class parish with Puritan and Nonconformist roots going back as far as the early years of the previous century. In 1639 its vicar had fallen foul of King Charles's ecclesiastical officials, and, being suspended from his duties, had left for New England taking some dozen like-minded local families with him. Huguenot lace-makers, fleeing from Catholic persecution in France, had arrived and settled in their place, bringing their trade with them, so that by the time Newton arrived, there were not only Baptist and Independent ministers already well established in the town, but there was also a strong Methodist element. With his background, Newton was the ideal incumbent, as Dartmouth probably realised, to reach out to such groups and to persuade them back into the fold of the Established Church. Such was Newton's success that by the middle of the following year the church building was not big enough to accommodate his congregation and a gallery had to be built.

His parishioners' admiration for their new curate grew even greater when his *Authentic Narrative* was published and went through five editions in its first six months. They found they now had a famous writer in their midst, but there were hardly any able to read the book for themselves. "The people stare at me," he wrote, "and well they may. I am indeed a wonder to many, a wonder to myself."[13] After his years in Liverpool, where he had associated with men like Wesley and Whitefield, there must have been times when

Olney seemed an intellectual backwater, so that the prospect of someone of Cowper's social standing and classical learning wanting to join him there must have been very exciting. He was certainly eager to help Cowper and Mrs Unwin, but he also admitted some years later that their arrival had provided him with

> two excellent friends whose company greatly enlivened my situation in a small country town where ... there was not a single person with whom I could converse with pleasure and profit.[14]

Some aspects of Olney have changed little since Cowper and Mrs Unwin first moved into the house known as Orchard Side. Its High Street is still its most distinctive feature, being not only long and straight but exceptionally wide, with a triangular market place on its left just before the road turns past the impressive fourteenth-century church of St Peter and St Paul, with its beautiful slender spire, and then crosses the bridge over the River Ouse. Orchard Side is a dour-looking place and with 21 windows in its flat, three-story frontage could still easily be taken for a factory rather than a house. In Cowper's day the imitation battlements on its roof added nothing to its beauty. He observed to William Unwin when they were leaving it in 1786 that his first impression was that it looked like a prison, yet he stayed there for 18 years. The house stands on the south side of the market place and so afforded Cowper a clear view of the three majestic elm trees which overshadowed the Town Hall, or Shiel Hall, as it was called then, and of a curious little hexagonal building with a pyramid-shaped roof which acted as the town jail. From his window he could keep a close eye on whatever happened to be going on in the town: goings-on which were to play a major part in the hundreds of letters he wrote from there.

Today Olney would still be a quiet market town were it not for the fact that its High Street is the main A509 carrying a non-stop flow of traffic between Milton Keynes and Wellingborough, but it is nevertheless a gracious town with a remarkable number of elegant houses. There is no evidence now of industry anywhere, yet writing of it in his book on Cowper in 1935, Gilbert Thomas described it as "a minor satellite of Northampton in the manufacture of shoes, and factory sirens disturb, at regular intervals, its ancient peace".[15]

Ancient peace? That was certainly not true of Cowper's day either. His letters paint a grim picture of the place. Writing to William Unwin he described it as "inhabited by the half-starved and ragged of the earth" (18th

November 1782). The chief industry then was lace-making. It is estimated that there were 1,200 lace-makers in the town, but it was an impoverished cottage industry under threat from imports and new machines. Cowper told Joseph Hill:

> I am an Eye-Witness of their Poverty, and do know that Hundreds in this little Town are upon the Point of Starving, and that the most unremitting industry is but rarely sufficient to keep them from it. (8th July 1780)

It was unremitting, and when daylight failed it had to be carried on by candlelight, yet the government was proposing a tax on candles, which prompted Cowper to wish that the taxman could "visit the miserable huts of our lace-makers of Olney, and see them working in the Winter months, by the light of a farthing candle, from four in the afternoon till midnight" (3rd July 1784) With most of the women working such hours, it is not surprising that that their children should run riot, but here Cowper did not seem to understand the situation; he blames the parents, not the conditions:

> Heathenish parents can only bring up Heathenish children; an assertion nowhere oftener or more clearly illustrated than here at Olney, where children, seven years of age, infest the streets every evening with curses and with songs to which it would be unseemly to give their proper Epithet. Such urchins as these could not be so diabolically accomplished unless by the connivance of their parents. It is well indeed, if in some instances, their parents be not themselves their instructors. (24th Septembr 1785)

The men were sometimes "so profane, so drunken, dissolute, and in every respect worthless" (18th November 1782). But given conditions such as these, the parish of Olney was just the place for an Evangelical like John Newton.

Always a man of prodigious energy, Newton nevertheless set himself a punishing workload: services every Sunday, morning and afternoon, with an informal lecture in the evening; sermons on two or three weekdays as well as meetings, some for children and young people and prayer groups for those "deeply serious about their faith". On top of this, as he said, "My afternoons are generally spent in visiting the people, 3 or 4 families a day."[16] Surprisingly, Cowper began to help him in all this and became, one might say, an unofficial lay curate. Newton tells us that

> ... he loved the poor, often visited them in their cottages, conversed with them ... sympathised with them, counselled them and comforted them in their distress.[17]

When we consider what we have already seen of Cowper's shyness, this does come as a great surprise, and we can see that it also surprised Newton, as he was well aware of his friend's disposition:

> While I remained at Olney we had meetings two or three times a week for prayer. These he constantly attended with me. For a time his natural constitutional unwillingness to be noticed in public kept him in silence. But it was not very long before the ardency of his love for the Saviour, and his desire of being useful to others broke through every restraint. He frequently felt a difficulty and trepidation in the attempt, but when he had once begun all difficulty vanished, and he seemed to speak, though with self-abasement and humiliation of spirit, yet with that freedom and fervency, as if he saw the Lord whom he addressed face to face.[18]

One of Newton's parishioners indeed observed that "of all men he ever heard pray, no one equalled Mr Cowper."[19] But these meetings were not only devoted to prayer. In a diary entry dated 27th January 1765 Newton wrote: "We spend an hour or more in prayer and singing, and part between six and seven."[20] Hymn singing was by no means a regular feature of Church of England services at that time, but out of Newton's meetings in that tiny Bedfordshire town came the *Olney Hymns*.

6

Olney Hymns

In 1765, shortly after leaving what he chose to call Dr Cotton's "Collegium Insanorum", Cowper subscribed to Christopher Smart's *A Translation of the Psalms of David*, an elegant volume which also included his 'Hymns and Spiritual Songs for the Fasts and Festivals of the Church of England', together with his more famous 'A Song to David'. It is interesting that Smart should have given precedence in the title to the Psalms and that it was the Psalms he expected to be sung, not his hymns. Indeed, John Walsh, the well-known music publisher, brought out a collection of forty-five separate melodies especially composed "by the most eminent Composers of Church Musick" to accompany Smart's versions. In contrast, although many of his 'Hymns and Spiritual Songs' are now accepted as among the finest religious verse written between Herbert and Hopkins, several are of such complexity that they could not possibly be sung by a congregation. His 'Easter Day', for example, is thirty-two verses long while the final line of each of the twenty elaborate stanzas of 'The King's Restoration' runs to a breathless twelve syllables. They are not hymns, they are poems. The words 'Hymns and Spiritual Songs', we need to remember, come from St Paul's Epistle to the Ephesians 5:18-19: " … be filled with the Spirit. Speaking to yourselves in psalms and hymns and spiritual songs, singing and making melody in your heart to the Lord." Paul's words clearly indicate that what he had in mind was not a church service, but an act of private worship.

What could and what could not be sung in church was a vexed question in the first half of the eighteenth century. Sternhold and Hopkins, whose version of the Psalter was first incorporated into the prayer book in 1562, holding sway with Church of England congregations for more than a century, had insisted in their Preface that psalms "are very mete to be used of all sortes of people privately for their solace & comfort: laying apart all ungodly Songs and Ballades, which tende only to the norishing of vyce, and corrupting of youth".[1] Luther, on the other hand, who had seen nothing wrong with singing German folk songs over a jug of ale, had not been afraid of the popular arts, and composed hymns which soon spread all over Europe until the priests complained that he was singing the people into Protestantism.[2] But then Calvin entered the debate, insisting that only the words of God himself were fit to be used in divine service, and this led to an exclusive concentration on the Psalms.

But as they were not sung in the original Hebrew, what rules were to govern translation? In his 'Essay Towards the Improvement of Church Psalmody' (1707) Isaac Watts made the initial breakthrough in Britain. He agreed with the conservatives that the Psalms should be read as God's word to us, and ought therefore to be translated as literally as possible, in prose in fact, because rhyme and metre are bound to change the meaning in some way. The significant word here however is *read*. When the Psalms are *read*, they are, Watts was arguing, God's word to us, but when we sing them to God our chief design is, or should be, to speak what is in our hearts, therefore using our own words. The argument is simple, but its implications were enormous. In his preface he claimed to be "the first who hath brought down the royal author into the common affairs of the Christian life, and led the psalmist of Israel into the Church of Christ".[3] It was an argument which would later allow Smart to go so far – perhaps too far for the times – as to take out all the Old Testament violence and anger and to put "Evangelical matter in their room". Watts too can surprise us. His version of the opening of Psalm 67 reads:

> Shine, mighty God! on Britain shine
> With beams of heav'nly grace.

A patriotic sentiment which neither God nor David could have had in mind.

Isaac Watts was an outstanding hymn-writer, and many he wrote are still in use today: 'When I survey the wond'rous cross' and, of course, 'Our God, our help in ages past'. If we look closely at the opening verse of this particular hymn we recognise what it is that makes his hymns so successful and what qualities a good hymn *needs* to have. The first thing we realise is that it is eminently singable:

> Our God, our help in ages past,
> Our hope for years to come,
> Our shelter from the stormy blast,
> And our eternal home.

The regularity of the common metre ensures that there will be no wobbles, elisions or uncertainties. There are no hard words to puzzle us and make us stumble. The language is plain, the syntax is straightforward and each line is a self-contained unit, so that it could be 'lined-out' if need be without any hiatus in the sense. There is a certain fervour to it, which would appeal to a congregation, but the sentiments it expresses are not over-personal; they have a universal appeal. It also has the merit of not being too long. But then Watts was recognised in his own day as a poet of sufficient stature to be included in Johnson's *Lives of the English Poets*.

Johnson's praise is perhaps rather surprising today: "As a poet, had he been only a poet, he would probably have stood high among the authors with whom he is now associated," but of the work for which he is still remembered Johnson is scathing:

> His devotional poetry is, like that of others, unsatisfactory. The paucity of its topicks enforces perpetual repetition, and the sanctity of the matter rejects the ornaments of figurative diction. It is sufficient for Watts to have done better than others what no man has done well.[4]

Repetition is inevitable, given Watts' didactic approach, and as he wrote over 600 hymns, but it was a floodgate he opened, and Charles Wesley, whose hymns are more emotional than doctrinal, is thought to have written more than 6,000.

Cowper himself had once been on the side of the conservatives. While admitting in an essay he contributed to *The Connoisseur* in 1756 that "The good old practice of psalm-singing is, indeed, wonderfully improved in many country churches since the days of Sternhold and Hopkins," he was clearly not in favour of some of the innovations:

> The tunes themselves have also been new-set to jiggish measures; and the sober drawl, which used to accompany the first two staves of the hundredth psalm with the *gloria patri*, is now split into as many quavers as an *Italian* air.[5]

There was, therefore, a long-established tradition of hymn-writing in existence by the time John Newton suggested that he and Cowper should collaborate on a new series of hymns intended for his parishioners in Olney. Watts had also written for his own congregation, but the Dissenters who gathered at his Mark Lane meetings were a relatively prosperous, sophisticated and homogeneous group who could be counted upon to understand and to respond to what he wrote for them; they were very different from the impoverished and ill-educated lace-makers of Olney.

When the *Olney Hymns* were first published in 1779, Newton explained in a preface that they had been divided into three books: the first contained hymns "formed upon select passages of the Scripture"; the second, "occasional hymns, suited to particular seasons, or suggested by particular events or objects"; the third being miscellaneous.[6] Among the particular events were some particular to Olney itself, for instance a fire which had swept through the town on the night of 22nd September 1777. With so many of the houses built of timber and thatch, and lit by candles, fires were a frequent hazard.

Cowper was later to describe one in a letter to Newton (17th November 1783) but on this occasion no one was hurt and there was a funny side to it, the only sufferer being one George Griggs. In the panic,

> He gave 18 guineas or nearly that sum to a woman whom in his hurry he mistook for his wife, but the supposed wife walked off with the money and he will probably never recover it.

Newton rarely saw the funny side to anything, and his hymn on the fire gave him the opportunity of warning his flock that it was in all probability sent by God as a punishment for their transgressions:

> For months and years of safety past,
> Ungrateful, we, alas! have been;
> Tho' patient long, he spoke at last,
> And bid the fire rebuke our sin. (13-16)

When he comes to describe the fire itself and the commotion it caused one might expect at least some show of vitality in the verse, but it is flat and lifeless:

> The shout of fire! a dreadful cry,
> Imprest each heart with deep dismay;
> While the fierce blaze and red'ning sky,
> Made midnight wear the face of day.

The throng and terror, who can speak?
The various sounds that fill'd the air!
The infant's wail, the mother's shriek,
The voice of blasphemy and pray'r!

But pray'r prevail'd, and sav'd the town;
The few, who lov'd the Saviour's name,
Were hear'd and mercy hasted down
To change the wind, and stop the flame.

Oh, may that night be ne'er forgot!
Lord, still encrease thy praying few!
Were OLNEY left without a Lot,
Ruin, like Sodom's, would ensue.
                                            (17-32)

Expressions such as "deep dismay" and "fierce blaze" are merely tokens, while "various sounds" is even less than that, and the nearest he comes to an image is "the face of day". Viewed as poetry, it is poor stuff, and it has to be acknowledged that there is plenty more of the same, but before it is condemned out of hand, we have to recognise that there may be a reason for writing such as this. In his preface, Newton makes a clear distinction between a poet and a versifier and suggests that hymns might be better coming from a versifier, particularly if they are intended for the use "of plain people". As he explains it,

> Perspicuity, simplicity and ease, should be chiefly attended to; and the imagery and colouring of poetry, if admitted at all, should be indulged very sparingly and with great judgment.[7]

He knew his own abilities, and he knew what he was doing:

> If the LORD whom I serve, has been pleas'd to favor me with that mediocrity of talent, which may qualify me for usefulness to the weak and the poor of his flock, without quite disgusting persons of superior discernment, I have reason to be satisfied.[8]

Newton has also been criticised for writing what have been called 'sermonettes'.[9] An early example of this is Hymn V, 'Lot in Sodom', which begins by narrating the story, follows with an explanation of it and concludes with lines giving it some local and contemporary relevance. Marshall and Todd accuse him of failing to "reconcile the instructive and the literary obligations of the hymn writer" and relying too heavily on "rhetorical question and pedantic pronouncement".[10] It could, however, be argued that by putting the ideas and words of a sermon into the mouths of his uneducated congregation he was encouraging them to look upon them as their own. It is as though they had thought of the examples and propositions for themselves. Far from failing, Newton is showing himself here to be the subtlest of educationalists. Particularly impressive, to my mind, is the hymn he wrote 'On the Eclipse of the Moon. July 30, 1776'. In the opening stanzas his description of the eclipse has a vivid immediacy:

> The moon in silver glory shone,
>   And not a cloud in sight;
> When suddenly a shade begun
>   To intercept her light.
>
> How fast across her orb it spread,
>   How fast her light withdrew!
> A circle, ting'd with languid red,
>   Was all appear'd in view.
>   (1-8)

And the parallels and precepts he draws from it follow with a pleasing naturalness. Nothing seems forced:

> How punctually eclipses move,
>   Obedient to thy will!
> Thus shall thy faithfulness and love,
>   Thy promises fulfill.
>
> Dark, like the moon without the sun,
>   I mourn thy absence, LORD!
> For light or comfort have I none,
>   But what thy beams afford.

> But lo! the hour draws near apace,
>   When changes shall be o'er;
> Then I shall see thee face to face,
>   And be eclips'd no more.
>   (21-32)

Newton composed more than 250 hymns, so the chances were that he would write one or two good ones at least, but he did more than that: he wrote some very great hymns which are still sung today and sung with as much enthusiasm as they have ever been. 'The Name of Jesus' appears in Book One which features hymns based "On Select Passages of Scripture", and it is the only hymn to take as its starting point a passage from the Song of Solomon. This is perhaps hardly surprising as the sensuality of the Song would no doubt have proved to be rather disturbing for his Evangelical congregation. Ostensibly, the chosen text is Song 1:3, "Because of the savour of thy good ointments thy name is as ointment poured forth, therefore do the virgins love thee." But this is no more than hinted at in the hymn we know so well:

> How sweet the name of Jesus sounds
>   In a believer's ear?
> It sooths his sorrows, heals his wounds
>   And drives away his fear.
>
> It makes the wounded spirit whole,
>   And calms the troubled breast;
> ' Tis Manna to the hungry soul,
>   And to the weary rest.
>   (1-8)

Here we do truly encounter "Perspicuity, simplicity and ease", and the words would strike a knowing chord with the "poor of his flock" who would have been only too familiar with sorrows, wounds, fear, despair, troubles, hunger and weariness. It is a hymn fraught with emotion, yet is nowhere sentimental or maudlin, even in its closing verse:

> 'Till then I would thy love proclaim
>   With ev'ry fleeting breath;
> And may the music of thy name
>   Refresh my soul in death.
>   (25-8)

Only a few pages later there is the jubilant 'Glorious things of thee are spoken' with its memorable and rousing finale:

> Fading is the worldling's pleasure,
> All his boasted pomp and show;
> Solid joys and lasting treasure
> None but Zion's children know.
> (37-40)

But, of course, more famous than either of these, and possibly the only hymn ever to have reached the top of the charts, backed as it was by the moody skirl of the pipes, is 'Amazing Grace'.

Newton's hymns, as we have seen, were directed to "the poor of his flock"; they were also, he said, "the fruit and expression of my own experience",[11] and when his parishioners were first shown the words of 'Amazing Grace' they would instantly have identified the *dangers* and *toils* with the hazards and adventures of Newton's own life. His *Authentic Narrative* had been published in 1764 and they were proud of their curate's fame. But while the success of the hymn clearly owes something to the life story of its author, it is not so specific that when sung, the singer cannot share in the experience and relate to the sentiments. Its theme is a simple one: the importance of grace:

> Amazing Grace! (how sweet the sound)
>   That sav'd a wretch like me!
> I once was lost, but now am found,
>   Was blind, but now I see.
>
> 'Twas grace that taught my heart to fear,
>   And grace my fears reliev'd;
> How precious did that grace appear,
>   The hour I first believ'd!
>
> Thro' many dangers, toils and snares,
>   I have already come;
> 'Tis grace has brought me safe thus far,
>   And grace will lead me home.

The Lord has promis'd good to me,
    His world my hope secures;
He will my shield and portion be,
    As long as life endures.

Yes, when this flesh and heart shall fail,
    And mortal life shall cease,
I shall possess within the vail,
    A life of joy and peace.

The earth shall soon dissolve like snow,
    The sun forbear to shine;
But God who call'd me here below,
    Will be for ever mine.

The simplicity here – there are fewer than twenty words with more than one syllable – can only be described as stately, and we notice how Newton has skilfully blended biblical reference with personal testimony: in lines 3 and 4 we find ourselves reminded of the Prodigal Son and also of the words of the man cured of blindness in John 9:25.

Converts sometimes exaggerate the sinfulness of their earlier lives in order to make their conversion seem the more remarkable, but *wretch* hardly seems adequate to describe the blasphemous atheist and insubordinate, libertine slave-trader he had been. It astounded and amazed Newton himself, and he was convinced – with good reason – that he had been personally favoured by divine providence.

One could never accuse Newton of lacking in self-assurance. He knew his strengths and his weaknesses. He knew that he was not a poet, but that William Cowper was.

In 1771 they had agreed that the *Olney Hymns* would be a collaboration between them both equally, but in 1773, when Cowper had written only 67 hymns, he suffered what Newton tactfully called an "affecting indisposition" and wrote no more. Newton was so disheartened by this that his first reaction was to abandon the project altogether, but he was persuaded to go on with it alone and in 1779 he published the collection "as a monument, to perpetuate the remembrance of an intimate and endeared friendship".[12]

If, as Newton says, and we have no reason to doubt his word, Cowper's hymn-writing came to an end because of an "indisposition", we might expect to find some evidence of it in those hymns which we do have. There are indeed lines which are indicative of sadness and depression, but we cannot draw any firm conclusions from this. We do not know in what order the hymns were written and it is always dangerous to infer biographical fact from an author's words.

Newton himself has been blamed for Cowper's breakdown. Lady Hesketh was in no doubt about it. Writing to William Hayley in 1801 she insisted that Newton's

> … unguarded proposal of composing Hymns from ev'ry Text of Scripture they cou'd Collect, did infinite injury to our friend! certain it is that he was well and in health when this idea was started. That he had been well for several years but he pursued the proposed Task with such eagerness and avidity that it heated his brain, Sunk his spirits and brought on that dreadful depression, which rendered him Miserable during the space of 7 years! – only imagine a man of his Genius dwelling incessantly on this one Subject! walking for Hours by himself in that great rambling Church at Olney, composing these Hymns! he has told me that the idea never quitted him night or day, but kept him in a *constant fever*; and add to that when he left the Church, it was to attend their prayer meetings, and all the enthusiastic conversation which these meetings were sure to occasion.[13]

It is hard not to believe that there may be an element of truth in what she says, but we need to bear in mind how violently opposed she was to the Evangelical movement – an opposition which would not have been helped in any way by the barrage of letters she received from Cowper during the summer months of 1765 when he first arrived in Huntingdon. Indeed, they were hardly letters; they were more in the nature of religious tracts:

> My dear cousin, a firm persuasion of the super-intendence of Providence over all our concerns is absolutely necessary to our happiness. Without it we cannot be said to believe in the Scripture, or practice any thing like resignation to his will. If I am convinced that no affliction can befall me without the permission of God, I am convinced likewise that he sees and knows that I am afflicted; believing this, I must, in the same degree, believe that if I pray to him for deliverance, he hears me. (4th September 1765)

By October, it would seem that she had read enough of this, and we find Cowper gently rebuking her for her "long silence". The correspondence was soon to come to a complete stop, and there was no further contact between them for almost 20 years. His sad observation regarding "the silence of many with regard to me" (6th March 1766) suggests that Lady Hesketh was not the only one his enthusiasm had alienated.

But he was not easily discouraged, and another of his cousins, Martin Madan's sister Maria, was to receive close on 3,000 words over two days in April on the subject of the afterlife and whether or not we shall recognise each other there.

It is excessive, but the reasoning shows that Cowper was not mentally disturbed. His emotional disturbance is, however, beyond doubt. He was still suffering from that excitement of the new convert which had led Dr Cotton to delay his release from St Albans. Surprisingly, whenever he considered his own situation, it was the sense of a great peace that he was at pains to emphasise: "At length, the storm being passed, a quiet and peaceful serenity of soul succeeded" (4th April 1776). It is this peace and serenity of soul which he describes so very feelingly in his 'Song of Mercy and Judgement', a poem written shortly after the death of his brother in 1770, and before any work on the *Olney Hymns* had begun.

The poem opens with an account of the suffering and despair he had once felt, and for three stanzas its sentiment and vocabulary could not be more conventional: "Shades of Night" and "Waves of deep Affliction". But then he gives us details of his confinement in St Albans such as we could never have expected from an eighteenth-century poet. He could not bring himself to touch food, he tells us, and so began to waste away until he was forcibly fed. He gibbered madly, had to be physically restrained for his own safety and was put on what we would now call suicide watch:

> Food I loath'd nor ever tasted
>   But by Violence constrain'd,
> Strength decay'd and Body wasted,
>   Spoke the Terrors I sustain'd.
> Sweet the Sound of Grace Divine,
> Sweet the grace which made me thine.

> Bound and watch'd lest Life abhorring
>> I should my own Death procure,
> For to me the Pit of Roaring
>> Seem'd more easy to endure.
> Grace Divine how sweet the Sound,
> Sweet the grace which I have found.
>
>   (19-30)

The closing two lines of each stanza are repeated as a refrain and varied in this way throughout the poem, thus adding to the remarkable discipline with which this frank confession is recalled. It is emotion – I think one can risk saying – recollected in tranquillity, and in the plainest of language.

He was reduced, he continues, "to moping Madness" and saw and heard the "Flames of Hell and Screams of Woe", as he was to do so often in the nightmares of his later life. But "the Word of Healing" saved him. It would have been difficult to avoid conventionalisms here, but Cowper skilfully manages to do so by having Christ speak to him directly:

> I, he said, have seen thee grieving,
>> Lov'd thee as I pass'd thee by,
> Be not faithless but Believing,
>> Look, and Live, and never Die.
> Sweet the Sound of Grace Divine,
> Sweet the grace which makes thee mine.
>
>   (55-60)

The closing stanza announces that, like a true Evangelical, he will tell his story for the sake of others, as he already had done in his memoir and was about to do in his hymns:

> Since that Hour in Hope of Glory,
>> With thy Follow'rs I am found,
> And relate the wondrous Story
>> To thy list'ning Saints around.
> Sweet the Sound of Grace Divine,
> Sweet the grace which makes me thine.
>
>   (73-8)

It is surprising that this poem is not to be found in every anthology of eighteenth-century poetry, but that it was not published in his own lifetime is not. Confessional poetry such as this – with the single exception of Christopher Smart's 'Hymn to the Supreme Being' – would have to wait until the middle of the twentieth century.

At the end of *Adelphi*, the narrative of his brother's conversion which Cowper added to the memoir he had written in Huntingdon in 1766, he wrote:

> I have added two Hymns, which I compos'd at *St. Albans*, not for the composition, but because they are specimens of my first Christian thoughts, being written very shortly after my first conversion, and I am glad to present them, because I cannot read them over now, without feeling *that joy of heart*, which the Lord gave me, *fresh'ning as it were*, upon my mind, at the perusal of them.[14]

The first of these two hymns, 'The Happy Change' is based on Revelation 21:5, "Behold I make all things new", and develops the traditional association of Sun and Son. Man's soul is a "barren soil" and a "dreary province" before conversion, but then the heart sends forth "the sweet smell of grace" and where Satan held his "dark domain" there is now a "new Empire" and a "heav'nly reign". And it ends very traditionally, saying that whereas the sun has "cheer'd the nations" from the beginning of time, only the light of Jesus can shine into our hearts.

According to Samuel Greatheed, who preached Cowper's funeral sermon, the second hymn, 'Retirement', was written when he first moved to Huntingdon, leaving the strife and tumult of the world for "the calm retreat and silent shade". It has a certain quiet charm to it, but rather than joy, the overall tone of both these hymns might better be described as contentment.

Without question, both meet the basic requirements which the poet Norman Nicholson, in his book on Cowper, laid down for a successful hymn:

> they keep strictly to their chosen metre and stanza form; the sense corresponds closely to the shape of the lines; the language is simple; they are direct in thought, broad in imagery, and unified in theme.[15]

But while they manage all this, they present us with no challenge, offer us no new insight or delight, and do not ask us to think, the attributes and qualities one would expect of a poem. Of course it is often argued that hymns are not poems, but it is surely not necessary for them to be quite so bland, so innocuous, and so easily forgotten. We are entitled to expect more than this, and more there certainly was in the verses Cowper wrote in 1767 when Mrs Unwin fell seriously ill.

He wrote to his aunt, Judith Madan, that "Her Disorder is a Nervous Atrophy attended with violent Spasms of the Chest and Throat." They had gone to consult Dr Cotton, but although she was probably suffering from nothing more than panic attacks, possibly brought on by the death of her husband and the emotional disturbance of the move to Olney, he had held out little hope that any medicine could help her. Cowper was in despair. "She is the chief Blessing I have met with in my Journey since the Lord was pleased to call me," he told his aunt. Yet, if God demanded this sacrifice of him, he was determined to accept it. At the end of the letter he wrote of the verses he was enclosing:

> I began to compose them Yesterday Morning before
> Daybreak, but fell asleep at the End of the first two Lines,
> when I awaked again the third and fourth were whisper'd to
> my Heart in a way which I have often experienced. (10th
> December 1767)

Which other poems he had in mind we cannot tell, but the verses he sent to Mrs Madan were 'Oh for a closer walk with God':

> Oh! for a closer walk with God,
> A calm and heav'nly frame;
> A light to shine upon the road
> That leads me to the Lamb!
> (1-4)

In the very first line there is something to challenge us: something rather unexpected about that word 'walk'. It gives us pause, until we recognise it as a conscious reminder of two verses from Genesis: 3:8, where Adam and Eve hear God walking in the garden, but hide from him, aware now that they have sinned; and 5:24, the text which heads the hymn and recalls the death of Enoch. Sin and death. In the hands of most hymn-writers, these two words would lend themselves readily to the direst of warnings and be couched in terms of a sermon. But Cowper's hymn is not a sermon. He does not preach. Unlike Watts, Wesley and Newton, he never climbed the steps into a pulpit. His place was among the congregation, sitting in a pew, and this is one of the factors which make his hymns so different from those of his predecessors. They are more personal and introspective. Here he recalls the joy and peace he experienced after his conversion, but recognises that such feelings do not last. Their first innocence fades. As he examines his own emotions he acknowledges that this is certainly so in his case. What he feels now is an "aching void":

> What peaceful hours I once enjoy'd!
>> How sweet their mem'ry still!
> But they have left an aching void,
>> The world can never fill.
>> (9-12)

He is aware that he has sinned, and that by loving worldly things – in this case, Mrs Unwin, it would seem – he has allowed idols to enter into his life. He prays for forgiveness and that any such idol should be torn from him, perhaps even his beloved companion. We may be inclined to shudder at such extremes, but we have to admire the quiet skill with which the analysis has been conducted and with which he brings the hymn to such a satisfying close by echoing, while deftly varying, the opening stanza:

> So shall my walk be close with God,
>> Calm and serene my frame;
> So purer light shall mark the road
>> That leads me to the Lamb.
>> (21-4)

Between them, Cowper and Newton wrote close on 350 hymns, a seemingly small output compared with Charles Wesley, yet quite enough to make us wonder whether all of them were sung. This is one of the many questions we would like answered about the hymn-singing at Olney. Even at the rate of a new hymn every week – itself a dizzying prospect for any congregation – there would have been enough to last them seven years. And if, as seems likely, many of the congregation were semi-literate at best, how did they 'learn' the words? Were they 'lined-out' to them, as had long been the fashion with psalms in the Church of England? It is difficult to imagine how enough copies could have been written out, by hand, and so frequently, even for those who were able to read.

But if the hymns were 'lined-out', that is sung echo-like by the congregation, one line at a time, after having first been sung to them, then Newton's 'The Lord will provide', which runs to 64 lines, would surely have ruled itself out on the grounds of length alone, while it would have been asking rather a lot of the lace-makers of Olney to cope with the convoluted syntax and bizarre vocabulary of Cowper's 'Self-Acquaintance':

> While unbelief withstands thy grace,
>> And puts the mercy by;
> Presumption, with a brow of brass,
>> Says, "Give me, or I die."
>> (13-16)

Some of their hymns we can be quite sure were sung as they were composed, as Newton explained in his preface, for particular occasions, such as 'On the Death of a Minister' (Hymn 31), and yet that is couched in such general terms that it could have been sung at the death of any minister. Far more specific. however, is Hymn 26, Cowper's 'On Opening a Place for Social Prayer', and this can be dated with some confidence. Newton's mission to Olney had met with such success that he was soon holding prayer meetings and Bible study groups on Tuesday and Sunday evenings. At first they were held in Molly Mole's cottage, but as the number joining in grew, they moved into the Great House, owned by Lord Dartmouth. Eventually, as many as 130 people were attending these gatherings, and permission was given to move into what was called the 'Great Room'. This was in April 1769.

It is a balanced and skilfully organised hymn, with contrasting concepts of space: interior/exterior, near/far, earth/heaven. And the couplet which opens stanza 5,

> Behold! at thy commanding word
> We stretch the curtain and the cord,

sounds so domestic that we could be led to believe it was a description of the very room in Olney they had moved into, though the words prove to be a direct quotation from Isaiah 54:2 ("Enlarge the place of thy tent, and let them stretch forth the curtains of thy habitation, spare not, lengthen thy cords and strengthen thy stakes") and show us the depth of Cowper's knowledge of the Bible, and his ability to find the perfect text for the occasion. And it is not only a biblical source which is quoted. "And bring all heaven before our eyes" (line 16) echoes a line from Milton's 'Il Penseroso' (l. 166)

Literary mixtures of this kind are not uncommon and present no problem, but there is also some apparent confusion in the theology. The brief reference to "thy chosen few" seems to reflect a standard Calvinistic view of the elect, but the overall tenor of this hymn is more in line with that of the Dissenters. In keeping with the opening of the Great Room it says that God is not confined to any one space, but is wherever people meet together. There is biblical precedent for this: "Wherever two or three are gathered together" (Matthew 18:20), but it had nevertheless been an argument which had led to the Quakers' denial of the need for 'Steeple-houses'. Stanza 2 not only asserts the belief that Christ is within each of us, but that people take him home with them after the meetings:

> For thou within no walls confin'd,
> Inhabitest the humble mind;
> Such ever bring thee, where they come,
> And going, take thee to their home.
>
> (5-8)

Few followers of the established Church of England would have liked the sound of that.

As John Newton explained, the hymns in the first book of *Olney Hymns* were written for the Bible study groups and were meant to teach. They are overtly didactic, frequently opposing such beliefs as that good works could lead to salvation:

> Works of man, when made his plea,
> Never shall accepted be;
> Fruits of pride (vain-glorious worm)
> Are the best he can perform.
>
> (Hymn 64, 5-8)

The emphasis – and a totally Evangelical one – is on the need for grace:

> Banish ev'ry vain pretence
> Built on human excellence;
> Perish ev'ry thing in man,
> But the grace that never can.
>
> (21-4)

These are among the hymns vilified by that most bigoted of Cowper's early biographers, Hugh l'Anson Fausset: "Evangelicalism suspected and hated the aesthetic instinct as it did the material world. There could be no truce between poetry and such warped sectarianism."[16] But even in the straightforward exposition of the parables – 'The Sower' (hymn 16) for example – there are moments when the material world is featured and celebrated in a very pleasing, if not starling manner:

> The watchful birds the spoil divide
>   And pick up all the grain.
>   (15-16)

"Watchful" is by no means one of those automatic eighteenth-century epithets; it has been *chosen,* and chosen because it is the right word.

Fausset's jaundiced eye blinded him to any such qualities. All he saw were hymns "strewed with all the barbarous concomitants of sacrificial suffering judiciously inflicted by the God of Evangelicalism for the purpose of redemption".[17]

In fact, even a hymn such as 'Ephraim Repenting', where God does hand down 'chastisement', ends with forgiveness and pity:

> My sharp rebuke has laid him low,
>   He seeks my face again;
> My pity kindles at his woe,
>   He shall not seek in vain.
>   (21-4)

It is not the exclusion of Calvinism we meet, but a Saviour whose love reaches out to all mankind.

Cowper's finest hymns are those where the personal element is strongest, but another of those questions we will never have answered is how the lace-makers who left their dingy, thatched cottages in the alleys of Silver End to sing in the Great House responded to the personal ecstasies and anxieties of the man they knew and addressed as 'Sir Cowper'.

And another question we have to face, though not perhaps to answer, is whether something can be both a hymn and a poem at the same time.

Cowper's most famous hymn is the one beginning 'God moves in a mysterious way', but it is not one whose meaning can be taken in at one reading, and certainly not at one hearing. Indeed, when we come to the end, the final stanza sends us back to reconsider the whole:

> Blind unbelief is sure to err,
> > And scan his work in vain;
> God is his own interpreter,
> > And he will make it plain.
> > > (21-4)

This is a rejection of the proposition held by the physico/theologians such as Ray and Derham that God can be seen and understood in and through nature. The only true revelation we have, this hymn insists, is through the Word, and a footnote refers us to John 13:7: "Jesus answered and said unto him, what I do thou knowest not now, but thou shalt know hereafter." Faith requires of us that Keatsian "negative capability". God moves in a mysterious way and we cannot expect definitive answers. The verb "moves" does not only imply motion here so much as intention as when a chess player considers his 'moves'.

The opening two stanzas present us with an instant problem:

> God moves in a mysterious way,
> > His wonders to perform;
> He plants his footsteps in the sea,
> > And rides upon the storm.

> Deep in unfathomable mines
> > Of never-failing skill;
> He treasures up his bright designs,
> > And works his sovereign will.

The "storm" and the "unfathomable mines" seem to suggest Neptune and Vulcan more than the God of the New Testament, and they are by no means comfortable images. But the hymn's title is 'Love Shining out of Darkness'. There are images of threatening clouds and frowns, but the clouds are "big with mercy" and the frown hides a "smiling face". Yet, while it is meant as a poem of hope, the images of threat seem the more powerful. Both sides of the problem are present here. Samuel Greatheed tells us that Cowper wrote the hymn in 1773 when he felt the imminent threat of another breakdown: " … and during a solitary walk in the fields he composed a hymn, which is so appropriate to our subject, and so expressive of the faith and hope which he retained so long as he possessed himself."[18]

It is a faith which is expressed in that fine image:

> The bud may have a bitter taste
>   But sweet will be the flow'r.
>   (19-20)

It is a poem which can be seen as posing the question: "Why me?" It is a question which we will all continue to ask, but one which the poem is telling us we can never expect to have answered; not in this world at least, and in this respect its universal appeal is beyond question.

Cowper was honest with himself. He knew that the joys of the newly converted are transitory, and it is in his voicing of the ensuing struggles and uncertainties that he reveals his strength as a religious poet.

By the standard of Newton's recommendation of "Perspicuity, simplicity and ease", Cowper's 'The Contrite Heart' has to be judged a failure as a hymn, but it is an outstanding poem:

> The LORD will happiness divine
>   On contrite hearts bestow:
> Then tell me, gracious God, is mine
>   A contrite heart, or no?
>
> I hear, but seem to hear in vain,
>   Insensible as steel;
> If ought is felt, 'tis only pain,
>   To find I cannot feel.
>
> I sometimes think myself inclin'd
>   To love thee, if I could;
> But often feel another mind,
>   Averse to all that's good.
>
> My best desires are faint and few,
>   I fain would strive for more;
> But when I cry, "My strength renew,"
>   Seem weaker than before.
>
> Thy saints are comforted I know
>   And love thy house of pray'r;
> I therefore go where others go,
>   But find no comfort there.

> O make this heart rejoice, or ache;
>   Decide this doubt for me;
> And if it be not broken, break,
>   And heal it, if it be.

Olney, having once been described as a place "inhabited by the half-starved and ragged of the earth", it is highly unlikely that words such as "averse" were part of their everyday vocabulary, and if the practice of lining-out was used, the penultimate line would, by itself, be meaningless. The probability is that it was never sung.

The opening statement made in the first two lines is clear and simple, but what follows is not only complex, it is also intensely personal. Hymns which use the generalised 'I', such as 'When I survey the wond'rous cross', present a congregation with no problem; it is a statement and an emotion with which they can all identify, but Cowper's 'I' is not only personal, it is individual. We know that there were times when he himself found little comfort in the Church, but it is hardly reasonable to attribute such a feeling to an entire congregation and expect them to join in singing:

> Thy saints are comforted I know
>   And love thy house of pray'r;
> I therefore go where others go,
>   But find no comfort there.

And how would their curate have reacted to such a protest?

Cowper's lines are giving voice to an intensely personal spiritual struggle. The dilemma facing him was: "is mine / A contrite heart, or no?" He hears the word of God, but seems unable to "feel" it. He is "inclin'd" to love Him, but then feels inside himself "another mind, / Averse to all that's good".

It is a spiritual struggle not unlike those we encounter in the poems of George Herbert, the only poet Cowper seems to have valued. In his memoir he wrote:

> This was the only author I had any delight in reading. I poured over him, all day long; and though I found not in them what I might have found, a cure for my malady, yet it never seemed so much alleviated as while I was reading him.[19]

And in a letter to William Unwin dated 14th November 1781, he claims, "I have not read an English poet these thirteen years, and but one these twenty years." Was that one poet George Herbert? It seems so. The easy conversational tone he adopts when speaking to God in ll. 3-4 is very Herbertian, recalling such opening gambits of his as "My God, I heard this day … "

The initial question the poem posed had been straightforward, but after many shifts of thought it concludes by leaving the answer ultimately to God, and Cowper does so in lines of an almost metaphysical complexity evident even in his syntax. Herbert had ended his poem 'Affliction I' with the line, "Let me not love thee, if I love thee not," and we are surely reminded of this when Cowper's poem ends:

> And if it be not broken, break,
>   And heal it, if it be.

One can only conclude that if 'The Contrite Heart' fails as a hymn, it fails only because it is such a fine poem and one which is not shamed by being put alongside the work of George Herbert.

There are hymns which it is difficult, even for confirmed believers to relate to today: most notoriously 'Praise for the Fountain Opened' which begins:

> There is a fountain fill'd with blood,
>   Drawn from EMANUEL'S veins;
> And sinners, plung'd beneath that flood,
>   Loose all their guilty stains.

There is no mention of blood in the text from Zechariah which this hymn purports to be expounding. Cowper has added "The Blood of the lamb" from the Book of Revelation. It seems grotesque today, but we have to look beyond the literal and see it as an image, a symbol of redemption. In this it has a long tradition, including Watts' "His dying Crimson like a Robe" and the baroque extravagances of Richard Crashaw.

Cowper's hymns have come in for some harsh comments. Added to Fausset's dismissal of them as "morbidly preoccupied with sin and luxuriat[ing] in self-abasement",[20] we have Lord David Cecil's patronising judgement that Cowper "dutifully carried out his part of the bleak task".[21] One wonders whether either critic had actually read them.

Cowper himself took great care and trouble in the writing of them. They were his apprenticeship as a poet and he was giving of his best, as can be seen from one of the late hymns, 'Grace and Providence' which concludes:

> Forgive the song that falls so low
> Beneath the gratitude I owe!
> It means thy praise, however poor,
> An angel's song can do no more.

7

Despair

A wretch like me

The strain of over zealous piety which had been such a feature of Cowper's letters to his aunt and to his cousin Harriot when he first left Dr Cotton's care eventually began to fade into that quiet contentment described in his letter to Maria Cowper of 20th October 1766. But zeal was never far below the surface and it came rising up again when his brother fell ill. John Cowper was six years younger than William and of a very different disposition. Educated at Felsted School rather than Westminster, he went up to Corpus Christi, Cambridge, where he served as both Praelector and Bursar. He was ordained in 1765 and appointed rector of Foxton, a village six miles south of Cambridge. William was very fond of him and wrote in *The Task*:

> I had a brother once, –
> Peace to the mem'ry of a man of worth,
> A man of letters and of manners too,
> Of manners sweet as virtue always wears,
> When gay good-nature dresses her in smiles.
> He graced a college in which order yet
> Was sacred, and was honor'd, lov'd and wept
> By more than one, themselves conspicuous there.
> (II.780-7)

But John was so far from sharing his brother's Evangelical views that they occasioned something of a rift between them, and on his visits to Olney he was never invited to preach from Newton's pulpit or even to take an active part in family prayers. And yet in a letter he wrote to his cousin a few months after John's death we find Cowper saying: "He told me that from the time when he was first ordained, he began to be dissatisfied with his Religious Opinions" (7th June 1770). Consistency was never one of Cowper's strong points, and here it is simply a different impression that he wishes to make.

95

John first became ill in 1769 and William hurried to Cambridge to care for him. He recovered quite quickly, but six months later, in February 1770, he suffered a relapse. Cowper described it in *Adelphi* as "an asthma and dropsy, supposed to be the effect of an imposthume [an abscess] in his liver".[1] It was clear that he was not going to recover this time. "His agony was dreadful," Cowper wrote, but his chief concern was his brother's spiritual state.

The distress, both physical and spiritual which John Cowper experienced is recounted in *Adelphi*, the sequel which William added to his own memoir, and which was published separately by John Newton in 1802. It too is a "conversion narrative" and therefore features instances and observations typical of the genre. When Cowper first visited his brother, he reported that, "His couch was strewn with volumes of plays", a sure sign in Evangelical discourse of a dissolute life, which that word "strewn" only serves to emphasise. On his second visit, a degree of flippancy is evident: " … nor could I find by his conversation that he had one serious thought."[2] This clashes somewhat with his observation a few paragraphs earlier:

> His outward conduct … was perfectly decent and unblameable. There was nothing vicious in any part of his practice, but being of a studious, thoughtful turn, he placed his chief delight in the acquisition of learning.[3]

Yet another inconsistency, and it soon becomes clear that there is a dual purpose behind the writing of *Adelphi*.

The published version is based on a transcript of the letters Cowper wrote to Newton and Mrs Unwin during the six weeks he was actually in Cambridge caring for his brother. When he first arrived, on 16th February, he was clearly shocked by John's physical condition. His hands and feet were swelling from the dropsy and he was suffering violent fits of asthma which Cowper described vividly:

> His agony was dreadful. Having never seen any person afflicted in the same way, I could not help feeling that that he would be suffocated, nor was the physician without fear of the same kind.[4]

Equally fearful to Cowper was the fate of his brother's soul. Writing to Mrs Unwin the week after he arrived (26th February 1770) he told her:

> In the mean while I am toss'd upon the Waves of Hope and
> Fear, I see my brother asleep upon the very Brink of Ruin,
> and the only Hand that can pluck him thence is not yet
> stretch'd out for his Deliverance.

But then, on 11th March, his wish came true; the great event took place and
he wrote ecstatically to Newton:

> Oh praise the Lord with me, and let us exalt his name
> together. My lamb that was lost is found, my child that was
> dead is alive again – the Lord has done it, he has given me the
> desire of my heart, my brother is born of God.

The words to notice here are "he has given me the desire of my heart." The
response is entirely self-centred, and from this point onwards his account in
the letters and in *Adelphi* is open to question. After the "light was darted into
his soul,"[5] Cowper left him for an hour "because I was afraid lest he should
fatigue himself by too much talking". But when he returns there is no sign of
fatigue, and John is recorded as delivering the first of what amount to several
short sermons, which are precise, eloquent and carefully structured. Writing
to Newton on 17th March, Cowper tells him that John is "so weak, he can
hardly move a limb, and for the most part rather delirious. His difficulty of
breathing returns, and the swelling in his legs is much as it was." Yet, for all
that, we are asked to believe that he asked:

> Alas! What must have become of me if I had died this day
> se'ennight? What should I have had to plead? My own
> righteousness? That would have been of great service to me to
> be sure. Well – Whither then? Why to the mercy of God.[6]

It is remarkable too how the mini-sermons he now delivers follow the
Evangelical line so closely. Good works are of no account, nor are the
teachings of the Church Fathers:

> There is but one key to the New Testament. I cannot describe
> to you, nor shall ever be able to describe what I felt in the
> moment when it was given to me.[7]

That a dying asthmatic should be capable of such sustained eloquence is
unlikely, and equally unlikely is Cowper's ability to recall it all, word for

word, and write it down for his friends in Olney. What makes the account even more suspect is a letter he wrote to William Unwin after he had returned to Olney. He tells him that John's "friends at College knew nothing of the Matter [his conversion]. He never spoke of these things but to myself, nor to me when others were within Hearing" (31st March 1770).

There was, therefore, no evidence for this conversion other than Cowper's own word. No one challenged it, of course, as it was exactly the sort of conversion the Evangelicals rejoiced in. John Newton was certainly delighted:

> When we shall meet on Tuesday evening I propose to impart
> it to the people in a body by reading your letter. My heart
> jumps at representing to myself how they will look, how they
> will feel, how they will pray and give thanks, when they hear
> what God has wrought.[8]

Fausset describes Newton here as writing "with a glee that strikes the modern mind as almost indecent".

Why would Cowper enact such a charade? If we look at the opening sentence of *Adelphi*, his state of mind and his motive are quite evident:

> As soon as it had pleased God, after a long and sharp season
> of conviction, to visit me with the consolations of his Grace,
> it became one of my chief concerns that my relations might
> be partakers of the same mercy."[9]

It is what he passionately *wanted* to happen, and, as is not uncommon with psychotics, he confused wishes with reality and managed to convince himself and others that it had really happened.

Once it was all over, his brother's death was not something which seems to have caused Cowper further grief. His letters to Joseph Hill, his financial adviser, are concerned with what he would inherit. He was planning to take out an annuity and is soon regretting that he had not been left more. Later in the year he is asking Hill to settle a "tedious affair" with a tailor to whom he owes over £40 and who is expecting not only payment but interest on it. He confesses (17th November 1770) that he is "likewise indebted for a Suit or two to Thomas Williams Taylor in Arundel Street". When all this had been settled he was glad to learn that he had enough left over for Hill to buy him "a dozen and a half red and white, small pattern handkerchiefs at half a crown apiece, and a yard and a half narrow striped Muslin for Gentlemen's

Ruffles" (12th January 1771). This is the people of Olney's 'Sir Cowper', dapper as ever, living elegantly and rather beyond his means. But there was a shadow of troubles about to come. In a letter he wrote in June 1772 to his aunt, Mrs Madan, about his "spiritual trials", he told her:

> I weary myself with ineffectual struggles against His will, and then sink into an idle despondence equally unbecoming a soldier of Christ Jesus. A seaman terrified at a storm who creeps down into the hold, when he should be busy amongst the tackling aloft, is just my picture.

The image of a sailor in peril was one he often used, and the words "idle despondence" are reminiscent of his mood immediately before the crisis of 1763.

His cousin Harriot was in no doubt what was the cause. As we have seen, she put the blame on Newton, and while her aversion to all things Evangelical probably conditioned and coloured her view, there may be some element of truth in it. But it is highly likely that it was local gossip, and not entirely his spiritual trials, which was at the root of what was soon to be his most serious breakdown.

People who attract attention – and Cowper would certainly have done so in Olney – are inevitably liable to attract gossip, which turned unpleasant when Mrs Unwin's daughter Susanna left home to marry the Rev. Matthew Powley in Huddersfield. Talk of 'impropriety' had been one of the factors which had led to the move from Huntingdon. Now, with Susanna no longer living with them, the relationship would have been seen as verging on the scandalous. We have to realise, though, that from the moment they had met in Huntingdon, William Unwin, a singularly devout young man, always had the greatest respect and admiration for Cowper, and he saw nothing untoward in his mother's position. This alone should have been enough to dispel suspicion. But once again, there was gossip, and the obvious solution was for Cowper and Mary Unwin to marry. They were devoted to each other and there was no great difference in their ages: Mary was 48 and William 41. There should have been no problem.

There was a problem, however, and it was Cowper's relationship with women. He always enjoyed close relationships with them. It could be said that he needed close relationships with women. But not too close. What he did not want was an intimate, sexual relationship. It is interesting that when he translated Horace's Ode II.ix, he omitted the slightly erotic last stanza, thus leaving it as a simple lyric in praise of winter. Biographers have not been slow to advance theories to 'explain' this – latent homosexuality or a physical deformity. The first is improbable; the second, as I have already argued, is impossible.

The relationship which he had enjoyed with Mrs Unwin for the previous eight years was exactly what he wanted: it was maternal. Not long after moving in with the family in Huntingdon he had written of her, "I could almost fancy my own Mother restored to Life again" (11th March 1766). And, "Mrs Unwin has an almost maternal affection for me, and I have something very like a filial one for her, and her son and I are brothers" (20th October 1766). In his book *Loss and Symbolic Repair*, Andrew Brink asserts that the death of Cowper's mother when he was six was a shadow which fell across the remainder of his life, "darkening it into periods of inhibiting fear and suicidal melancholy".[10] He goes on to argue that all Cowper's relationships with women were quests for a mother figure. It may be, then, that marriage to Mrs Unwin would seem almost incestuous. For whatever reason, it was not what he wanted. But in rejecting it, he would be rejecting her, and they would have to separate. There was no alternative. He had rejected Theadora, and a few lines in a Latin poem written at the end of 1774 suggest that she was still on his mind:

> Et praeter omnes te mihi flebilem,
> Te cariorem luce vel artubus,
>   Te vinculo nostrum jugali,
>   Deserui tremulam sub ense.

> [And you above all are a cause of sadness to me, you, dearer
> than light or limb, you united in our nuptial bond, whom I
> deserted and left trembling under the sword.]

But rejecting Theadora had been different and far simpler. He was older now. He would be alone and he had a great fear of that. In his poem 'Doom'd as I am' he had written:

> See me neglected on the world's rude coast,
> Each dear companion of my voyage lost!
> Nor ask why clouds of sorrow shade my brow!
> And ready tears wait only leave to flow!
>   (17-20)

Change was something Cowper always hated, and he hated having to make decisions. Now what faced him was a replica of the dilemma in which he had found himself in 1763: he must either follow a path he dreaded, or betray someone close to him by drawing back. The dilemma was the same and the outcome was the same.

During the first weeks of 1773 his mental state was beginning to give cause for alarm. On 2nd January Newton wrote in his diary: "My time and thoughts much engrossed today by an afflicting and critical dispensation at Orchard Side." Later he says: "My dear friend still walks in darkness. I can hardly conceive that anyone in a state of grace and favour with God can be in greater distress; and yet no one walked more closely with Him, or was more simply devoted to Him in all things."[11] Then on the 24th he was sent for at four in the morning. Cowper had had a dream in which he heard the words "Actum est de ti, periisti" ("It is all over with thee, thou has perished"). The memory of it never left him. Twelve years later he wrote of it to Newton as something "before the recollection of which, all consolation vanishes" (16th October 1785) In April, with Olney's annual fair day about to take place, it was thought that the noise might upset him, and Newton wrote, "April 12th. Annual fair day: the noise of which made my dear friend willing to seek a retreat with us till it shall be over; and now he is here, he seems desirous to stay."[12] And stay he did, until May of the following year. Newton has come in for some harsh criticism where Cowper is concerned. Saintsbury put it very bluntly:

> I am nearly sure that Cowper would have been not only immeasurably happier, but a greater figure in English literature, if the Reverend Mr. Newton had been early consigned to the sharks to whom, no doubt, he had chucked so many (let us hope dead) slaves.[13]

Fausset firmly believed that Newton and his religious beliefs were responsible for Cowper's madness, but to have cared for him, in such circumstances and for so long, under his own roof, must count as an exemplary act of Christian charity.

Early in 1786, in two long letters to his cousin Harriot, Cowper described those months in great detail. They are remarkably frank letters, made all the more remarkable because he tells her that he goes into such detail because she has not asked him about it: "Because you *do not*, and because your reason for not asking consists of a delicacy and tenderness peculiar to yourself, for that very cause I will tell you" (16th January 1786). Like his "conversion narratives", this too reads as a polished and considered piece of prose, even beginning with a narrator's phrase: "Know then that in the year '73 … I was suddenly reduced from my wonted rate of understanding to an almost childish imbecility." He thought his food was poisoned and that everyone hated him, especially Mrs Unwin, though he would have no one but her to care for him, and, as he could not be left alone, "She therefore ordered a bed to be spread for her in a corner of the chamber, and slept upon it in her cloaths. For a long time my nights were disturbed to a great degree, and bad as my days were, were still worse than they."

This continued, according to his own confession, for 12 years. As Cowper said, "It is a long time for a Lady to have slept in her cloaths, and the patient at first sight seems chargeable with much inhumanity who suffers it" (9th February 1786). It is difficult to know how to respond to such a statement, as he does not seem to feel any real remorse. He seems to think he was entitled to be so pampered, adding, "But God knows how great has been the occasion."

The "occasion" was the fear that he might try to commit suicide again. An entry in Newton's diary reads, "Our hopes of a speedy deliverance damped today by a return of the temptation."[14] Their fear seems to have abated, but in October, when Newton thought it was safe to leave him, Cowper did try to hang himself. The oddest aspect of this attempt on his own life is that he regarded it as a direct command from God to offer himself up as a sacrifice. Having failed to do so, he was doubly damned. He had directly refused to obey God's word. His failure to commit suicide he now saw as the unpardonable sin, the sin against the Holy Ghost. There is no way of arguing against such irrationality. His own Evangelical teaching told him that once a believer had received the grace of God, it would never be taken from him. His friend William Bull tried to reason with him, but to no avail. Cowper assured him that he was not mad, only in despair that "there is no encouragement in the Scripture so comprehensive as to include my case, nor any consolation so effectual as to reach it" (27th October 1782). His belief that his case was unique, it must be said, suggests an astonishing degree of vanity.

He explained his situation to Newton very clearly and at some length in a letter written a few months after his friend had moved to London:

> All that is Ænigmatical in my Case would Vanish, if you and
> Mrs. U. were able to avail yourselves of the Solution I have so
> often given You. That a Calvinist in principle, should know
> himself to have been Elected, and yet believe that he is lost,

is indeed a Riddle, and so obscure that it Sounds like a Solecism in terms, and may well bring the assertor of it under the Suspicion of Insanity. But it is not so, and it will not be found so.

I am trusted with the terrible Secret Myself but not with the Power to Communicate it to any purpose. In order to gain credit to such a Relation, it would be necessary that I should be able to produce proof that I received it from above, but that power will never be given Me. In what Manner or by whom the denouement will be made hereafter, I know not. But that it will be made is certain. In the mean time I carry a load no Shoulders Could Sustain, unless underpropped as mine are, by a heart Singularly & preternaturally hardened. (10th May 1780)

What must be remembered is that Cowper genuinely believed what he said. He insists that he was not mad, and indeed he wasn't *all the time*. His letter continues with some chit-chat about his paintings and concludes with the poem 'A Fable', which tells of a raven whose nest survived a storm only to be robbed by "neighbour Hodge" the next morning. It is a poem, however, whose moral, so appropriate here, stresses the precarious nature of existence:

> Fate steals along with silent tread,
> Found oft'nest in what least we dread,
> Frowns in the storm with angry brow,
> But in the sunshine strikes the blow.

Cowper firmly believed that he was damned. This would all be beyond our comprehension were it not that he has told us what it felt like in his poem 'Hatred and Vengeance', which dates from 1774.

Like Isaac Watts' ode, 'The Day of Judgement', which Cowper almost certainly knew, 'Hatred and Vengeance' is written in English sapphics, a verse form which takes its name from the Greek poet Sappho of Lesbos:

> Hatred and vengeance, my eternal portion,
> Scarce can endure delay of execution,
> Wait, with impatient readiness, to seize my
> > Soul in a moment.

Damn'd below Judas; more abhorr'd than he was,
Whom for a few pence sold his holy master.
Twice betray'd Jesus me, the last delinquent,
      Deems the profanest.

Man disavows, and Deity disowns me.
Hell might afford my miseries a shelter;
Therefore hell keeps her ever-hungry mouths all
      Bolted against me.

Hard lot! Encompass'd with a thousand dangers;
Weary, faint, trembling with a thousand terrors;
I'm call'd, if vanquish'd, to receive a sentence
      Worse than Abiram's.

Him, the vindictive rod of angry justice
Sent, quick, and howling, to the centre headlong;
I, fed with judgements, in a fleshly tomb, am
      Buried above ground.

The stressed syllable with which each line begins gives the poem an unstoppable impetus driving it forward to that terrifying conclusion, "Buried above ground". It is the appalling uniqueness of his situation that Cowper is emphasising. The story of Abiram is told in Numbers 16. He was one of the rebels who opposed Moses and in consequence so provoked God that the earth opened up and swallowed them "quick into the pit". Cowper dearly wished such a judgement, with its speed and finality, for himself, but that, he acknowledges, would have been too good for him. His sin is such that he is damned below Judas, who was consigned to the lowest circle of Dante's hell. This could be seen as a somewhat extravagant, even arrogant claim, but the alliteration of "Man disavows, and Deity disowns me" punches it home. Neither man nor God wanted anything to do with him, and as hell would be far better than the state he found himself condemned to, even those gates had been bolted against him. The nightmare quality of the poem is there from the outset: the possibilities of that word "execution" reminding us how often Cowper suffered from dreams of being led off to his own execution. The violence of the language, contrasting with the imposed discipline of the verse form, enacts for us the torture he had to endure, as do the twists in the syntax, especially that of lines 7 and 8. It is an emotional and technical tour de force, unequalled in English poetry until the "terrible sonnets" of Gerard

Manley Hopkins.

But the despair eventually faded just as the earlier ecstasy had, and as it did so Cowper learned a lesson: that to keep the Black Dog away he had to keep busy. Surprisingly for a man of his class, the first hobby he took up was carpentry:

> As soon as I became capable of action, I commenced carpenter, made cupboards, boxes stools. I grew weary of this in about a twelvemonth, and addressed myself to the making of birdcages. To this employment succeeded that of gardening, which I intermingled with that of drawing, but finding that the latter occupation injured my eyes, I renounced it, and commenced poet. (16th January 1786)

8

Some Light Verse

The poems which Cowper composed during the early years of his recovery were mostly written for his own amusement, or for a few close friends, and while some dealt with sombre topical events such as the eruption of Mount Etna and the burning of Lord Mansfield's library during the Gordon Riots, they were not things which Cowper himself made any great fuss about. He knew his limitations and expressed them memorably in a letter to William Unwin:

> I have no more Right to the Name of a Poet than a Maker of Mousetraps has to That of an Engineer, but my little Exploits in this way have at times amused me so much, that I have often wish'd myself a good one. Such a Talent in Verse as mine, is like a Child's Rattle, very entertaining to the Trifler that uses it, and very disagreeable to all beside. But it has served to rid me of some melancholy Moments, for I only take it up as a gentleman Performer does his Fiddle. (7th February 1779)

Perhaps a little more could be claimed for one or two of these "mousetraps". 'Verses, Supposed to be Written by Alexander Selkirk, during his Solitary Abode in the Island of Juan Fernandez' proved to be one of Cowper's most popular poems and was frequently reprinted, once under the illusion that it had actually been written by Selkirk himself. It is hard to believe that anyone could have been so deluded, as the connection with Selkirk (or Crusoe) is at best tenuous. The second stanza does give some indication of what it might be like to be marooned on an uninhabited island:

I am out of humanity's reach,
    I must finish my journey alone,
Never hear the sweet music of speech,
    I start at the sound of my own.
The beasts that roam over the plain,
    My form with indifference see,
They are so unacquainted with man,
    Their tameness is shocking to me.

                    (9-16)

That the tameness of the animals could be seen as shocking is an interesting paradox, as is the suggestion that the sudden sound of the castaway's own voice could make him jump. But for the most part this is not an island; it is a symbol for a state of mind, and the mind is unquestionably that of Cowper himself. The isolation is his own. Cowper tended to see everything in his own terms, something which would always prove a limitation.

The regal optimism of the opening line, "I am monarch of all I survey," backed by the cheery energy of its anapaests, soon proves to be an illusion. The solitude has no charms, and the stanza ends:

Better dwell in the midst of alarms
    Than reign in this horrible place.

                    (7-8)

In the way that these lines recall, while reversing, Satan's assertion in *Paradise Lost* that it is "Better to reign in hell than serve in heaven", they remind us of Cowper's fixed belief in his own damnation. It was not a belief he ever voiced openly in his poems, however, which is hardly surprising. Here instead he imagines himself returning to "Society, friendship, and love":

My sorrows I then might assuage
    In the ways of religion and truth.

                    (21-2)

This Evangelical note seems quite out of keeping with Alexander Selkirk, as do the lines which follow:

> Religion! what treasure untold
>> Resides in that heav'nly word!
> More precious than silver and gold,
>> Or all that this world can afford.
>> (25-8)

They are lines which came in for some sharp criticism from Wordsworth in his appendix to the second edition of *Lyrical Ballads*: "Some Critics would call the language prosaic: the fact is, it would be bad prose, so bad, that it is scarcely worse in metre." And he dismissed as "vicious poetic diction" the stanza's last lines:

> Ne'er sighed at the sound of a knell,
>> Or smil'd when a Sabbath appear'd.

Cowper had stopped going to church after his mental collapse of 1773 and the isolation here is personal. Religion could no longer offer him any consolation, and the longing for friendship which we see in so many of his letters is there in lines which Wordsworth thought were "admirably expressed":

> Ye winds that have made me your sport,
>> Convey to this desolate shore,
> Some cordial endearing report
>> Of a land I shall visit no more.
> My friends do they now and then send
>> A wish or a thought after me?
> O tell me I yet have a friend,
>> Though a friend I am never to see.
>> (33-40)

He regarded Cowper, he said, as a "chaste writer", and these lines, he felt, "would be equally good whether in prose or verse, except that the Reader has an exquisite pleasure in seeing such natural language so naturally connected with metre". His own debt to Cowper is clear in his affirmation that " ... in works of *imagination and sentiment* ... in proportion as ideas and feelings are valuable, whether the composition be in prose or verse, they require and exact one and the same language." But imagination is no help to Cowper/Selkirk in this situation. Imagination can carry him back to his "own native land", but it is not enough; it "Soon hurries me back to despair". The logic of the poem is full of uncertainties as Cowper tries to think himself into a situation other than his own, and as he fails to do so the comfort of the concluding stanza lacks conviction. Just as the birds and the beasts go safely to their rest, so mercy comes to the rescue of man:

> There is mercy in every place,
>   And mercy, encouraging thought!
> Gives even affliction a grace,
>   And reconciles man to his lot.
>   (53-6)

The generalisation would hardly have been true of Selkirk, and was certainly not applicable to Cowper. He may later have acquiesced in his lot, but he was never completely reconciled to it.

The uniqueness of Cowper's position, as he saw it, is touched on in a seemingly innocuous little poem 'The Shrubbery'. Initially the tone appears to be pastoral in the most conventional manner, celebrating "happy shades" that "offer rest"; but the subtitle is "Written in a Time of Affliction" and the first stanza ends with a skilfully balanced pair of lines which topple the convention:

> How ill the scene that offers rest,
>   And heart that cannot rest, agree!
>   (3-4)

There is nothing amiss with nature, nor with the scene before him, though curiously the shrubbery has now acquired a glassy stream and some woodland:

> This glassy stream, that spreading pine,
>   Those alders quiv'ring to the breeze,
> Might sooth a soul less hurt than mine,
>   And please, if any thing could please.
>   (5-8)

The problem lies in Cowper's soul. His status is fixed and unalterable, and no scene of any kind, he says, can ever help:

> But fixt unalterable care
> > Foregoes not what she feels within,
> Shows the same sadness ev'ry where,
> > And slights the season and the scene.
>
> (9-12)

But although his belief in the inevitability of his damnation was as constant as ever, his thoughts of suicide must have left him, and by the end of the 1770s Newton felt it was safe to take up a position he had been offered in London and to leave Cowper in the care of Mrs Unwin.

Much had changed in Olney since Newton's first arrival there in 1764, and he was no longer held in the same high regard or shown the same deference. It has been suggested that he brought this on himself by encouraging his parishioners to take a more active part in church services. A Church of England parson in the eighteenth century ranked second to the squire and kept himself somewhat aloof from the local community. Over time, Newton's egalitarian attitude gradually undermined his position, particularly in the eyes of the younger members of his congregation. Familiarity, one could say, does seem to have bred contempt.

In 1777 a potentially nasty event took place. In the September (most biographers have it as October, but Newton's hymn for the occasion is dated 22nd September 1777) a fire broke out in Olney destroying over a dozen houses. Newton had been in London at the time, but he hurried back to give whatever help he could. He opened a relief fund and composed a hymn for the occasion (see p. 75), but in it he blamed the outbreak on the people's sins. Then, fearful of a recurrence of the carelessness with candles which had actually started the blaze, he prohibited the annual Guy Fawkes candlelight procession. His caution was understandable, but he was spoiling the fun, and people were not going to put up with that. Newton described what happened:

> Many put candles in their windows who had not done so in former years; and some who had, doubled their number. This gave encouragement to the sons of Belial, and when night came on there was much riot and confusion. A wild, lawless mob paraded the streets, breaking windows, and extorting money from one end of the town to the other.[1]

They marched on the vicarage. Newton, the sometime slave-trader, had faced trickier situations before, and he was determined to stand up to the mob, but Mrs Newton, who was not in good health, persuaded him otherwise and he sent out a servant to buy them off:

> I was forced to send an embassy and beg peace. A soft message and a shilling to the captain of the mob secured his protection and we slept in peace. Alas, "tell it not in Gath." I am ashamed of the story.[2]

After that his position as curate in Olney was untenable, and when he was offered the curacy of St Mary Woolnoth, a church in the heart of the City of London, he did not hesitate. He preached his farewell sermon in St Peter and St Paul on 13th January 1780. Olney was too small a stage for Newton to act on. The City was just what he needed and it was not long before he was recognised in the capital both as an inspiring preacher and as a leading figure in the abolitionist movement. Cowper, for his part, soon found that the pace of life without Newton was rather more to his liking.

In a community as small as Olney, Cowper's melancholy, if not his breakdown, could not be kept secret for long. His absence from church would in itself have been conspicuous. To cheer him up a local family hit upon then idea of making him a present of a pet hare. An odd thing to do, one might have thought, yet so closely has the creature since become associated in our minds with Cowper that the museum in Olney adopted it as their symbol, and in the market place, just outside Orchard Side, is a weathervane showing a silhouetted quill pen and a hare. Hares also feature in the memorial stained-glass window in the church of St Nicholas in East Dereham, where Cowper is buried.

It was in a letter published in *The Gentleman's Magazine* in June 1784 that Cowper famously gave the world a full account of the part that hares had played in his life.

Ten years previously, he explained. when he was "much indisposed both in mind and body", a neighbour had given him a leveret his children had grown weary of and were beginning to neglect. Cowper gladly took it in, and word soon got around, so that before very long he had as many leverets offered him "as would have stocked a paddock". He kept three which, despite their names, Puss, Tiney and Bess, were all males. They each had distinctive personalities. Puss was so tame and so loved human society that Cowper often carried it about in his arms. Tiney could be playful but had a surly nature and was liable to bite if handled too much. Bess was tame but the boldest of the three and not afraid to attack the cat if it felt the need. They were individuals, and he loved them all to the extent that

> my intimate acquaintance with these specimens of the kind has taught me to hold the sportsman's amusement in abhorrence; he little knows what amiable creatures he persecutes, of what gratitude they are capable, how cheerful they are in their spirits, what enjoyment they have of life, and that, impressed as they seem with a peculiar dread of man, it is only because man gives them peculiar cause for it.[3]

In the days of the hunting squires such sentiments were by no means usual, but there always was, as will be seen, a strong humanitarian side to Cowper. He cared for the creatures and he cleaned them out himself, not leaving tasks like that to the servants. It was this which gave him such an understanding of them:

> I discovered by accident that fine white sand is in great estimation with them; I suppose as a digestive. It happened that I was cleaning a bird-cage while the hares were with me; I placed a pot filled with such sand upon the floor, to which being at once directed by a strong instinct, they devoured it voraciously; since that time I have generally taken care to see them well supplied with it.[4]

Written as a letter and not an essay, the account has all the colloquial ease of his correspondence and ends with a practical and rather charming postscript:

> I should not do complete justice to my subject, did I not add, that they have no ill scent belonging to them, that they are indefatigably nice in keeping themselves clean, for which purpose nature has furnished them with a brush under each foot; and that they are never infested by any vermin.[5]

Of an evening the hares had the run of the downstairs parlour, and one of Cowper's letters to Newton is a vivid and hilarious account of when his favourite, Puss, gnawed through a window blind and made a bid for freedom. The narrative reads like a farce quite the equal of 'John Gilpin'. The whole town, men, women, children and dogs go off in pursuit of the runaway. One man tries to catch it with his hat but fails. Eventually after many twists and turns it falls into one of the pits in the Tan Yard and is pulled out by its ears, washed in a bucket and brought home in a sack.

Stories of Cowper and his hares must have become widely known, as among the hare memorabilia in the Olney Museum is a fob consisting of three seals, each carved with the name and image of the three hares. It had belonged not to Cowper but to Lady Hesketh, and she had been given it by none other than Princess Elizabeth, the daughter of George III. There is also a small circular snuff-box which was sent to him by Lady Hesketh with the three hares painted on the lid. As Cowper recognised, they closely resembled the three originals in that one was sprightly, one fierce and one gentle (letter of 9th February 1786). The design was by George Romney, whose reputation stood high at the time, and the snuff-box was probably costly. It was another gift from 'Anonymous', and further poignant evidence, as he must surely have recognised, of the love Theodora still felt for him. Indeed there is an interesting ambiguity in his thank-you letter to Harriot. He acknowledges his "nameless benefactor" but continues "I therefore thank you my Cousin for a most elegant present" (31st January 1786). Which cousin, we would like to know, did he have in mind?

One of the sad things about keeping pets is that we tend to outlive them and on 7th March 1783 Cowper ended a letter to his friend William Bull: "You know that I kept two hares. I have written nothing since I saw you but an Epitaph on one of them, which died last week. I send you the first impression of it." It is a very straightforward poem, a simple poem one could call it, but a closer reading shows that it was not an easy poem to write. Its achievement lies in the overall tone which Cowper has managed to strike. There is, to start with, the problem of composing an epitaph of any kind on a hare. Epitaphs are for people, not animals. It might be possible and acceptable to write an epitaph for a dog: dogs are after all man's best friend. But not a hare. The very idea of keeping a hare as a pet is eccentric enough in itself. Thomas Gray got away with writing an 'Ode on the Death of a Favourite Cat, Drowned in a Tub of Gold Fishes', but he began by recognising that it was a ridiculous thing to have happened and not a suitable subject for an ode. And so, by treating it as though it were, and decking it out with inappropriately extravagant language he brought off a brilliant little mock-heroic, a gem of its kind. But that was not Cowper's aim. This hare had been important to him. It was not to be ridiculed. He wanted to celebrate its life and lament its death: to write an epitaph in fact. The first stanza, however, is defensively comic. A quatrain of eight- and six-syllable lines (common metre) is frequently found in hymns and has some dignity, but lines of eight and seven syllables have almost none:

> Here lies, whom hound did ne'er pursue,
>   Nor swifter Grey-hound follow;
> Whose foot ne'er tainted morning dew,
>   Nor ear heard Huntsman's hallo'.

The poem continues in common metre, but the heavily weighted rhymes of the second and fourth lines have something of a pantomime effect:

> Old Tiney, surliest of his kind,
>   Who, nurs'd with tender care,
> And to domestic bounds confin'd,
>   Was still a wild Jack-hare.
>
> Though duly from my hand he took
>   His pittance ev'ry night,
> He did it with a jealous look,
>   And, when he could, would bite.
>   (5-12)

Having admitted in this way that his epitaph cannot be serious, but then by giving us specific, not generalised, details of its diet and habits, he invites us to see Tiney not simply as a hare, but as one particular hare:

> His diet was of wheaten bread,
>   Of milk, and oats, and straw,
> Thistles, or lettuces instead,
>   With sand to scour his maw.
>   (13-16)

And while the lack of decorum in the fifth stanza does invite laughter, it is laughter of delight:

> A Turkey carpet was his lawn,
>   Whereon he lov'd to bound,
> To skip and gambol like a fawn,
>   And swing his rump around.
>   (21-4)

Cowper brings his own feelings into the poem and tells us why he so valued the creature:

> I kept him for his humour' sake
> > For he would oft beguile
> My heart of thoughts that made it ache,
> > And force me to a smile.
> > > (33-6)

But to dwell on such things would make him look sentimental, or just plain silly, and Cowper avoids this with a clever change of direction. He misses Tiney, but transfers his feelings to his one remaining hare called Puss:

> But, now beneath this walnut-shade
> > He finds his long, last home,
> And waits in snug concealment laid,
> > 'Till gentler Puss shall come.
>
> He, still more ancient, feels the shocks
> > From which no care can save,
> And part'ner once of Tiney's box,
> > Must soon partake his grave.
> > > (37-44)

Without our noticing, Cowper has become Puss. It is the kind of simplicity that belies the skill which has gone into the writing, and it is a skill which is evident in so many of Cowper's shorter poems.

The death of another pet – probably belonging to the dissolute Dick Coleman who was living next door (letter of 9th November 1780) – features in a short poem, 'On a Goldfinch Starved to Death in his Cage'. The speaker in the poem is the dead bird itself, and it begins by reminding us of the freedom it once had:

> Time was when I was free as air,
> The thistle's downy seed my fare,
> > My drink the morning dew;
> I perch'd at will on ev'ry spray,
> My form genteel, my plumage gay,
> > My strains for ever new.

It then tells us how it was caught, caged, neglected and starved to death. At this point we would normally expect a brief moral on man's cruelty to poor defenceless creatures, but instead the goldfinch thanks the "gentle swain" responsible for its death for bringing its woes to an end. Death, it says, is preferable by far: a disturbingly dark thought in view of what we know of Cowper's suicidal tendency.

Death seems to have been much on his mind. In his 'Colubriad', a poem about the killing of a snake, death appears, superficially, to be treated rather light-heartedly. *Colubra* is the Latin for a serpent, and the title, copied from the *Iliad*, suggests a mock-heroic approach, which is what we are given. Cowper mocks his own heroics by exaggeration in verse which is deliberately (and ingeniously) clumsy. He finds the snake threatening his three little kittens who are oblivious of the danger, and so:

> On to the hall went I, with pace not slow,
> But swift as lightning, for a long Dutch hoe:
> With which well-arm'd I hasten'd to the spot ,
> To find the viper, but I found him not.
> (18-21)

With "heroic ardour", he pursues, then finds and eventually kills the beast:

> With out-stretch'd hoe I slew him at the door,
> And taught him NEVER TO COME THERE NO MORE.
> (40-1)

If, however, we look at the letter he wrote to William Unwin on 3rd August 1782 in which he relates the same story, it is far less humorous and he prefaces it with a very different observation. "It is a sort of paradox but it is true. – We are never more in danger than when we think ourselves most secure, nor in reality more secure then when we seem perhaps to be most in danger." His own anxieties are never far from his mind, and a similar thought is behind his poem 'On the Loss of the Royal George'. The ship sank on 29th August 1782 with the loss of 800 lives. The disaster was reported in *The Gentleman's Magazine*:

> The ship was careening at Spithead, and many of her guns
> being removed to one side, some of her upper ports being
> open, and near the water's edge, a sudden gust of wind overset
> her, and she went to the bottom with about 400 of her crew,
> and, it is supposed, at least as many women and children.[6]

Cowper's words, while unremarkable for the most part, would be rousing enough when sung, as intended, to the tune of Handel's March in *Scipio*, but what is worth noting is the brief reference to the vessel's commander, Admiral Kempenfelt. He too was unprepared for the terrible event which was to strike him down. He was below deck and "His sword was in the sheath / His fingers held the pen."

Also of note is the poem's subscript telling us that it was written "By desire of Lady Austen who wanted Words to the March in Scipio". So many of Cowper's poems, we realise, and certainly all his more substantial works, were written at the direct instigation of someone else – something surely unique in the history of poetry:

> Toll for the brave –
> The brave! that are no more:
>   All sunk beneath the wve,
> Fast by their native shore …
>
> Toll for the brave –
> Brave Kempenfelt is gone,
>   His last sea-fight is fought,
> His work of glory done.
>   It was not in the battle,
> No tempest gave the shock,
>   She sprang no fatal leak,
> She ran upon no rock;
>   His sword was in the sheath,
> His fingers held the pen,
>   When Kempenfelt went down
> With twice four hundred men.

9

Moral Satires

That taught my heart to fear

One of the odder members of Cowper's family was his cousin, Martin Madan. Six years older than Cowper, he too had been at Westminster, admitted to the Inner Temple in 1747 and called to the Bar a year later, but during these years he was also "a deep-drinking, all-night reveller at the Poetical Club".[1] Then came his conversion, which was as dramatic as any. A brilliant mimic, he had gone along with a group of friends to hear John Wesley preach, intending to return with them to their coffee house afterwards and impersonate him to everyone's delight and amusement. But the first words he heard as he entered the church were "Prepare to meet thy God," and he left converted. He was asked by his cronies if he had taken off the old Methodist, to which he replied, "No, Gentlemen, but he has taken me off."[2] In 1750 Wesley granted him a licence to become an itinerant preacher, and in 1757 he was ordained, proving to be a powerful speaker with a strong voice and a charismatic personality. His reputation spread, and he had soon acquired a devoted following.

It was Martin Madan whom Cowper sent for after his suicide attempts in 1763 and who persuaded him that all mankind was guilty of sin. For a while he convinced him that his case was "less desperate" than he thought, and when he held forth on the gospel of atonement, Cowper wrote in his memoir, "I had not the least doubt within me but that this was the Gospel of Salvation." But the certainty did not last. Next morning he awoke "with ten times a stronger sense of my alienation from God than ever".[3]

They remained friends, and later, when he was living in Huntingdon, Cowper went on a brief preaching tour with Madan and in 1776 he wrote to thank him for sending him his *Collection of Psalms and Hymns*. "Mrs Unwin plays well on the harpsichord, and I doubt not those Songs of Sion will sound sweetly in the ears of one so lately escaped from the thunders of Sinai" (10th February 1766).

In 1762 Madan was appointed chaplain of the Lock Hospital, which had opened in 1747 as the first clinic in London for the treatment of venereal disease. Later it was to become the Lock Asylum for the Reception of Penitent Female Patients. It was an odd establishment, as Madan's preaching had become so popular that a chapel was built for him. 'Seat-holders' were admitted to it as well as the patients, so that it came to be filled partly by the destitute and partly by some of the wealthiest Evangelicals in the country.

Madan must have seen and dealt with some wretched young women there and, to his credit, he decided that something needed to be done to help them. Unfortunately his decision was calamitous. His reading of the Bible showed him that polygamy had not always been regarded as a sin and that any man who took a woman's virginity had, according to Old Testament law, married her and was therefore responsible for her care and support. If such a law were to be instituted in Britain, it would, in his view, halt the spread of prostitution and ensure that male seducers and adulterers would have to accept their responsibility. The intention was good, but it paved the way to hell for him. In 1780 he advanced his ideas in a three-volume work, *Thelyphthora or, a Treatise on Female Ruin Considered on the Basis of Divine Law*. Newton tried to persuade him not to publish it, but Madan, who was never lacking in self-belief, went ahead. The result was inevitable: widespread moral outrage. To advocate polygamy, the man must be either an incorrigible lecher or a madman. Such was the general opinion. Yet we have to remember that there was some Old Testament authority behind the notion: it is there in the opening lines of Dryden's *Absalom and Achitophel*:

> In pious times ere priest-craft did begin,
> Before polygamy was made a sin;
> When man on many multiplied his kind,
> Ere one to one was, cursedly, confined …

It was out of the question of course in Georgian England, and Newton was insistent that Cowper should write a refutation of it, but Cowper was reluctant. It seems that at first he found it difficult to take his cousin's wild ideas seriously. In a reply to Newton he added a four-line squib:

> If John marries Mary, and Mary alone,
> 'Tis a very good match between Mary and John.
> Should John wed a score, oh the claws and the scratches!
> It can't be a match: – 'tis a bundle of matches.

Cowper's sense of humour should never be underestimated, but neither should Newton's persistence. Cowper thought again, but came to the conclusion that lust would always be prevalent among mankind and that Madan had found "nothing but a new way to expose himself to the censure of those who Think, & the laughter of those who do not". He was puzzled by the title page and the "hard name the Author has Baptized his Book with" (6th February 1780), but before the end of the year he had done as he was told, and his reply, *Antithelyphthora*, appeared as an anonymous pamphlet. Anonymity always added an extra spice to skirmishes in the literary world, and in any case Cowper's was not a name that people knew. Added to which, he would hardly have wished to upset his aunt, Madan's mother.

Rather than sermonise and castigate as, it is tempting to believe, Newton might have preferred, Cowper chose to pen a sprightly little allegory, Spenserian in concept, but in couplets which have more than a touch of Alexander Pope to them. Because Madan's ideas were thought very fanciful, if that is not too weak a word, he is introduced to us as Sir Airy del Castro, or the Knight of Castles in the Air, and is seen as wooing the fair maid Hypothesis (but as that is something of a mouthful her name is changed to Posy). She is an enchantress who has already seduced others into folly, among them Bishop Berkeley, whom she convinced

> That Forms Material, whatsoe'er we Dream,
> Are not at all, or Are not what they seem,
> That Substances and Modes of ev'ry Kind,
> Are but Impressions on the passive Mind,
> And He that Splits his Cranium, breaks at most
> A Fancied Head against a Fancied Post.
>
> (40-5)

But she convinced Sir Airy of something even stranger:

> That lewd Incontinence and lawless Rape
> Are Marriage in its true and proper Shape,
> That Man by Faith and Truth is made a Slave,
> The Ring a Bauble, and the Priest a Knave.
>
> (64-7)

And so, in keeping with such beliefs, they go off into an arbour of thickest yew where their passion is consummated – or presumably so, as Cowper ironically insists that a direct statement is not acceptable:

> But what Old Chaucer's merry Page befits,
> The chaster Muse of Modern Days, Omitts.
>
> (84-5)

Young women everywhere "wept in throngs" that they could no longer count on man being faithful to his marriage bond. In despair they called out for some knight to save them and so up steps Sir Marmadan, who can be counted upon to *mar* Martin Madan.

A trumpet sounds. Sir Airy buckles on his armour to defend his cause. The "insidious witch" mounts behind him, thus allowing Sir Marmadan to skewer them both with his lance, just as Phinehas did the adulterers in Numbers 25, whereby "the plague was stayed from the children of Israel." Thus, true love and marital fidelity prevail:

> Then sang the Married and the Maiden Throng,
> Love Graced the Theme, and Harmony the Song.
>
> (201-2)

It is a slight piece, but not without a certain charm and must have amused his contemporaries.

In the summer of 1780, with Newton now established in his London parish, life in Olney was becoming noticeably more relaxed. This is evident from Cowper's letters. His cousins are no longer at the receiving end of those long religious tracts. He is even prepared to joke with Mrs Newton: 'When I write to Mr. Newton he Answers me by Letter. When I write to you, You Answer me in Fish' (5th June 1780). And William Unwin is treated to a riddle on, of all things, a kiss. When Hayley published it, he omitted the last two lines, probably considering them rather risqué:

> Alike the delight of the Poor and the Rich,
> Tho' the Vulgar are apt to Present me his Breech.

It is certainly a side to Cowper we have not seen before.

During those summer months he regularly went on long walks with Mrs Unwin. He took drawing lessons from James Andrews, a local engraver and artist, and he spent hours in the garden, tending his melons and cucumbers. Writing always took second place to gardening, he told Newton: " … my Appetite for fame is not keen enough to combat with my Love of fine weather, my Love of Idleness, and my Love of Gardening Employments" (8th April 1781).

But as the fine weather drifted into the darker days of winter so his mood changed. It was the time of year when he was always most prone to melancholy. Mrs Unwin knew this, and to keep his mind occupied she suggested he should "devote his thoughts to poetry".[4] Cowper himself was well aware of the effect that winter had on him, as he confessed to Newton when he wrote to him in late December telling him that he was writing a poem to be called 'The Progress of Error':

> At this season of the year, & and in this gloomy, uncomfortable climate, it is no easy matter for the owner of a mind like mine, to divert it from sad subjects, & fix it upon such as may administer to its amusement. Poetry, above all things, is useful to me in this respect. While I am held in pursuit of pretty images, or a pretty way of expressing them, I forget everything that is irksome, &, like a boy that plays truant, determine to avail myself of the present opportunity to be amused, & to put by the disagreeable recollection that I must after all, go home & be whipt again. (21st December 1780)

Despite the levity of the image, his despair is evident in that closing sentence.

The title, 'The Progress of Error', which had been Mrs Unwin's suggestion, is not as remarkable as it now seems to us. The 'progress poem' had become an accepted genre, made famous by Gray's 'Progress of Poetry', which traced the history of poetry from Greek and Roman times. William Collins had already constructed a history of the theatre in his 'Epistle: Addressed to Sir Thomas Hanmer', and Goldsmith's 'The Traveller' followed the course of 'Liberty' as it progressed through the countries of Europe.

From the outset Cowper makes it clear to his readers that his intention is to teach, but they would have expected no less at that time:

> Take, if ye can, ye careless and supine!
> Counsel and caution from a voice like mine.
>
> (9-10)

In true Augustan fashion he then pens portraits of the various sinners he sees around him, leading off with that familiar eighteenth-century figure, the hunting parson:

> Oh laugh, or mourn with me, the rueful jest,
> A cassock'd huntsman, and a fiddling priest;
>
> (110-11)

Curiously, music, especially if played in church, was something Cowper was particularly averse to. Not even wine, he argued, "does more debauch and befool the natural understanding than Music" (9th September 1781):

> If he, the tinkling harpsichord regards
> As inoffensive, what offence in cards?
> Strike up the fiddles, let us all be gay,
> Laymen have leave to dance, if parsons play.
>
> (148-51)

It is not easy to see the connection between a harpsichord and a game of cards. but he is opposed to all forms of what the world at large regarded as socialising and argues for a return to simpler values:

> Has time wore out, or fashion put to shame,
> Good sense, good health, good conscience, and good fame?
>
> (245-6)

We are reminded of his description of the life he lived with the Unwins in Huntingdon.

William Cowper was one of Jane Austen's favourite poets, but he himself had no time at all for novelists:

> Ye novelists who marr what ye would mend,
> Sniv'ling and driv'ling folly without end,
> Whose corresponding misses fill the ream
> With sentimental frippery and dream,
>
> (309-12)

His muse, "eagle-pinioned", then swoops down on a new prey, another writer, Lord Chesterfield. Chesterfield was subjected to attacks from many different directions. His *Letters*, according to Samuel Johnson, taught "The morals of a whore and the manners of a dancing master". Cowper's lines here have no such bite to them, but thinking of Chesterfield's letters to his son leads him to a consideration of education, and in particular the follies of that gap year of the eighteenth century, the Grand Tour, observing:

> How much a dunce that has been sent to roam,
> Excels a dunce that has been kept at home.
>
> (415-16)

Couplets as pointed as this are by no means common, however, and it was rare for Cowper to be prepared to attack an individual. For the most part the targets of his satire are the obvious ones: scholars who misread sacred texts, and the press with its "ever-bubbling spring of endless lies", but the attacks are too generalised to make any great impression. The conclusion, when it is reached, is, as one would expect, that all can be put to rights by following Christ:

> I am no preacher, let this hint suffice,
> The cross once seen, is death to ev'ry vice:
> Else he that hung there, suffer'd all his pain,
> Bled, groan'd and agoniz'd, and died in vain.
>
> (621-4)

Newton, the preacher, may have been miles away in London, but his influence is to be heard throughout, so much so that there may be some truth in Norman Nicholson's suggestion that writing this poem allowed Cowper "to work out of his system some of the obsessions and preoccupations which were left over from the days of Newton".[5]

Eventually Cowper himself seems to have come to the conclusion that an undiluted diet of religious moralising would not be pleasing to the general palate, and in December 1781 he sent Newton "a few lines on a thought which struck me yesterday". The lines were entitled 'The Flatting-Mill'. A flatting-mill was a device for gilding unpleasant-tasting pills, and Cowper saw a useful analogy. Poets likewise needed to sugar the pill of didacticism:

> If he wish to instruct he must learn to delight,
> Smooth, ductile, and even his Fancy must flow,
> Must tinkle and glitter like gold to the sight
> And catch in its progress a sensible glow.
>
> After all he must beat it as thin and as fine
> As the leaf that enfolds what an invalid swallows,
> For Truth is unwelcome, however divine,
> And unless you adorn it, a Nausea follows.
>
> (17-24)

He thought of using the poem as an introduction when the *Moral Satires* were published as a whole, but Newton persuaded him against it. Cowper did, however, have his own way in opening the collection with 'Table Talk', a poem almost totally lacking in religious content. It was more directly connected with contemporary events, and as he explained to Newton, there was "some froth here and there" which he hoped would "decoy people into my Company". Despite his modest disclaimers he wanted to be read and wanted to be recognised as a poet, as we can see from the image he chooses to describe his muse:

> I do not know, but am inclined to suspect that if my
> Muse was to go forth clad in Quaker colour, without
> one bit of Ribband to enliven her Appearance, she
> might walk from one End of London to the other as
> little noticed as if she were one of the Sisterhood indeed.
> (18th February 1781)

The poem is prefaced by a light-hearted motto from Horace: "If by chance the heavy burden of my poem should chafe you, throw it away … " The form is that of a conversation between two unnamed individuals, both of whom seem to be poets. B has been identified as Cowper himself, but as A says he was at Westminster, the piece can be read as Cowper debating with himself.

Without being politically specific, the opening paragraphs touch on the role and position of the monarchy, a sufficiently topical issue as George III was often thought to take too much interest in politics, and in the early years of his reign was suspected of seeking to reassert royal authority. The debate, if it can be called that, offers nothing new, and when A suggests that liberty might be a theme "more pertinent, if less sublime", Cowper follows that well-worn path which James Thomson had laid out in his progress poem 'Liberty' half a century before. In his lines on the abuse of liberty he glances at the Gordon Riots, but again only in the most generalised of terms.

Where, we begin to ask ourselves, is the froth he promised us? We would be glad of a little. When he turns to England's faults and failings, it is no more than a catalogue of abstract nouns: effeminacy, lust, venality, perjury, avarice. When A asks B what he, as a poet, intends to do to rectify this sad situation the interest level, for us, is instantly raised as B's response begins to read like Cowper's own literary manifesto.

His dislikes are, as might be expected, many and various, but his account of them in what we might call his own 'Progress of Poetry' is decidedly chaotic. The earliest epics he seems to approve of, for while they dealt with heroes and kings, mortal themes, the "song was moral" (l. 599); but then "luxury seduced the mind" and "wild imagination" took over. Anacreon and Horace are summarily dismissed, but no reason given, and from there we leap precipitously forward to the days of Cromwell when there was apparently no poetry at all. The Restoration is marked by "rank obscenity", but eventually this is mercifully cleansed by a school of virtuous satirists led by Addison. Pope is mentioned, and while his advocacy of virtue and morality is accepted, he too is dismissed. He had

> Made poetry a mere mechanic art;
> And ev'ry warbler had his tune by heart.
> (654-5)

Cowper was apparently unaware of his own debts to Pope's 'Essay on Criticism' in this section. The "clock-work tintinabulum of Rhime" had come in for criticism earlier, as had "creamy smoothness". The one positive quality he celebrates is in:

> the line, that plows its stately course,
> Like a proud swan, conqu'ring the stream by force.
> (522-3)

A similar ambition had been voiced in a letter to Joseph Johnson:

> Give me a manly, rough line, with a deal of meaning in it, rather than a whole poem full of musical periods, that have nothing but their oily smoothness to recommend them.
> (15th January 1781)

But ambition is not the same as achievement, and if we were to put the magnificent sweep and momentum of the opening lines of Dryden's *Absalom and Achitophel* against any paragraph in Cowper's *Moral Satires* we would see how 'tintinnabulous' and frankly dull his verse can be.

Nothing, however, prepares us for Cowper's astonishing assertion that there is one contemporary poet who surpasses all others, and that is Charles Churchill. Even that they went to Westminster School together hardly explains his partiality. They could not be more unlike. Although an ordained priest, Churchill only narrowly escaped jail for debt, was a member of the Hell Fire Club, deserted his wife, befriended and supported the libertine radical John Wilkes, wrote for the 'seditious' *North Briton*, eloped with a girl half his age, was obliged to resign from the priesthood and died of a fever in France at the age of 33. Cowper, though living quietly in Olney, was not blind to his faults, describing him as

Surly and slovenly and bold and coarse,
Too proud for art, and trusting in mere force,
Spendthrift alike of money and of wit,
Always at speed and never drawing bit.

(682-5)

Yet still he asserts that he "Contemporaries all surpassed". Viewed solely in the context of the poem, such an assertion regarding a poet of whom even (the few) modern readers of eighteenth-century poetry know next to nothing, might seem absurd. But it was, even though eccentric, a considered opinion, as we can tell from a long letter to William Unwin in which he gives a detailed and reasoned evaluation, and one which is even more extravagant: "Such natural unforced Effusions of Genius, the World I believe has never seen since the Days of Shakespeare." His reason for thinking so is "that bold Masculine Character, which I believe is the great Peculiarity of this Writer". This, I would suggest, is not only what he admires in his friend, but what he envies, as even the most superficial comparison of them shows up the lack of force in Cowper's satires. They are more moral than satirical. He refers to Churchill's 'The Times' and is full of admiration for it, except, as he says, "that the Subject is disgusting to the last Degree". The subject of Churchill's entire poem is homosexuality. Cowper himself had declared his own aversion to 'effeminacy', but went no further. He could never have penned such lines as:

Women are kept for nothing but the breed,
For pleasure we must have a GANYMEDE,
A fine fresh HYLAS, a delicious boy,
To serve our purposes of beastly joy.

(331-4)

It is not only that Cowper would not have had the nerve to write something of that sort, and have Mrs Unwin read it; he did not have the lived experience to *know,* except in the most general terms, what it was he was denouncing. There is therefore not the vehemence and passion that there undoubtedly is in Churchill.

In closing, poet B regrets that it is a

Pity! Religion has so seldom found
A skilful guide into poetic ground

(716-17)

adding:

> 'Twere new indeed, to see a bard all fire,
> Touch'd with a coal from heav'n assume the lyre,
> And tell the world, still kindling as he sung,
> With more than mortal music on his tongue,
> That he who died below, and reigns above
> Inspires the song, and that his name is love.
>
> (734-9)

Such verses would outweigh all others, he says, which prompts poet A to interpose with:

> Hail Sternhold then and Hopkins hail!

to which B, much to our surprise, answers: "Amen", and then goes on to say, "One Madrigal of their's is worth them all." To extol Charles Churchill may be looked upon as simply odd, but a poet praising Sternhold and Hopkins asks to have his critical faculties seriously called into question.

Cowper seems to have been unaware of the change of direction in poetry which was being urged by the likes of Warton, Collins and Gray in the middle years of the century. In the preface to his first collection Warton had been adamant that "the fashion of moralising in Verse has been carried too far, and he looks upon *Invention* and *Imagination* to be the chief Faculties of a Poet, so he will be happy if the following Odes ... bring back Poetry into its right channel."[6] As far as Cowper was concerned, moralising was the right channel, indeed the only channel, and he would probably not even have understood what Keats meant by saying: "We hate poetry that has a palpable design upon us."[7] The problem is that, as he said in 'Table Talk', "Whate'er we write, we bring forth nothing new" (l. 733). In 'Truth' there is not only nothing new, the design is bluntly palpable. It is a sermon on those familiar Evangelical themes: the sin of pride and the erroneous belief in justification by good works, and after close on 600 lines it is all summed up in the closing triplet:

> Angelic gratulations rend the skies,
> Pride falls unpitied, never more to rise,
> Humility is crown'd, and faith receives the prize.
>
> (587-9)

Cowper's fundamental tenet is there in his description of the teachings of Scripture as "Heaven's easy, artless, unincumber'd plan" (l. 22), and this simplicity is portrayed in the surprising suggestion that an Olney lace-maker "Shuffling her threads about the live-long day" (l. 320) has a clearer understanding of the Gospels than Voltaire:

> Oh happy peasant! Oh unhappy bard!
> His the mere tinsel, her's the rich reward;
> He prais'd perhaps for ages yet to come,
> She never heard of half a mile from home;
> He lost in errors his vain heart prefers,
> She safe in the simplicity of hers.
>
> (331-6)

He may of course have been fleshing out Christ's words in Luke 10:21: "thou hast hid these things from the wise and prudent, and hast revealed them unto babes." In keeping with this, he himself has perhaps aimed at a verse which is equally artless, but in the process he has come close to being simply pedestrian. The verse could be classified as Augustan, but it is Augustan verse diluted, having none of the wit and energy of Pope.

There is one passage, a character sketch of an "ancient prude", which stands out from all the rest, being especially vivid:

> Yon ancient prude, whose wither'd features show
> She might be young some forty years ago,
> Her elbows pinion'd close upon her hips,
> Her head erect, her fan upon her lips,
> Her eye-brows arch'd, her eyes both gone astray
> To watch yon am'rous couple in their play,
> With boney and unkechief'd neck defies
> The rude inclemency of wintry skies,
> And sails with lappet-head and mincing airs
> Duely at clink of bell, to morning pray'rs.
> To thrift and parsimony much inclin'd,
> She yet allows herself that boy behind;
> The shiv'ring urchin, bending as he goes,
> With slipshod heels, and dew drop at his nose,
> His predecessor's coat advanc'd to wear,
> Which future pages are yet doom'd to share,
> Carries her bible tuck'd beneath his arm,
> And hides his hands to keep his fingers warm.
>
> (131-48)

However, vivid as it is, it proves to be, point by point, a recreation in words of William Hogarth's print *Morning*, the first in his *Times of the Day* series. There could have been no such scene enacted in Olney of course: Cowper's was the only household to have a servant. He could not have seen it, but it also seems that he could not imagine it. Every detail is borrowed. His experience of the outside world, unlike Charles Churchill's, came to him at second hand. But it also has to be recognised that it was not in his nature to be as caustic as Churchill. Nevertheless, he has made very skilful use of his material here; he avoids preaching and allows the picture to speak, clearly and eloquently, for itself.

When we look at Cowper's letters of around this time and notice the dates of his first mention of the individual poems, we cannot but be astonished at the speed with which he was writing. It was a creative outburst without precedent or explanation. He first mentions 'The Progress of Error' in a letter to Newton on 21st December 1781. A month later 'Truth', he says, is almost finished. By the beginning of February 'Table Talk' is nearing completion and by the end of the month so is 'Expostulation'. In eight weeks he has composed close to 3,000 lines of rhyming couplets. Remembering Pascal's apology to a friend for having written such a long letter with the excuse that he had not had time to make it shorter, one could wish that Cowper had taken more time and revised more carefully. Towards the end of 'Expostulation' (one could wish likewise that he had had a better ear for a title) he admits:

> I know the warning song is sung in vain,
> That few will hear, and fewer heed the strain.
>
> (724-5)

And few would care to argue with this assessment.

Cowper's editors have shown that 'Expostulation' belongs to a well-established homiletic tradition (vol. I, p.522) while Bill Hutchings is prepared to take it further back than that, rightly calling it "Jeremiah rendered into heroic couplets".[8] Jeremiah? According to Vincent Newey, "in a poem like *Expostulation* his piety issues in a torrent of zealous condemnation washing into every conceivable nook and cranny of the nation's sinful state, so that, far from being redeemed, poetry grows bloated and incontinent on an excessive diet of righteousness."[9]

'Expostulation' begins by recounting at length the history of the rise and downfall of the Jews, concluding that such a story should be seen as a warning to all nations to "keep wisdom or meet vengeance", and that this warning ought to sound shrillest in British ears. He details the troubles besetting Britain and bluntly asserts that they are the vengeance of divine providence.

He touches on the various sins which have invited God's anger, and various they are indeed: the imperial exploitation of India, homosexuality, the abuses of the Test Act, and discredited priests. He then launches into another 'progress poem'. This time it is an outline of British history and again is totally haphazard. It damns the Druids, but praises Caesar who tamed a savage people and left behind the legacy of Latin. After celebrating the downfall of Woden and Thor he weighs in against the Church of Rome, rather surprisingly choosing to single out the papal crusades for special condemnation. Coming closer to his own times he records the defeat of the Armada and the suppression of the Jacobite rebellion, and ends by seeming to suggest that Georgian England had never had it so good:

> Peculiar is the grace by thee possess'd,
> Thy foes implacable, thy land at rest;
> Thy thunders travel over earth and seas,
> And all at home is pleasure, wealth and ease.
>
> (580-3)

He accuses the nation of ingratitude, reminds his readers of the heroes and worthies who died for the true religion's sake, but ends by doubting, as we have seen, if anyone is ready to listen to his warning.

Cowper sent a completed copy of 'Expostulation' to Newton on 8th April and was then perhaps kept busy in his garden, as we can see that he took a few weeks off from writing and it was not until 13th May that he mentions having begun work on 'Hope'.

It is hard to account for the lack of consistency in this poem. It is as if Cowper was now capable of writing at such a rate that he set off at a sprint each morning without always looking back on what he had written the day before. How else are we to account for the solemn retelling of that already grim parable in Matthew 22 of the guests who failed to turn up for the wedding of a king's son, and where a gatecrasher is cast into outer darkness, being followed immediately by a genuinely funny debate conducted between a colonel, an ensign and a priest about the respective merits of faith and good works, which the colonel opens with:

> Adieu to all morality! if grace
> Make works a vain ingredient in the case.
> The Christian hope is – waiter, draw the cork –
> If I mistake not – blockhead! with a fork!
> Without good works, whatever some may boast,
> Mere folly and delusion – Sir, your toast.
>
> (359-64)

The way such inelegant vernacular is slipped into the argument is brilliant, and Cowper manages to sustain the joke at some length, but just why he does so is by no means clear, and a few lines after the debate is over we are surprised by a description of the bleak and barren landscape of Greenland and praise for the Moravian missionaries who sailed to its shores to save the souls of the atheists and heathens they found there. This is followed by a celebration of the life of George Whitefield. It reads like a stream of unconsciousness.

It is a disappointing poem in other respects too. The doctrinaire sections on Hope itself are little more than platitudes, and the portraits, which are so often the strength of eighteenth-century satire (we think of Dryden's Zimri and Pope's Sporus) have no flesh on them. Except, that is, for a picture near the end of the poem of a Christian sunk into the depths of despair.

We can sense that something important is about to be related. Cowper addresses Truth directly as though it were his muse, and asks:

> That while I trembling trace a work divine,
> Fancy may stand aloof from the design.
>
> (671-2)

What follows does indeed owe vey little to fancy. This man, he says, deserves our pity. Once he was happy:

> Politely learn'd, and of a gentle race,
> Good-breeding and good sense gave all a grace,
> And whether at the toilette of the fair
> He laugh'd and trifled, made him welcome there,
> Or, if in masculine debate he shar'd,
> Insur'd him mute attention and regard.
>
> (682-7)

On a first reading there is nothing remarkable here until we realise that every detail applies to Cowper himself, a classical scholar who could trace his ancestry back to Henry III. The laughter reminds us of those days in Southampton Row with his cousins when he "giggled and made giggle", and the masculine debate could refer either to his days in the Temple or in the meetings of the Nonsense Club.

The change which comes over him is also depicted in terms which remind us of his account of his own despair in his memoir:

> His eyes are sunk, arms folded, head reclind,
> Those awful syllables, hell, death and sin,
> Though whisper'd, plainly tell what works within,
> That conscience there performs her proper part,
> And writes a doomsday sentence on his heart;
>
> (689-94)

Some of the detail seems beyond imagination:

> He hears the notice of the clock, perplex'd,
> And cries, perhaps eternity strikes next.
>
> (700-1)

And where in the memoir we read, "My ears rang with the sound of the torments that seemed to await me," in the poem we have, "laughter sounds like madness in his ears."

The Christian's recovery, just when all hope seemed lost, is presented to us as of a felon in prison, expecting to be executed, but then granted his freedom at the last moment. This too is prefigured in the memoir: "No convicted criminal ever feared death more or was more assured of dying."[10]

Safe in the knowledge that such details of his personal life were known only to members of his family and a few close friends, Cowper could use them as illustrative of what might pass for a versified sermon. The interest for us lies in the immediacy of these passages. They read like events which have been lived through and 'felt', whereas when treating of Faith and Hope the language is more that of the hymns. Much has changed. The passion of the early days after his conversion is no longer there. There is what seems like an intellectual acceptance of religion, but the despair had been lived through, and, one suspects, still was present. In a letter to Newton not long after the *Moral Satires* had been published, he wrote:

No man upon earth is more sensible of the unprofitableness of a life like mine than I am, or groan more heavily under the burthen; but this too is vanity, because it is in vain; my groans will not bring the remedy, because there is no remedy for me. (20th April 1783)

As was only to be expected, 'Hope' was soon followed by 'Charity', a poem which, though over 600 lines long, he seems to have written in two weeks.[10] In a rhyming letter to Newton (12th July 1781) he took a very light-hearted approach to it:

I have writ Charity, not for popularity, but as well as I could, in hopes to do good. And if the Reviw'r, should say to be sure, the Gentleman's Muse, wears Methodist shoes, you may know by her pace, and talk about grace, that she and her bard, have little regard, for the tastes and fashions, and ruling passions, and hoyd'ning play, of the modern day … and has baited her trap, in hopes to snap, all that may come, with a Sugar plumb …

In truth there is no more "sugar plumb" here than in any of the previous poems. Averaging over 40 lines a day suggests that Cowper was on auto-pilot by this time, and the approach certainly has that familiar blend of the rambling and the formulaic. As James Thomson had already, and famously, done before him, he argues that the arts can only flourish where there is liberty, and he celebrates commerce, believing it to be a force for good in its ability to spread not only material goods but the good news of Christianity throughout the world. Interestingly, one aspect of commerce which he castigates at length in 'Charity' is the trade in slaves.

10

Lady Austen

How precious did that grace appear

While Cowper was writing the rather gloomy 'Charity', an event took place in Olney which was to change the whole course of his life and, in the way it was narrated by William Hayley, firmly caught the imagination of several later biographers. Looking out of his parlour window one morning in July 1781 Cowper saw, according to Hayley, two ladies coming out of the draper's shop on the High Street. One of them he knew to be Mrs Jones, the wife of Thomas Jones, curate of the nearby village of Clifton. But who was the other lady? Lord David Cecil, after picturing for us "the bulging, bow-windowed little draper's shop" tells us that "there was something about her appearance by which he was immediately and strangely attracted."[1] Then, as Gilbert Thomas has it, "With characteristic impulsiveness, innocent as a child's, he requested Mrs. Unwin to ask the two ladies to tea,"[2] but when they came in he was so shy that he could hardly bring himself to speak to them.

Shyness? Yes. But *impulsiveness*? That was never a characteristic one would attribute to Cowper. It is a charming story, but like other colourful incidents which have been passed down from book to book, there is almost certainly no truth in it. Mrs Jones' companion was her sister, Lady Austen, and news of the imminent arrival in the area of a titled lady would have been talked of excitedly, not kept secret. Cowper's own account of their first meeting is very different. He wrote to Newton on 7th July 1781 that "Lady Austen, waiving all forms, has paid us the first Visit, and not content with showing us that proof of her Respect, made handsome Apologies for her Intrusion."

Lady Austen was 44 when they first met, five years younger than Cowper. She had been only 19 when she married Robert Austen, who was twice her age. In 1760 he had succeeded to the baronetcy and for many years they lived in the small town of Sancerre in the Loire valley, to which she returned for several more years after his death in London in 1772. In 1778, when France entered the war with America against England she came back to London, but soon decided that a simpler life in the country would be more to her taste.

She once described herself as "the ugliest of all women"[3] but Romney's sensitive portrait of her suggests otherwise. In Cowper's first mention of her to Newton she is

> a lively, agreeable Woman, who has seen much of the World and accounts it a great Simpleton as it is, she laughs and makes laugh, and keeps up a Conversation without seeming to labor at it.

There is a good deal of speculation and imagination in Lord David Cecil's description of her as "all quick-silver and electricity, a live, high-strung, compelling personality with an intense desire to please and considerable powers of doing so".[4] But he is probably not far from the truth. What is certain is that within days she had taken control of life at Orchard Side and so transformed it that she even organised what Cowper himself called a *fête champêtre* (29th July 1781), no doubt echoing the words of this elegant lady who had lived so long in France. Dick Coleman and one of Lady Austen's servants pushed a wheelbarrow full of "eatables and drinkables" for more than a mile to a spinney on the Throckmorton estate at Weston. A plank across the barrow served for a luncheon table, and at six the servants, who had dined elsewhere, boiled the kettle for tea. It was after eight o'clock before they reached home, having spent the day together "from noon 'till Evening, without one cross occurrence, or the least weariness of each other". It is hard to imagine Mrs Unwin arranging such an outing, a fact she might have been very conscious of herself.

When he first mentioned Lady Austen to Newton he had noted her skill in conversation, and within a few weeks of her arrival he had completed a poem whose title – it cannot have been coincidence – was 'Conversation'.

One cannot overestimate the importance of conversation in eighteenth-century polite society. Dr Johnson was justly famous for his enjoyment of the rough and tumble of argument and debate, but *conversation* meant something altogether different to him: "That is the happiest conversation where there is no competition, no vanity, but a calm quiet interchange of sentiments."[5] Addison had written a *Spectator* paper on it (no. 557), and in 1757, when he was 26, Cowper had contributed a witty essay to *The Connoisseur* in which he listed the "pests and nuisances of society": those who grimace and gesture while they speak; who mimic others; who shout at you or whisper in your ear; together with the whistlers, tune-hummers, tattlers, half-swearers, and humbuggers. Some 26 years later, when he re-visited the theme in verse, he was at first less concerned with these social nuisances than with moral failings: blasphemous oaths and prurience where speech is "the pamperer of lust". In his essay he had said that he was not going to attempt to "lay down any particular rules for conversation, but point out such faults in the discourse and behaviour, as render the company of half mankind rather tedious than amusing".[6] And here, to begin with, it is the faults he concentrates on. There are some people, he tells us, who can never make up their minds, while others will bully you into submission. Some tell long, tedious stories:

> But sedentary weavers of long tales,
> Give me the fidgets and my patience fails.
>
> (207-8)

Others bore their listeners with narratives so preposterous that no one could possibly believe them. Among other things he can't abide are pipe-smokers, and fops who drench themselves in perfume. There are those who insist on telling you about their ailments – we have all met them – and the huntsmen who boast about how well they rode and how magnificent their horses are. The car-bore would be our modern equivalent, I think.

Midway through the poem, Cowper turns to consider the positive aspects of conversation. It is a familiar line of argument: speech is what distinguishes us from the beasts. It is a God-given gift and should therefore be used "to praise the pow'r that bids it flow" (l. 444). Rather than providing us with a contrasting list of virtues, however, Cowper relates the story of the two disciples being joined by Christ as they walked to Emmaus, of which as early as 1765 he had written to Lady Hesketh that "if the stamp of divinity was any where to be found in Scripture, it was strongly marked and visibly impressed upon that passage."

Cowper's own retelling of the story is marked by a tone of quiet authority, and we begin to realise that a change has been taking place during the composition of the poem itself. We are no longer being harangued and lectured as in previous satires. In the opening paragraph there was that distinctly workaday image, asserting that conversation was as distinct from mere talking as "harmony divine" was from "The constant creaking of a country sign" (l. 10). There were colloquialisms like "Give me the fidgets" (l. 209) and "Faint as a chicken's note that has the pip" (l. 356). It is altogether less formal, and those positive values which he has been suggesting to us increasingly become features of his own verse:

> A tale should be judicious. clear, succinct,
> The language plain, and incidents well-link'd ...
>
> (235-6)

> But Conversation, chuse what theme we may,
> And chiefly when religion leads the way,
> Should flow like waters after summer show'rs,
> Not as if rais'd by mere mechanic pow'rs.
>
> (703-6)

Religion now appears to be holding somewhat less sway, and gradually the focus centres on what has perhaps been hovering near the forefront of his mind all along: poetry. He opens the debate – for debate it is – by casting some old aspersions on the rigidity of the Augustan couplet and claiming a new freedom:

> A poet does not work by square or line,
> As smiths and joiners perfect a design,
> At least we moderns, our attention less,
> Beyond th'example of our sires, digress,
> And claim a right to scamper and run wide,
> Wherever chance, caprice, or fancy guide.
>
> (789-94)

But he moderates the claim 60 lines later, objecting to the overuse of digression and especially of "fancy so profuse". (l. 856). In 1763, in an essay published in the *St James's Magazine* he had ridiculed the ode, which was so much in vogue at that time:

> It requires a strength of fancy, sublimity of sentiment,
> curious elegance of diction, and though it seems perpetually
> flying off from its subject, an artful connexion of parts, so as
> to make together one beautiful whole.[7]

His views had not changed. Allusions to the "heathen train" (l. 821) of Greek and Roman gods were also severely frowned on. Simplicity and directness were what he favoured, referring to the poets who shared his opinion as "us plain folks" (l. 548). All extremes were to be avoided in favour of the middle way:

To find the medium asks some share of wit,
And therefore 'tis a mark fools never hit.
(879-80)

Having completed his list of the "rude injuries" the lyre of poetry has suffered, he returns to a familiar theme and looks forward to the time when

tun'd at length to some immortal song,
It sounds Jehovah's name, and pours his praise along.
(907-8))

The feeling that the gaiety and light-heartedness of Lady Austen may be heard in the more relaxed tone of 'Conversation' is supported by the fact that the next poem he wrote in this series was called 'Retirement', and we remember that in his letter to Newton (21st August 1781) he explained that she had decided to settle in Olney as she was "very desirous of Retirement", and that she had "seen much of the World and accounts it a great Simpleton, which it is" (7th July 1781). The joys of retirement and the evils and perils of city life are among the poem's main themes:

From cities humming with a restless crowd,
Sordid as active, ignorant as loud,
Whose highest praise is that they live in vain,
The dupes of pleasure, or the slaves of gain,
Where works of man are cluster'd close around,
And works of God are hardly to be found.
(21-6)

These are of course commonplace themes. In *The Spectator* 465, Addison had stated it very succinctly: "In our Retirement every thing disposes us to be Serious. In Courts and Cities we are entertained with the Works of Man, in the Country with those of God." At first glance Cowper would seem to have very little new to add. The wonders revealed by the microscope and the telescope have been brought to our attention before, and our power to

trace in Nature's most minute design,
The signature and stamp of pow'r divine
(53-4)

suggests we are once again about to be regaled with the ideas of the 'physico-theologians' John Ray and William Derham, whose immensely popular works catalogued examples demonstrating "the Being and Attributes of God from his works of Creation". But a closer look at the poem gives us something of a surprise. We find that it is not at all a celebration of the traditional joys of retirement, of the familiar Horatian ideal; it is in fact a reasoned and rational analysis of what such a life actually involves, which turns some of the conventions on their head.

Among the instances of people who retire to live a quiet life in the country, that of the statesman (ll. 365-480) is the most telling. We feel on safe ground here. It is meant, it would seem clear, to call to mind Horace's second Epode, the archetypal *Beatus ille*. And it does, but in more ways than we might at first have expected. Horace pictures the idyllic life for us:

> How pleasant to rest, sometimes beneath an old oak,
>   sometimes on a carpet of grass;
> and all the while the brook glides by between its high banks,
>   the birds are trilling in the trees,
> and the splashing waters of springs play counterpoint,
>   a summons to easy slumber.
>   (trans. Joseph P Clancy)

Cowper follows suit with an idealised English landscape:

> Her hedge row shrubs, a variegated store,
> With woodbine and wild roses mantled o'er;
> Green baulks and furrow'd lands, the stream that spreads
> Its cooling vapour o'er the dewy meads,
> Downs that almost escape th'enquiring eye,
> That melt and fade into the distant skie.
>   (419-24)

But his English statesman finds it hard to settle. The squire and the parson are not the sort of company that appeals to him: one too coarse, the other too obsequious. Riding about on his pony, then coming home to read a book or play billiards; it all begins to pall. He wants to know what is going on in the city and before very long he

> Flies to the levee, and receiv'd with grace,
> Kneels, kisses hands, and shines again in place.
>   (479-80)

At this point we recall that Horace's praise of rural life is in fact in inverted commas. It is spoken by Alfius the money-lender who gives the delights of a rural prospect some thought, then in the closing lines calls in all he is owed and heads back to the stock exchange. Cowper and Horace both sincerely love the countryside, but both are mocking the sort of person who

> likes the country, but in truth must own,
> Most likes it, when he studies it in town.
>
> (573-4)

And he cites Thomson's *Seasons* and Pope's 'Windsor Forest' as having most likely been the townsman's chief studies.

Cowper had a "great respect" (10th March 1792) for Thomson, considering him "admirable in description", even if there was "somewhat of affectation in his style" (19th June 1788). But that respect was for Thomson as a poet; his beliefs Cowper totally opposed. Thomson had begun his 'Hymn on the Seasons' with the lines:

> These, as they change, Almighty Father! these
> Are but the varied God. The rolling year
> Is full of thee. Forth in the pleasing Spring
> Thy beauty walks.

To approach God through nature – indeed to identify God with nature – rather than through the revelation of his word was anathema to Cowper. Early in 'Retirement' he had plainly stated:

> Instruct me, guide me to that heav'nly day,
> Thy words, more clearly than thy works display.
>
> (94-5)

Some poets, he even suggests – and he may have had Thomson in mind – wrote about nature because it was the fashionable way to enhance their literary reputation:

> The snowy robe her wintry state assumes,
> Her summer heats, her fruits and her perfumes,
> All, all alike transport the glowing bard,
> Success in rhime his glory and reward.
>
> (195-8)

"Snowy robe" does sound very much like Thomson.

There is far more about poetry itself in 'Retirement' than in any of the previous poems. Writers of love poetry also have a cold eye cast upon them. It is not simply their habit of moping about in the fields and woods sobbing and sighing for love – though this is unmanly enough. The trouble is that they claim to worship and adore their mistresses, and as far as Cowper is concerned worship and adoration can have only one object, and it is not woman. She "Deserves to be belov'd, but not ador'd".

There is far less emphasis on asserting the Evangelical message in this final poem in the sequence, but it still has a serious purpose. Before he had even begun work on it he had a clear idea of the direction it was to take, as he explained to William Unwin:

> The name of it is Retirement, and my purpose, to recommend the proper improvement of it, to set forth the requisites for that end, and to enlarge upon the happiness of that state of life when managed as it ought to be. In the course of my journey through this ample theme, I should wish to touch upon the Characters, the deficiencies and the Mistakes of thousands who enter on a scene of Retirement, unqualified for it in every respect, and with such designs as have no tendency to promote either their own happiness of that of others. (25th August 1781)

Retirement, the poem says, is something to be enjoyed, but it should not be seen as a time for idleness and self-indulgence. It should be dedicated to God, as, of course, should poetry itself. But, as the final section declares,

> Religion does not censure or exclude
> Unnumber'd pleasures harmlessly pursued.
> (783-4)

Among these pleasures he includes his own harmless pastimes of gardening and painting and there were also some earlier passages which delight without having any palpable design on us, passages which in fact give us brilliant and unexpected snapshots of the age. There is, admittedly, an air of snobbish contempt in his portrayal of those who cannot afford a rural retreat and so have to be content to move out into "suburban villas" (l. 481). "Tight boxes", he calls them, where "ignorance of better things" leads people to live

There prison'd in a parlour snug and small,
Like bottled wasps upon a southern wall.

(493-4)

Rather less snobbish, but still condescending, is his portrayal of sea-bathing, which had become fashionable among a certain sort of people:

Your prudent grand mammas, ye modern belles,
Content with Bristol, Bath and Tonbridge-Wells,
When health requir'd it would consent to roam,
Else more attach'd to pleasures found at home.
But now alike, gay widow, virgin, wife,
Ingenious to diversify dull life,
In coaches, chaises, caravans and hoys,
Fly to the coast for daily, nightly joys,
And all impatient of dry land agree
With one consent to rush into the sea.

(515-24)

The alliteration in the lists speeds up the lines and adds greatly to the jollity of it all. This is not a snapshot. It is a saucy seaside postcard.

It is the type of acutely wry observation which was becoming a feature of the letters he was writing to his friends about life in Olney. At one point in the poem he had addressed us directly as "Friends" and the lines begin to sound more and more like someone talking to us. By the end of the poem he is taking himself seriously, though modestly, as a poet:

Me poetry (or rather notes that aim
Feebly and vainly at poetic fame)
Employs, shut out from more important views,
Fast by the banks of the slow-winding Ouse,
Content, if thus sequester'd I may raise
A monitor's, though not a poet's praise,
And while I teach an art too little known,
To close life wisely, may not waste my own.

(801-8)

Cowper is finding his own self and his own voice, which will soon be powerfully heard in his greatest work, *The Task*.

Meanwhile, Lady Austen was enjoying her retirement and Cowper was enjoying her company. He was eager to explain to William Unwin that she would be a valuable companion for his mother (28th August 1781). The thought that he did protest too much might cross a suspicious mind. The plan was that she should move into the other half of Orchard Side once Dick Coleman, his wife, their child and a thousand rats had been got rid of, and in October she left for London to dispose of her property there. They would write to each other. Mrs Unwin would not, however, be included in this as "At her departure she herself [not him, we notice] proposed a correspondence, and because writing does not agree with your Mother, proposed a correspondence with me" (9th February 1782). We do not know whether Mrs Unwin ever saw the verse letter he wrote to Lady Austen on 17th December 1781. He addresses her as "Dear Anna" – Mrs Unwin always called him *Mr Cowper*. The letter is, ostensibly, about friendship, but there are several instances when the language might easily suggest rather more to a lady of sensibility. When he picks up his pen to write to her he says he feels

> that itching, and that tingling,
> With all my purpose intermingling,
> To your intrinsic merit true,
> When call'd to address myself to you.
>
> (25-8)

He repeatedly suggests that their meeting was brought about by God:

> Mysterious are his ways, whose power
> Brings forth that unexpected hour,
> When minds, that never met before,
> Shall meet, unite and part no more.
>
> (29-33)

The meeting he sees as "An harbinger of endless good". And the closing lines are certainly open to question – more than one question indeed. Theirs is a friendship

> That has cemented us in one;
> And plac'd it in our power to prove,
> By long fidelity and love,
> That Solomon has wisely spoken;
> 'A three-fold cord is not soon broken.'
>
> (102-6)

If this sounds uncomfortably like a *ménage à trois*, what might Lady Austen have thought if she recollected – and she knew her Bible, they both did – the verse in Ecclesiastes which preceded it? "Again, if two lie together, then they have heat: but how can one be warm alone?" Taken in this context, it sounds very much like a proposal – almost an indecent one.

She lost no time in replying, but, to Cowper's astonishment, her letter, as he explained to Unwin (9th February 1782), "expressed a sort of romantic idea of our merit, and built such expectations of felicity upon our friendship, as we were sure nothing human could possibly answer." This use of the 'royal we' here is rather indicative of his self-righteousness. He in turn replied very promptly to put any such romantic ideas out of her head. "Your Mother heard me read the letter, she read it herself, and honour'd it with the warmest approbation," he told William Unwin. One can be quite sure of that.

Cowper does not, to my mind, come out of this very well. There is no suggestion that he himself may have been to blame in any way. His tone is not only self-righteous, it is bumptious:

> When persons for whom I have felt a friendship disappoint
> and mortify me by their conduct, or act unjustly towards me,
> though I no longer esteem them friends, I still feel that
> tenderness for their character that I would conceal the
> blemish if I could.

His letter gave "mortal Offence". Lady Austen sent him her answer, "but such an one as I could by no means reply to". And that, for the time being, was the end of the affair.

He had plenty to keep him busy though. In May 1781, Joseph Johnson, who had published *Olney Hymns*, agreed to issue a collection of Cowper's poems, and in the following months letters and galley proofs passed to and fro. Cowper expected the volume to appear that summer, but had to learn, as writers before and since have also had to learn, that 'Printers and Booksellers are born to be the most dilatory and tedious of all Creatures' (23rd May 1781). Johnson explained to him that the summer was not a good time to bring out a new book, and the delay gave Cowper the opportunity to add the later satires. The book finally appeared in February 1782 with the title *Poems by William Cowper, of the Inner Temple, Esq.* The title was his own choice and it is hard to understand why he wanted to be known as *of the Inner Temple* as he had had no direct connection with the place for almost 20 years. But he was always at pains to be seen as a gentleman.

Unwisely, he had asked Newton to contribute a preface, which his friend was only too happy to do, but Joseph Johnson quickly realised that it would be damaging and advised against it. Newton had almost nothing to say about the poetry. Instead he gave a personal account of how Cowper had once "lived without God", then had suffered an "affliction" and undergone a "long indisposition". One of the few things he did say about the poems was that 'Table Talk' had been put first "with some regard to the prevailing taste, and that those who are governed by it may not be discouraged at the very threshold from proceeding farther". He concludes with a rampaging sermon of his own on the necessity of reading the Bible. (vol. I, p. 569). And Cowper had thought that Newton's preface might "obviate prejudices"! He also made the mistake of not telling William Unwin about the publication until the last moment. Unwin naturally felt aggrieved, both at not being been told earlier, and at not being asked to write the preface. Cowper's self-righteous apology (10th May 1781), does not seem to have made amends and had to be quickly followed by a poem expressing a fulsome profession of his friendship. He assured Unwin that it had not been "occasion'd by your gentle Remonstrance" (11th May 1781), though its timing makes that hard to believe, and its position at the end of the collection suggests that it was an "Afterthought" despite his insistence to the contrary.

He also insisted to Newton that "No man ever wrote … with so much indifference about the Event, or rather with so little ambition of public Praise" (16th August 1781), but once he had been published it was, as he himself recognised, a different matter:

> By the way, Magazines are publications we have but little respect for, 'till we ourselves are chronicled in them, and then they assume an importance in our esteem which before we could not allow them. (12th June 1782)

The response in the magazines was mixed. *The Critical Review* praised Cowper as a man with "a sober and religious turn of mind, with a benevolent heart, and a serious wish to inculcate the precepts of morality", but was unimpressed by him as a poet:

> He says what is incontrovertible and what has been said over and over again with much gravity, but says nothing new, sprightly or entertaining, travelling on a plain level flat road, with great composure almost through the whole long and tedious volume, which is little better than a dull sermon in very indifferent verse.

The London Magazine was kinder saying that his poems showed "good taste, and no small share of wit and humour". The writer in the influential *Monthly Review* was perceptive:

> Anxious only to give each image its due prominence and relief,
> he has no unnecessary attention on grace or embellishment:
> his language, therefore, though neither strikingly harmonious
> nor elegant, is plain, forcible, and expressive.[8]

Even more pleasing would have been the news that someone had sent the book to Benjamin Franklin, who replied that although the relish for reading poetry had long since left him,

> there is something so new in the manner, so easy and yet so
> correct in the language, so clear in the expression yet concise,
> and so just in the sentiments, that I have read the whole with
> great pleasure, and some of the poems more than once. (27th
> May 1782)

Cowper had sent a copy to Edward Thurlow, a close friend during his early days in London and now Lord Chancellor. It was accompanied by an uncomfortably unctuous letter expressing "affectionate remembrance of a connection which did me so much honor" (25th February 1782). But the Lord Chancellor did not even acknowledge receipt of it. Cowper claimed that

> When I sent my book to the Chancellor, I meant no more by
> it than to pay him that respect I thought he had a right to. If
> it had procured me a line from him in return, I should have
> been pleased perhaps and flattered by the notice of so great
> a man; but my expectations went no farther. (1st April 1782)

But he was clearly hurt by the silence, as several of his letters around that time show. And there is a degree of real bitterness in the poem 'Valediction' which he sent to Unwin on 10th November 1783. In it he bids farewell to Thurlow and also to his sometime friend George Colman, who had similarly failed to acknowledge the gift of his poems. Neither man ever saw the poem of course; Cowper wrote it to release his own feelings, and to Thurlow he says:

I sent you verse, and, as your Lordship knows,
Back'd with a modest sheet of humble prose,
Not to recall a promise to your mind,
Fulfill'd with ease had you been so inclin'd,
But to comply with Feelings, and to give
Proof of an old affection still alive –
Your sullen silence serves at least to tell
Your alter'd heart – and so my Lord – farewell.

(19-26)

The 'promise' was still niggling him over two years later when on 11th February 1786 he explained to Lady Hesketh that when he and Thurlow were both young men and had been drinking tea with some friends in Bloomsbury, he had said:

> Thurlow – I am nobody, and shall be always nobody, and you will be Chancellor. You shall provide for me when you are. He smiled and replied – I surely will … But alas! 24 years have passed since the day of the date thereof, and to mention it to him now would be to upbraid him with inattention to his plighted troth. Neither do I suppose that he could easily serve such a creature as I am, if he would.

That he should expect such a casual conversation, and one instigated by himself, to be a binding obligation is both surprising and revealing. The "high disdain [and] sense of injured merit"[9] are very evident here; it is yet another instance of Cowper expecting to be provided for by others and resentful when he is not.

But news of Cowper's success seems to have reawakened Lady Austen's interest in him. She sent him three pairs of worked ruffles, and he in turn sent her his poems. She was proposing to move to Weston, only a few miles from Olney, with two friends. Cowper was very disparaging about them. One, he said, was "a dissipated woman of fashion", the other a "haughty beauty" (24th February 1782). He was not at all sure that he wanted to renew the connection, but once they met again, the old attraction was evident, particularly on her side. She had taken up residence on Clifton Hill, and as it was a particularly wet summer, when it was too muddy for him to visit her, she would ride to Olney on an ass.

But how to get closer? At the risk of seeming unchivalrous, one might suggest that feminine wiles came into play. One evening in church she was seized by the excruciating pain of a bilious colic and had to be helped to

Orchard Side where it was all she could do to grasp Cowper's arm and be seated by the fireside. After a period of unutterable anguish she managed to climb the stairs and be put to bed. The doctor was summoned next day and she was soon cheerful again, but at bedtime she had another violent fit and as she had not begun to undress Cowper was allowed into her room. In about an hour she was feeling much better and next day was able to ride back to Clifton on the ass. But her trials were not over. A few weeks later villains tried to break into the house in Clifton, and the ladies were prevailed upon to take refuge in Orchard Side. Men with firearms were lodged in the house and so it was safe for them to return, but Lady Austen had been too much disturbed and had to stay with Cowper until the rector moved out of the vicarage and she could move in there. There was now only the orchard between them, and before long he was writing to Unwin:

> Lady Austen and we pass our days alternately at each other's Château; in the morning I walk with one or other of the Ladies, and in the afternoons wind thread – thus did Hercules, and thus probably did Samson. (19th January 1783)

That both Hercules and Samson were brought to their ends by women seems to have been an irony which escaped him.

Meanwhile he had struck up a friendship with someone of an entirely different disposition: William Bull, the pastor of the Independent church in Newport Pagnell. It was an unlikely friendship, as Bull was not only a Dissenter, but also an inveterate smoker. Cowper had condemned tobacco in 'Conversation' as a

> Pernicious weed! whose scent the fair annoys
> Unfriendly to society's chief joys.
>   (251-2)

But such was his feeling for Bull that he was prepared to make an exception in his case:

> My Greenhouse fronted with Myrtles, and where I hear nothing but the pattering of a fine shower and the sound of distant thunder, wants only the fumes of your pipe to make it perfectly delightful. Tobacco was not known in the Golden age. So much the worse for the Golden age. (3rd June 1783)

A few days later he wrote a letter to William Unwin in which there was a brilliant pen portrait of Bull, and one which might be read as an unconscious self-portrait:

> A Dissenter, but a liberal one; a man of Letters and of Genius; master of a fine imagination, or rather *not* master of it; an imagination, which when he finds himself in the company he loves and can confide in, runs away with him into such fields of speculation as amuse and enliven every other imagination that has the happiness to be of the party. At other times he has a tender and delicate sort of melancholy in his disposition, not less agreeable in its way. No men are better qualified for companions in such a world as this, than men of such a temperament. Every scene of life has two sides, a dark and a bright one, and the mind that has an equal mixture of melancholy and vivacity, is best of all qualified for the contemplation of either. It can be lively without levity, and pensive without dejection. Such a man is Mr. Bull. But he smokes tobacco – nothing is perfect. (8th June 1783)

Small wonder they became such firm friends.

A great admirer of Cowper's work, Bull sent him three volumes of the works of the French poet Mme Guyon, with the suggestion that he might care to translate a few of them; yet another instance of Cowper writing at someone else's suggestion.

Mme Guyon (1648-1717) was a controversial figure and when Cowper first mentioned the project to William Unwin he was aware of what might be said:

> A Quietist say you and a Fanatic, I will have nothing to do with her. 'Tis very well, you are welcome to have nothing to do with her, but in the mean time her verse is the only French verse I ever read that I found agreeable. (3rd August 1782)

Her valuation of grace above works would have found favour with Cowper, but Quietism was a different matter. It was a system of religious mysticism which taught that perfection and spiritual peace could be attained by an annihilation of the will and a passive contemplation of the divine. As followers of such a doctrine would ultimately have no need of priests, or indeed of the Church, it was condemned by the Inquisition in 1685, and for what was seen as her passionate incitement of it Mme Guyon spent seven years in jail, much of the time in the Bastille. But how often literature has benefited from the existence of jails and lunatic asylums: Cervantes, Bunyan, Clare, Smart, and in more recent times, Robert Lowell and Ivor Gurney. During her time in the Bastille Mme Guyon wrote almost 900 poems.

Cowper soon became aware that there were certain features and characteristics of her poems which it would be best not to translate too closely. He accepted an objection raised by William Unwin that she had sometimes been over-familiar in the way she addressed God, and assured him that in his versions there would be "a more sober and respectful manner of expression" (7th September 1783).

When we find Mme Guyon exclaiming:

> O vous mon Amour et ma vie,
> Possédez-moi la nuit seul à l'écart

Cowper has neutered the eroticism:

> My Saviour! occupy me still
> In this secure recess.

And whenever the nihilism inherent in the doctrine of Quietism is too evident, Cowper carefully turns it aside:

> L'amour qui m'instruit au silence,
> M'enseigne aussi de ne désirer rien;
> Et m'apprend que l'indifférence
>   Non le choix, est le plus grand bien …

becomes:

> Love this gentle admonition
> Whispers soft within my breast;
> "Choice befits not thy condition,
> Acquiescence suits thee best."

In his preface to the edition eventually published in 1801, Bull spoke very firmly on this issue of Mme Guyon's beliefs:

> To infer that the peculiarities of Madame Guion's theological sentiments were adopted either by Mr. Cowper or by the editor, would be almost as absurd as to suppose the inimitable translator of Homer to have been a pagan.

However, Bull has been criticised for putting into Cowper's hands verses which might have only added to his melancholy and there are stanzas in 'The Vicissitudes Experienced in a Christian Life' which stand out in Cowper's version as autobiographical:

> Has Hell a pain I would not gladly bear,
>   So thy severe displeasure might subside?
> Hopeless of ease, I seem already There,
>   My life exrtinguish'd, and yet death denied.
>
> *   *   *
>
> My claim to life, though sought with earnest care,
>   No light within me or without me, shows;
> Once I had faith; but now in self-despair
>   Find my chief cordial and my best repose.

Cowper found much that he admired in Guyon's work, praising its "strain of simple and unaffected Piety", but remembering that Lady Austen had lived for many years in France, and that her command of the language, we may assume, was greater than his, it is hard to believe that she did not offer her assistance, and so, sitting side by side while discussing the niceties of translation may well have been one of the project's additional pleasures.

She was directly responsible at this time for Cowper's work suddenly becoming the talk of the country. What he had said of Bull's mind having an "equal mixture of melancholy and vivacity" was equally true of himself, and when he was in one of his more gloomy moods Lady Austen set out to cheer him up. She told him a story she had heard in her youth, and at first he was not impressed, but then began to smile and the smile soon became a laugh. He was so intrigued by what he heard that when he retired for the night he didn't sleep, but wrote, and next morning presented her with the first draft of 'The Diverting History of John Gilpin'.

The story itself is a simple one. John Gilpin, a London linen-draper, has been married, as his wife bluntly puts it, "these twice ten tedious years", but they have never had a holiday, and she plans an excursion to The Bell, an inn in Edmonton, which at that time was a village ten miles north of the City. She and several of her relatives would travel there in a chaise, but John would have to ride behind them on horseback. Unfortunately the horse he has borrowed bolts, and his hat, wig and cloak go flying off. Dogs bark, children scream and in the commotion the turnpikes fling open their gates assuming he is taking part in some sort of race. The "snorting beast" gallops past Edmonton and does not stop until it reaches its own stable. Not discouraged, Gilpin decides to try once more, but it is the same all over again and the horse only stops when it gets back to Gilpin's shop.

The poem is a ballad, a verse form Cowper described to Unwin as "a species of poetry, I believe, peculiar to this country, equally adapted to the drollest and the most tragical subjects. Simplicity and ease are its proper characteristics" (4th August 1783). Imitations of medieval ballads had been much in vogue, but Cowper chose instead to imitate the eighteenth-century popular street ballads. He worked at the poem meticulously, and we can see from the changes he made that what he was aiming for was a deliberate coarseness. Stanza 24 had initially been smooth and innocuous enough in its first printing:

> The Horse who never had before
> Been handled in this Kind,
> Affrighted fled and as he flew
> Left all the World behind.

But it was changed to:

> His horse, who never in that sort
>   Had handled been before,
> What thing upon its back had got
>   Did wonder more and more.

To this end the changes are quite brilliant: the syntax has become tortuously clumsy, the vocabulary common, and the last line is a classic example of redundant padding out. Deliberately bad verse is not easy to write. Throughout the poem there is a good deal of imagery equally lacking in 'decorum', together with a fine mixture of pseudo-romance and the downright prosaic, and Cowper frequently shows himself to be an expert in bathos:

> Stop, stop, John Gilpin! – Here's the house
> > They all at once did cry,
> The dinner waits, and we are tired,
> > Said Gilpin – so am I.

But some kinds of clumsiness he would not stoop to. In the first printing he had rhymed *Horse* with *worse*, but that, as he admitted to Unwin, was "a false rhyme" and quite unprofessional, so had to be changed (1st November 1784).

'John Gilpin' was first published anonymously in the *Public Advertiser* on 14th November 1782 and was an instant success, a success greatly enhanced by a public recitation in Freemasons Hall by John Henderson, one of the most popular actors of his day. It was soon being reprinted in newspapers, chapbooks, broadsides and with countless illustrated editions for years to follow. The sheer high spirits of the story-telling were such that before long Cowper could rightly claim to Unwin that " … now all the world laughs, at least if they have the same relish for a tale ridiculous in itself, and quaintly told, as we have" (18th November 1782).

In more recent times that "same relish" has been somewhat lacking among critics. Norman Nicholson, usually a sensitive reader of Cowper, confessed he was "quite unable to appreciate it. I can raise scarcely a grin at the antics of the miserable linen-draper," adding in a rather curmudgeonly tone: " I am surprised that Cowper could laugh at the misfortunes of a rider on a frantic, runaway horse without, apparently, giving one thought to the horse."[10] Others have ingeniously connected it with 'The Castaway' and discovered darker elements in it, elements of Cowper's melancholy. William Norris Free reads it as a satire on bourgeois attitudes and speech habits.[11] James King tells us that Mrs Gilpin's attempt is "an emblematical representation of Cowper's deepest fears about the futility of human compassion when compared with the scorn of God".[12] And Morris Golden, while disclaiming any suggestion that he is uncovering unintended allegory, finds that "something of Cowper's attitude towards the rush towards death, the unreliability of God, the meaningless violence of the world is at the root of these jokes."[13]

Jokes, viewed in this dim academic light, would indeed be hard to laugh at, and while such arguments may be plausible, they are hardly convincing. After all, though Gilpin had an uncomfortable ride and lost his wig and his hat and coat, and missed having dinner with his wife, he got home safe and sound, and the poem ends on a happily triumphant and appropriately discordant note:

Now let us sing, long live the king,
    And Gilpin long live he,
And when he next doth ride abroad,
    May I be there to see!

It is a relief to find Vincent Newey saying he thinks it is Cowper's happiest poem and a "masterpiece of all such humorous writing".[14]

In the letter he wrote to Unwin about 'John Gilpin' Cowper told him that " … strange as it may seem, the most ludicrous lines I ever wrote have been written in the saddest mood, and but for that saddest mood perhaps had never been written at all." Then reverting to shipwreck imagery once again, he added: "To say truth it would be but a shocking vagary, should the mariners on board a ship buffeted by a terrible storm, employ themselves in fiddling and dancing. Yet sometimes, much such a part act I" (18th November 1782).

For the most part, however, he was perfectly content with his way of life and a few days later contrasted it with Joseph Hill's in London:

> How different is the complexion of your Evenings and mine! Yours spent amid the ceaseless Hum that proceeds from the inside of 50 noisy and busy periwigs, mine by a domestic fireside, in a retreat as silent as retirement can make it, where no noise is made but what we make for our own amusement. For instance, here are two Ladies and your humble Servant in company; one of the Ladies has been playing on the Harpsichord, while I with the other have been playing at Battledore and Shuttlecock. A little dog in the mean time howling under the chair of the former, performed in the Vocal way to admiration. (7th December 1782)

Cowper seemed to be quite unaware of the tension which might exist between two ladies in such circumstances, but Thomas Scott, the curate of Olney at that time and Lady Austen's landlord at the vicarage, was in a position to witness closely what was going on and tactfully observed: "Who can be surprised that two women should be continually in the society of one man, and quarrel sooner or later with each other?"[15] Inevitably, the relationship came to a second, sudden and final breakdown in the early summer of 1784. Accounting for it to his cousin, Lady Hesketh, in 1786, Cowper was, one might say, economical with the truth. He fails to mention Lady Austen's first visit, or the quarrel of 1782, and implies that being

155

obliged, out of simple good manners, to spend so much time in her company got in the way of his writing, and that her ill-health had obliged her to go to Bristol.

Samuel Greatheed, a pupil of William Bull, who helped Hayley with his biography of Cowper, gives a very different view of Lady Austen:

> Her mind afforded as great a contrast to Mrs U's as can well be conceived; she entertained no small contempt and aversion for her; and frequently indulged her unequalled turn for satire at Mrs U's expense, sometimes in her company, but oftener in Mr C's. At length Mrs U. who was not always aware of the ridicule designed against her, became apprehensive (perhaps not wholly without occasion) that some ideas were formed of a permanent union between her two Companions; and at her request Mr C. drop'd all Correspondence with Lady A. upon her removal.[16]

Mrs Unwin might well have been *apprehensive*. Cowper had given Lady Austen a lock of his hair which she mounted in a diamond brooch and wore pinned to her breast, and as if this were not enough, he composed a poem to celebrate the fact:

To a Lady
Who wore a Lock of his Hair Set
With Diamonds

The star that beams on Anna's breast
    Conceals her William's hair,
'Twas lately severed from the rest
    To be promoted there.
The heart that beats beneath the star
    Is William's well I know,
A nobler prize and richer far
    Than India could bestow.
She, thus his favoured lock prefers
    To make her William shine.
The ornament indeed is hers,
    But all the honour mine.

Hayley, as was his wont, chose to see nothing wrong in such words. "To me they appeared expressive of that peculiarity in his character, a gay and tender gallantry, perfectly distinct from amorous attachment." But he was prepared to admit that Lady Austen "may easily be pardoned , if she was induced by them to hope, that they might possibly be a prelude to a still closer alliance".[17] *Possibly?*

There is no way of knowing for certain how the final break came about, but, while Lady Austen was in Bristol, Mrs Unwin's daughter and son-in-law went to stay at Orchard Side. Susanna had always disliked Cowper and it is possible that a family conference was held. Perhaps Mrs Unwin was invited to return to live with them in Dewsbury, thus forcing Cowper into making a decision. This was something he never had been good at, but if forced, there was never any doubt which way he would jump. A letter to William Unwin dated 12th July 1784 begins "Your sister leaves us this Evening" and the second paragraph reads:

> You are going to Bristol. A Lady, not long since our very near
> neighbour, is probably there. She *was* there very lately. If you
> should chance to fall into her company, remember if you
> please that we found the connexion on some accounts an
> inconvenient one; that we do not want to renew it, and
> conduct yourself accordingly. A character with which we
> spend all our time should be made on purpose for us. Too
> much or too little of any single ingredient, spoils all. In the
> instance in question, the dissimilitude was too great not to be
> felt continually, and consequently made our intercourse
> unpleasant. We have reason however to believe that she has
> given up all thoughts of a Return to Olney.

It is the coldness of his sentiments here – he will not even bring himself to mention her name – which is unpleasant.

Kenneth Povey, who has written extensively on the relationship between Cowper and Lady Austen, suggests that she herself provided a way out of the difficulty by writing to Cowper as she had done once before, and in terms which allowed him an excuse for breaking off the friendship. She told Hayley many years later that his final letter to her, if she had kept it, would have proved that she was willing to devote her life and fortune to him.[18] She returned to Clifton the following year where she remained, one might say defiantly, until 1790, but there was no contact with Cowper. She then settled in London and in 1796 married Count Claude Tardiff du Granger, a French nobleman who was himself a poet.

To her lasting credit, however, before she left Olney she had imposed a task on Cowper, which became his most celebrated poem, *The Task*.

11

The Task

His word my hope secures

Readers who opened Cowper's 'The Task' when it was first published in July 1783 might well have been taken aback a little by the unusually personal tone of its brief 'Advertisement':

> The history of the following production is briefly this. A lady,
> fond of blank verse, demanded a poem of that kind from the
> author, and gave him the SOFA for a subject. He obeyed.

Interestingly, four years previously, on being asked to write a birthday poem, he had declined, telling William Unwin, "I am not good at Writing upon a given Subject" (9th November 1780). In truth, as we have seen, he rarely did otherwise, and in this instance, when Lady Austen (for it was she again) issued her demand he was quick to obey. But the real point at issue here has sometimes been missed. The debate with Lady Austen was not about the topic, the subject of the poem at all. Her suggestion was probably more a cry of desperation. It was the first thing she thought of – it was *there*, before both their eyes. The debate between them – and it seems to have been a long-standing one and not just a matter of that moment – was about *verse form*: what could and could not be accomplished in blank verse. We have to remember that Cowper had recently published seven long poems covering a wide variety of topics in *couplets*. It was a form he was comfortable in. Cowper had, I believe, been insisting that blank verse has its limitations. With the example of Milton still so dominant, he was arguing that blank verse is only appropriate for epic or matters of serious import, such as Christopher Smart's 'Seatonian Poems' on the Attributes of the Supreme Being, with which Cowper would have been familiar. Lady Austen's counter-argument was that you can write about anything in blank verse: the sofa for example. But when Cowper took up her challenge it is was as though he was determined to prove her wrong, that you can *not* write about such an everyday object in blank verse without it becoming burlesque or mock-heroic. Burlesque does seem to have been exactly what he was intending in the opening one hundred lines or so, which in all probability he was proposing to present to Lady Austen to clinch his argument.

At first glance these opening lines seem entirely and unusually personal, referring to the titles of three of the poems in his previous collection:

> I sing the SOFA. I who lately, sang
> Truth, Hope, and Charity, and touch'd with awe
> The solemn chords ...

There is an assumption here that we know and are familiar with this writer who seems to be taking us into his confidence. At the same time there is a deliberate echo of the lines added to the opening of Virgil's *Aeneid* "Ille ego qui quondam gracili modulatus avena carmen" ("I who once tuned his song upon a slender reed"). And this is quickly followed by a glance in the direction of *Paradise Lost*:

> ... and with a trembling hand,
> Escap'd with pain from that advent'rous flight,
> Now seek repose upon a humbler theme.
> (I.3-5)

Milton had referred to his "adventurous song / That with no middle flight intends to soar", but in deliberate contrast Cowper tells us that he is aiming for something even lower than the middle flight – a "humbler theme". He is, I would suggest, determined from the outset to lose this bet with Lady Austen, and to do so by way of a joke.

However, what had at first looked like setting out as a mock-heroic, then changes tack and becomes a progress poem, indeed a mock-georgic, relating the history of seats, beginning with the "hardy chiefs" who had no other clothing than "their own painted skins" and sat on "the rugged rock" until "the birthday of invention" saw the arrival of the joint stool:

> On such a stool immortal Alfred sat,
> And sway'd the sceptre of his infant realms.
> (I.22-3)

Three legs then became four and a later generation, splendidly and heroically, gave them a "twisted form vermicular". The Miltonics are skilfully maintained as the history is continued and the stools become chairs, first acquiring backs, then arms, but the arms were

> rude at first, and not with easy slope
> Receding wide, they press'd against the ribs,
> And bruised the side, and elevated high
> Taught the rais'd shoulders to invade the ears.
>
> (I.63-6)

The ladies, rightly, "Gan murmur", and so the soft settee was devised and eventually the sofa itself:

> Thus first necessity invented stools.
> Convenience next suggested elbow chairs,
> And luxury th'accomplished Sofa last.
>
> (I.86-8)

But it had not all been gain. *Luxury* was a loaded word in the eighteenth century. Barbarism may have given way to civilisation, but hardihood had been exchanged for indolence, and in this Cowper already seems to have in mind one of the major themes of the poem as a whole.

Having reached a point where he is no longer sure that the sofa is a subject to be celebrated at all, one can sense Cowper's uncertainty. He cannot stop here, but neither is it obvious how he can continue. Tentatively he starts to disassociate himself from it all:

> Oh may I live exempted (while I live
> Guiltless of pamper'd appetite obscene)
> From pangs arthritic that infest the toe
> Of libertine excess. The Sofa suits
> The gouty limb 'tis true; but gouty limb,
> Though on a Sofa, may I never feel.
>
> (I.103-8)

What is he to do? The answer is suddenly quite simple: he gets up and walks outside. And this was not a convenient piece of literary fiction or a poetic device. Cowper and Mrs Unwin were, as we know, both keen walkers, and the path he is about to take us on was one of their favourites. Nothing, however, has prepared us for this abrupt change, which will be followed by many more. Readers in the latter half of the eighteenth century expected logical and regular progression in their poems, and a critic writing in *The Monthly Review* in 1786 complained of its "want of unity and design", adding that the poem was "composed of reflections that seem independent of one another". But Cowper knew what he was doing. The word 'Walk' is in the titles of the last two books of *The Task*, and the poem as a whole can be seen as one long ramble. We are being invited to go along with him and to stop and reflect with him as one thing after another occurs to him or catches his attention. It may seem casual and artless but there is method to it, and as early as 10th October 1784, while still working on the poem, he had explained to William Unwin: "If the work cannot boast a regular plan ... it may yet boast that the reflections are naturally suggested always by the preceding passage." "Suggested" is the crucial word here. Cowper had read and greatly admired Beattie's *Dissertations* in which, in a chapter entitled "Of the Association of Ideas", he had written:

> When we give full scope to our thoughts and permit them to shift, as imagination or accident shall determine, one idea brings in another, which gives way to a third, and that in turn is succeeded by others.[1]

Cowper had himself advised his readers in his 'Advertisement' that although he had begun by writing, as he had been told to, of the sofa,

> Having much leisure [he] had connected another subject with it: and pursuing the train of thought to which his situation and turn of mind led him, brought forth at length, instead of the trifle which he at first intended, a serious affair – a Volume.

The association of ideas, as propounded by Locke, suggests that one idea will always be followed by the same sequence of ideas, but there is nothing so mechanical or methodical in Cowper's approach. *The Task* could, it might be argued, be seen as a very early instance of a stream of consciousness.

What he is conscious of as he sets out on this initial ramble is remarkable in that it is the very *unremarkable* landscape around Olney. James Thomson is credited with having been the driving force behind the description of natural scenery in the eighteenth century, but his landscapes are very different. It was the panoramic view he favoured, the grandiose and sublime rather than the local and particular. The sublime, that astute if somewhat irascible critic John Dennis tells us, consists of "thunders, tempests, raging seas, inundations, torrents, earthquakes, volcanoes, monsters, serpents, lions, tigers, fire, war and pestilence",[2] and Thomson availed himself of every one of them. Cowper admired Thomson, but with reservations: " ... it always seemed to me that there was somewhat of affectation in his style," he told his friend Mrs King (19th June 1788). He realised how often the detail was second hand and added: " ... when he describes what he never saw, one is forced to read him with some allowance for misrepresentation."

For his own part, Cowper claimed in a letter to Unwin, "My descriptions are all from nature; not one of them is secondhanded" (10th October 1784). It is a valid claim. What is more, his descriptions are of the actual, the ordinary, the commonplace things and events of every day, and for the most part in the language of every day – language such as men really use. He was, one might hazard, on the verge of a literary revolution, and aftercomers, as we shall see, found much to learn from him.

But before he describes the scenery around Olney, there is another jump in his thinking – a jump in time which takes him back to his school days when he would play truant from Westminster School and go wandering along the banks of the Thames, happily picking blackberries and crab apples as he went. He regrets the passage of time since then, time that has taken the spring out of his step, robbed him of some of his teeth and turned his auburn locks to grey. But it is not total regret. In words which again bring Wordsworth to mind, he enjoys the comfort of a recreating memory:

> My relish of fair prospect; scenes that sooth'd
> Or charm'd me young, no longer young, I find
> Still soothing and of power to charm me still.
>
> (I.141-3)

Even more arresting, if we have 'Tintern Abbey' in mind, are the words which follow, for just as Wordsworth stressed the importance of Dorothy's company on such occasions, so Cowper expresses his happiness at having Mrs Unwin, "the dear companion of my walks", beside him. It is not only the sofa which has been put to the back of his mind. So, it would seem, has Lady Austen, and this is made quite clear in some of the closing lines of Book VI:

It shall not grieve me, then, that once when called
To dress a Sofa with the flow'rs of verse,
I play'd awhile, obedient to the fair
With that light task, but soon to please her more
Whom flow'rs alone I knew would little please,
Let fall th'unfinish'd wreath, and roved for fruit.

(VI.1006-11)

He has finished playing, but before he gets down to the business of describing their walk together, he assures Mrs Unwin and so, indirectly, us too, that

Thou know'st my praise of nature most sincere,
And that my raptures are not conjured up
To serve occasions of poetic pomp,
But genuine.
(I.150-3)

Poetic pomp, and we know what he means, is certainly not present here, and yet to some extent what he gives us is in the tradition of formal eighteenth-century landscape verse. The spectator had, over the preceding years, been educated, as it were, first to appreciate landscape painting and then landscape itself. As a result, the landscapes most in favour were those which struck the viewer as "picturesque", a term defined by William Gilpin as "that kind of beauty which would look well in a picture".[3]

Initially Cowper is viewing the scene before him as though it were a picture. The Ouse, he says, "Conducts the eye along his sinuous course", and, as with molten glass, it "inlays the scene", but it is not long before we are convinced that this is an actual landscape he is presenting to us. There are not only rural sights, but rural sounds: birdsong and the wind in the trees. Then a startling non-sequitur in praise of whoever invented the weather-house allows him to say that once, when it was wet, he went out by himself – like the weather man – as it was too treacherous for Mrs Unwin, and so, taking an unfamiliar path, he discovered a tiny thatched cottage on a hilltop surrounded by trees. He called it the Peasant's Nest, and the snugness – one of Cowper's favourite words – of it seemed absolutely ideal:

Here, I have said, at least I should possess
The poet's treasure, silence, and indulge
The dreams of fancy, tranquil and secure.
                    (I.234-6)

Generations of poets – from Horace down to Elizabeth Bishop – have entertained the same fantasy, but Cowper was a realist, recognising that the nearest water supply was a "weedy ditch" and that the cottage was too far out of town for the baker to call. Writing later from the comfort of Weston Lodge he observed to Lady Hesketh once:

> You must always understand, my Dear, that when poets talk of Cottages, hermitages, and such like matters, they mean a house with 6 sashes in front, two comfortable parlours, a smart stair-case, and three bed-chambers of convenient dimensions; in short, exactly such a house as this. (26th November 1786)

Just how precise and accurate Cowper's descriptions of the area are we can see by comparing a few brief lines which tell how

Hence ancle-deep in moss and flow'ry thyme
We mount again, and feel at ev'ry step
Our foot half sunk in hillocks green and soft,
Rais'd by the mole, the miner of the soil
                    (I.271-4)

with an account in *Cowper Illustrated* (1803):

> The ascent is difficult, being thickly tufted by mole-hills, incrusted by verdant moss, and mingled with flowery thyme, the scattered sweets of which, regaling the scent, deceive the labour of the stumbling walk; for here the firmest footstep in continually eluded by the yielding earth. (p.36)[4]

When he comes to writing about the country people there is less of the sentimentality in which we find Thomson so often indulging. At harvest time, when the empty hay-wains are being held up by the slower progress of the fully laden ones, the "boorish" drivers fall out and begin shouting at each other:

There, from the sun-burnt hay-field homeward creeps
The loaded wain, while lighten'd of its charge
The wain that meets, it passes swiftly by,
The boorish driver leaning o'er his team
Vocif'rous, and impatient of delay.

(I.295-9)

This is a scene, we feel sure, that Cowper has witnessed himself more than once.

Examples of hard work lead to a condemnation of idleness and of those who prefer looking at landscape paintings to going out into the fresh air to see the beauty of nature for themselves. The natural world is infinitely various, he says. There is beauty to be found everywhere, even on the "common overgrown with fern, and rough / With prickly gorse". This thought prompts one of those narrative digressions found in Thomson's *Seasons*. In this instance it brings to Cowper's mind the sad and true story of Kate, the serving maid, whose lover drowned at sea, and who ever afterwards roamed "the dreary waste", heartbroken, her clothes reduced to rags and "craz'd" in mind. They are lines which ought to be granted a place in any history of English literature. No one had written on a subject like this before, and many years later when Wordsworth followed Cowper's example, critics were still not quite ready for such a thing.

Also to be found on the common were the gypsies, "A vagabond and useless tribe" he has no time for. They eat vermin and dead dogs. They steal and prefer "squalid sloth to honourable toil". He looks upon them as savages, and follows this by dismissing the whole idea, so popular at the time, of the 'noble savage'. With one exception, however, and that, as his own note tells us, is Omia. It is here that we first see the deeply humane side to Cowper's nature. Omia had been born in Tahiti, and brought back to England in 1774, where he was pampered, made much of by London society and then taken back home on Cook's third voyage two years later. It was a cruel thing to do, in Cowper's view, and he imagines how unhappy Omia must have been there having once seen and enjoyed the material luxuries of England. As he put it to Newton,

> We brought away an Indian, and having debauched him, we
> sent him home again to communicate the infection to his
> country – fine sport to be sure, but such as will not defray the
> cost. Nations that live upon bread-fruit, and have no mines
> to make them worthy of our acquaintance, will be but little

visited for the future. So much the better for them; their
poverty is indeed their mercy. (6th October 1783)

He pictures Omia forlornly scanning the horizon in the hope of seeing a
British vessel, but warns him:

> Alas! expect it not. We found no bait
> To tempt us in thy country. Doing good,
> Disinterested good, is not our trade.
> We travel far 'tis true, but not for nought;
> And must be brib'd to compass earth again
> By other hopes and richer fruits than yours.
>
> (I.672-7)

There is real bitterness in these lines and anger at the behaviour of his own
country. We have come a long way from the gentle self-mockery of the
poem's opening. The moral judgements which had featured so prominently
in Cowper's 1782 collection surface again, and it was at about this stage in
the composition of the *The Task* that he explained to William Unwin:

> ... the whole has one tendency. To discountenance the
> modern enthusiasm after a London life, and to recommend
> rural ease and leisure, as friendly to the cause of piety and
> virtue. (10th October 1784)

He is realistically prepared to allow that cities in general and London in
particular have contributed much to man's well-being and especially his
cultural well-being. He cites Sir Joshua Reynolds and the fashionable
sculptor John Bacon. He also celebrates the scientific discoveries which had
been made, but in the balance against all this go the number of "petty
robbers" who are hanged while officers of the East India Company, who
amass fortunes through extortion and corruption, not only go free, but are
honoured:

> That thieves at home must hang; but he that puts
> Into his overgorged and bloated purse
> The wealth of Indian provinces, escapes.
>
> (I.736-8)

Book I concludes, as stated in the 'Argument', "with a reflection on the fatal effects of dissipation and effeminacy upon our public measures" or, as he put it more succinctly in one of his most famous lines:

> God made the country, and man made the town.
>
> (I.749)

When we reach the close of Book VI and look back, we feel as though we have had the privilege of spending several hours in the company of a benign and cultured gentleman, a wonderful conversationalist who has allowed us to share the simple pleasures of his domestic life, but if this is so, then it is only because we have momentarily forgotten the Evangelical rantings which so often brought us up short in Book II. Book II is called 'The Time-Piece' and readers might have been tempted to believe that it referred to another item of furniture, a long-case clock perhaps which stood behind the sofa. In which case they would have been mightily puzzled as they read on, for no one could have guessed what he meant by it, and we know only because John Newton wrote and asked him directly. Cowper's somewhat assertively self-defensive reply reads:

> The Time-Piece appears to me, (though by some accident the import of that title has escaped you) to have a degree of propriety ... The book to which it belongs is intended to strike the hour that gives notice of approaching judgment; and dealing pretty largely with the *signs* of the *times*, seems to be denominated as it is with sufficient degree of accommodation to the subject. (11th December 1784)

The signs of the times he had in mind were a series of natural disasters, beginning with the hurricane and tsunami which had devastated Jamaica in 1780, a spectacular meteor which had terrified people in August 1783, the dense fog which had blanketed most of Europe that same summer and the massive earthquake of the year before which had killed at least 40,000 people in Calabria.

These are the kinds of event – with a touch of the sublime to them – which would have so appealed to James Thomson, and it is not long before Cowper is in correspondingly rhetorical mode:

When were the winds
Let slip with such a warrant to destroy,
When did the waves so haughtily o'erleap
Their ancient barriers, deluging the dry?
(II.53-6)

There is no indication that Cowper empathised in any way with the people who had been killed or left destitute by these calamities. He might have been recounting stories from the Old Testament, not recent disasters. To him they seem to have been no more than events brought about by an angry god to punish sinful mankind. God sends an earthquake and the earth:

quakes at his approach. Her hollow womb
Conceiving thunders, through a thousand deeps
And fiery caverns roars beneath his foot.
(II.88-90)

He is not only an angry god, he is a tyrannical god and, even more disturbingly, as envisaged by Cowper, shows no more concern for people than Cowper does himself. He is not concerned with the level of guilt, and if he decides to punish the innocent, it is, as Cowper sees it, to warn the truly guilty of what is in store for them. It comes as no surprise to learn that it is the sinful and guilt-ridden English who should take most heed.

It is hard to square any of this with his claim (letter of 10th April 1784) that none of his descriptions are second-hand and that none of his delineations of the heart are borrowed from books, as all the details of the Sicilian earthquake come from *The Gentleman's Magazine*. Nor does there seem to be any way in which, as he had claimed, his ideas follow on from each other: a scornful account of English aristocrats forgetting the recent treachery of France in the American wars and happily going horse-racing in Fontainebleau, is followed by a passage on the writing of poetry.

He enjoys, he tells us, the challenge that comes with the complexities of writing, added to which there is a therapeutic value to it, for while he is writing,

He feels th'anxieties of life, denied
Their wonted entertainment, all retire.
(II.302-3)

He doubts, however, whether the writing of satire has ever changed anything of significance and insists instead that it is the pulpit one should look to, but his tone becomes increasingly shrill and the language and syntax more and more Miltonic as he realises the futility of that hope, finding all too often not the "legate of the skies" there, but hypocrisy and affectation. His examples of hypocrisy and affectation happily provide us with two of the few memorable passages in Book II. The first of his clergymen is

> loose in morals, and in manners vain,
> In conversation frivolous, in dress
> Extreme, at once rapacious and profuse.
> Frequent in park with lady at his side,
> Ambling and prattling scandal as he goes,
> But rare at home, and never at his books,
> Or with his pen, save when he scrawls a card ...
> (II.378-84)

And then comes the brilliantly envisaged performance of another cleric after he has delivered his sermon:

> Forth comes his pocket mirror. First we stroke
> An eye-brow; next, compose a straggling lock;
> Then with an air, most gracefully perform'd,
> Fall back into our seat; extend an arm
> And lay it at its ease with gentle care,
> With handkerchief in hand, depending low,
> The better hand more busy, gives the nose
> Its bergamot, or aids th'indebted eye
> With op'ra glass, to watch the morning scene,
> And recognise the slow-retiring fair.
> (II.445-54)

Following on from this he laments, in an extended personification, the downfall of discipline in schools and colleges, and then by way of contrast presents us with a very different kind of clergyman and scholar, as exemplified by his brother John, whom despite their religious disagreements, he describes as "a man of worth, / A man of letters and of manners too".

It is also significant that after the extended attack on the lack of discipline in schools and colleges – it runs to over 80 lines – the one college he exempts – "in which order yet / Was sacred and was honoured" – is the one in which his brother was a fellow. And this is not an isolated instance. Very often we find that friends and relatives are allowed to escape censure. Deans of the Church of England are full of pride, except for his cousin Spencer Cowper, who was dean of Durham from 1746 until his death in 1774. The officers of the East India Company were a corrupt bunch, but not Warren Hastings, who had been at Westminster with Cowper. Pipe-smoking was a disgusting habit, unless the pipe belonged to his friend William Bull. And all Roman Catholics were dreadful people, except for his neighbours, the Throckmorton family, who allowed him access to their park. A satirist who does not want to upset his friends can hardly claim to have strong principles. In truth Cowper was often didactic, but he was no satirist, even though he claimed to be: "In some passages, especially in the second book," he told Unwin, "you will observe me very satirical" (10th October 1784).

In the opening paragraph of Book III it seems as if Cowper looks back over Book II and admits to himself, and to his readers, that he had really lost his way. It presents us with an extended image of a rider who

> long in thickets, and in brakes
> Entangled, winds now this way and now that
> His devious course uncertain …
> (III.1-3)

Admitting that he too has "rambled wide", certainly from an encomium on the sofa, he now compares himself with the horseman when at last he discovers a "green-sward smooth", and so finds his way safely home:

> But now with pleasant pace, a cleanlier road
> I mean to tread.
> (III.17-18)

Giving further thought to Book II, he doubts the efficacy of satire, and, in any case, who is he, he asks himself, to think people would take notice of what he had to say? Instead, he decides to approach from a different angle and to concentrate on what he knows best: that "domestic happiness" which is "the nurse of virtue". Before doing so he fires one more broadside at cities with their prostitutes and card-sharps, then, at this point, and quite out of the blue, come those lines which take every reader by surprise and which none ever forgets:

I was a stricken deer, that left the herd
Long since; with many an arrow deep infixt
My panting side was charged when I withdrew
To seek a tranquil death in distant shades.
There was I found by one who had himself
Been hurt by th'archers. In his side he bore
And in his hands and feet the cruel scars.
With gentle force soliciting the darts,
He drew them forth, and heal'd, and bade me live.
Since then, with few associates, in remote
And silent woods I wander, far from those
My former partners of the peopled scene;
With few associates, and not wishing more.
Here much I ruminate, as much I may,
With other views of men and manners now
Than once, and others of a life to come.
I see that all are wand'rers, gone astray
Each in his own delusions; they are lost
In chase of fancied happiness, still wooed
And never won.
  (III.108-27)

These lines are often read as a personal statement. We remember the paranoia he felt as his public examination at the bar of the House of Lords drew closer. He felt driven out of society and sought refuge with Dr Cotton in St Albans where he underwent an Evangelical conversion and was saved by the crucified Christ. There is perhaps a reference also to his attempted suicides. But no reader outside the immediate circle of his family and friends would have recognised this, nor would he have wanted them to.

These lines give the *impression* of being personal, but it can be argued that they go beyond that. We have, in addition to Cowper himself, a poet/persona here and strong biblical echoes which suggest it be read in a different light. The "stricken deer" and the "panting side" recall Psalm 42:1 "As the hart panteth after the water brook, so panteth my soul after thee, O God." The arrows recall Job 6:4 "For the arrows of the Almighty are within me." Most significant, however, is the Song of the Servant of God in Isaiah 53:3-8 where we find the key words "stricken" and "gone astray":

He is despised and rejected of men; a man of sorrows, and acquainted with grief: and we hid as it were our faces from him; he was despised, and we esteemed him not. Surely he hath borne our griefs, and carried our sorrows; yet we did esteem him *stricken*, smitten of God and afflicted. But he was wounded for our transgressions ... *All* we like sheep have *gone astray*; we *have turned every one to his own way*; and the Lord hath laid on him the iniquity of us all ... for he was cut off out of the land of the living: for the transgression of my people was he *stricken*.

The most significant aspect of this Song is in the first verse which reads: "Behold my servant shall deal prudently, he shall be exalted and extolled, and be very high." These lines suggest that the poet/persona will succeed. He will be the chosen of God. Viewed in this light, Cowper can be seen as re-writing his own spiritual biography. The rejected will be glorified. In the context of the poem he revises God's sentence of eternal perdition. Salvation will come at last to the poet/persona and this is how the poem comes to a close in Book VI.

Among the "wand'rers gone astray", he dismisses those historians, geologists and astronomers who waste their lives trying to solve the mysteries of creation, insisting, as he has done so frequently before, that such answers will only ever be found in the Word of God, not in his works. The only intellectual pursuits worth following are those which lead to virtue and to truth, and which, he says, returning to his earlier theme, will only be found in "Domestic life in rural leisure pass'd" (III.293).

At first he is somewhat hesitant. He had confessed to Newton how useless he felt: "crippled and made useless in the church just at that time of life when my judgement and experience being matured, I might be most useful" (letter of 13th January 1784). We notice that he says he has been "*made* useless". He cannot understand why this is so. God's ways are mysterious, he says, but concludes, "in time it shall be explained."

He recognises that the outside world may look upon him as idling his time away, but retaliates by insisting that it is in that world – i.e. in the city – where idleness is to be found. He, in contrast, has *various* employments: "Friends, books, a garden, and perhaps his pen". It may not look as though he labours, but he is not slothful. His is a "laborious ease".

Mindful, it would seem, of the parable of the talents, he declares that he will not waste his life, but use the mind God has given him, and use it in the service of mankind. And he will achieve this, he indicates, through the very poem he is writing, and stresses its autobiographical element:

He that attends to his interior self,
That has a heart, and keeps it; has a mind
That hungers, and supplies it; and who seeks
A social, not a dissipated life,
Has business. Feels himself engaged t'atchieve
No unimportant, though a silent task.
                                    (III.373-8)

It cannot be coincidence that the word with which he ends this statement is the title of the poem.

An account of how he does spend his time then follows. If the weather is inclement he will stay indoors, drink his tea and read, sometimes reading aloud to Mrs Unwin, "her who shares his pleasures and his heart" (l. 390). If it is a nice day then he is off out into his garden. But the class distinction which was so taken for granted then does grate on our ears. He cannot, he says, trust his gardener:

conscious how much the hand
Of lubbard labour needs his watchful eye.
                         (399-400)

"Servile employ" such as digging is quite beneath a gentleman and best left to the *lubbard*, but when some skill and brainpower may be involved then Cowper takes over, and he explains at length how expert he is at pruning his fruit trees.

In the middle years of the eighteenth century a minor genre of neo-georgics – imitations of Virgil – had grown up: Dyer's 'The Fleece', Grainger's 'The Sugar-Cane' and Christopher Smart's 'The Hop-Garden' are the chief examples. These three can be said to cover wide-ranging topics of some economic importance, so that it is hard to know what to make of Cowper's georgic on *cucumbers*. Many of his readers may have been aware of the entry in Johnson's Dictionary which reads, "A cucumber should be well sliced, and dressed with pepper and vinegar, and then thrown out, as good for nothing." In the lead-up to the passage, his mention of John Phillips, the author of 'The Splendid Shilling', suggests that it will be a burlesque, and the splendidly ludicrous expression he uses for a manure heap, "a stercorarious heap", would seem to confirm this. But there are dissenting voices. In his extended study of *The Task*, Martin Priestman complains that so few critics have seen the cucumber-georgic as anything more than a joke. His argument is that "It is a mark of the poem's cock-eyed consistency that its whole development from beginning to end is explained, apparent inconsistencies and all, in this extraordinary passage."[5] But when he asserts that "without forcing a specifically Freudian interpretation, the horse-manure can easily be seen as standing for something like the state of mind in which the poet knew he wanted to write a poem without knowing what,"[6] one wonders who is joking. Weirder still is his suggestion that "Cowper is producing this history of a soul out of his own manure but not necessarily for his own consumption."

At the close of the passage, Cowper is able to laugh at himself:

> The learn'd and wise
> Sarcastic would exclaim, and judge the song
> Cold as its theme, and like its theme, the fruit
> Of too much labor, worthless when produced.
>
> (562-5)

But a change had taken place while he was writing it. Growing cucumbers out of season provided gardeners with a challenge, as he explained to Hill:

> I raise Cucumbers which I cannot eat, merely because it is difficult to raise them. And the conquest of difficulties is one of the most amusing things in the world because it is one of the most flattering to our pride." (13th February 1783)

It was a challenge he took seriously, and first-hand detail replaces the comic.

We learn of the seriousness with which he took his gardening from a letter he wrote to Mrs King in October 1788, when he was living in Weston Underwood. Looking back on his days in Olney he told her:

> But Gardening was of all employments that in which I succeeded best, though even in this, I did not suddenly attain perfection. I began with Lettuces and Cauliflowers, from them I proceeded to cucumbers; next to Melons. I then purchased an Orange tree, to which in due time I added two or three Myrtles ... To defend them from the frost in a situation that exposed them to its severity, cost me much ingenuity and much attendance. I contrived to give them a fire heat, and have waded night after night through the snow with the bellows under my arm, just before going to bed, to give the latest possible puff to the embers ... I became

ambitious of a Greenhouse, and accordingly built one, which, Verse excepted, afforded me amusement for a longer time than any expedient of all the many to which I have fled for refuge from the misery of having nothing to do.

Gardening not only kept Cowper busy enough to hold despair at bay, it also allowed him to achieve something which otherwise was lacking in his life. His garden was something over which he had control, something which he could order and shape to his own wishes, and it would not be going too far to say that he became quite an expert.

Curiously, he once claimed in a letter to Walter Bagot (18th March 1791) to be "a poor man who has but twenty books in the world", but this was certainly not true. Sir Geoffrey Keynes reckoned that when he died "he was possessed of several hundred volumes,"[7] and among them were a good number of books on gardening, including Philip Miller's classics the *Garden Calendar* and *Garden Dictionary*. He also possessed a copy of *The Clergy-Man's Recreation: Shewing the Pleasure and Profit of Gardening* by John Lawrence, AM, rector of Yelvertoft in Northamptonshire. It is an unpretentious book containing a good deal of sensible and practical advice. For example, addressing his readers directly he writes: "I need not tell you here, that 'tis perfect murdering of a young Tree to set it in the same Place and Soil where an old one had grown."

Cowper's copy, signed and dated 1797 (the year when Johnny Johnson persuaded him to sign and date all his books), is in the Cowper and Newton Museum in Olney and contains marginal comments. There are a few dozen, clearly in Cowper's own handwriting. Something about the book got under his skin, or rather something about its author, as the comments – contemptuous and angry – are aimed directly at him. Even in the first pages of the preface, the Rev. Mr Lawrence is told that he is conceited and bluntly bidden to stop bragging. On the subject of grafting, when Lawrence innocently remarks that " … in some cases a disappointment is very undesirable," Cowper has underlined the words and alongside has written, "Is it not so in all cases? Blockhead!" And when Lawrence refers to a "cistern for rainwater" he is told that it is a "Reservoir, ignorance of terms! Insufferable." What provoked his rage we can only surmise, but it is a side of Cowper not seen elsewhere, yet it is Cowper "undressed" as it were, writing for himself, talking to himself, with no other audience intended.

Even more remarkable are the marginalia in Lawrence's *The Fruit-Garden Kalender*. It is fulsomely dedicated to "Most High, Puissant, and Most Noble Prince Henry, Duke, Marquis and Earl of Kent". Cowper would seem to have known or suspected something irregular about the earl's private life, and where Lawrence extols his "Grace's comprehension, knowledge and experience of Men and Things", *Men* has been crossed out and *women* written underneath. On the next page, where it reads: "Your Grace will draw Multitudes after you, to pursue things that are innocent and useful," Cowper adds alongside *Multitudes,* "whores d'ye mean?" Once again we are brought up sharply against a side of Cowper's nature very far removed from the accepted public image, but it is a side we cannot choose to ignore.

To return to *The Task*, it is but short step back from the lines on gardening to his recurrent theme, the celebration of rural life:

> What could I wish that I possess not here?
> Health, leisure, means t'improve it, friendship, peace
> (III.690-1)

contrasted with the debauched life people lead in the city. But the countryside is being debauched too, he claims, and the villain responsible is the "omnipotent magician" Capability Brown. Cowper clearly has no time for landscape gardening:

> He speaks. The lake in front becomes a lawn,
> Woods vanish, hills subside, and vallies rise,
> And streams as if created for his use,
> Pursue the track of his directing wand
> Sinuous or strait, now rapid and now slow,
> Now murm'ring soft, now roaring in cascades
> Ev'n as he bids.
> (III.774-80)

And in achieving all this Brown bankrupts the owner:

> Estates are landscapes, gaz'd upon a while,
> Then advertis'd. and auctioneer'd away.
> (III.754-5)

Ancestral homes are passed on to the *nouveau riche;* the former owners must leave and head for London, which, Book III concludes somewhat shrilly, is

> more obnoxious, at this hour
> Than Sodom in her day had pow'r to be.
> (III.846-7)

Books IV, V and VI of *The Task* are called 'The Winter Evening', 'The Winter Morning Walk' and 'The Winter Walk at Noon'. Winter was always a mixed blessing for Cowper. It brought with it, as we have seen, some of his most acute depressions, but it was also the time when, to rid himself of despair, he wrote some of his finest verse. As he explained to Lady Hesketh,

> Dejection of Spirits, which I suppose may have prevented many a man from becoming an Author, made me one. I find constant employment necessary, and therefore take care to be constantly employ'd. Manual occupation does not engage the mind sufficiently ... but Composition, especially of verse, absorbs it wholly. (12th October 1785)

Bad weather would also keep him indoors more, and more time would be spent at his desk. The winter of 1783/4, when he was at work on *The Task*, was one of the most severe of the whole century. *The Gentleman's Magazine* recorded temperatures constantly below freezing from 19th December until 21st February, and the following day Cowper wrote to Newton: "I gave you joy of a Thaw that has put an end to a frost of nine weeks' continuance with very little interruption," but then told William Bull that "The Ice in my Ink however is not yet dissolved. It was long before the frost seized it, but at length it prevailed" (22nd February 1784).

Such weather must have been particularly hard on the post-boy whose arrival in Olney is announced in the opening lines of Book IV:

> He comes, the herald of a noisy world
> With spatter'd boots, strapp'd waist, and frozen locks,
> News from all nations lumb'ring at his back.
>
>   (IV.5-7)

We never doubt for a moment that this depicts a real event, one which Cowper has seen time and again. He is writing of what knows.

Letters were always a delight to him, but so were the newspapers which brought him word from the "noisy world". He subscribed to the *Morning Chronicle and London Advertiser*, which was published six days a week, and to the *General Evening Post* which appeared on Tuesdays, Thursdays and Saturdays, so there was never any shortage of news. While he felt safe and snug in Olney and glad to be far away from the corruptions of the city, he still had a keen interest in the world at large, and he quickly lets us know of his contempt for the English generals' lack of fight in the war against America, and of his disgust at the exploitation of the native population by the East India Company. He held strong political views, especially about the state of affairs in India, once writing to Unwin: "That Government therefore is bound to interfere and to Unking these tyrants, is to me self-evident" (31st January 1784).

Now that the newspapers have arrived, we are invited, in some of Cowper's most famous lines, to join him in reading them:

> Now stir the fire, and close the shutters fast,
> Let fall the curtains, wheel the sofa round,
> And while the bubbling and loud-hissing urn
> Throws up a steamy column, and the cups
> That cheer but not inebriate, wait on each,
> So let us welcome peaceful evening in.
> (IV.36-41)

The tone is intimate. It does not matter that Berkeley had already used the words "cheer but not inebriate". Cowper made far better use of them. They are his words now, and what we are hearing is what Coleridge called his "divine chit-chat", that distinctive note of conversational ease which was something new in English verse. It is the simplicity which is so appealing, and so notoriously difficult to achieve. Hugh Blair understood this:

> A writer of Simplicity expresses himself in such a manner, that every one thinks he could have written in the same way … it seems the very language of nature … it shows us a man's sentiments and turns of mind laid open without disguise … reading an Author of Simplicity, is like conversing with a person of distinction at home, and with ease, where we find natural manners, and a marked character.[8]

Cowper himself explained to William Unwin:

> Every man conversant with verse-writing knows, and knows by painful experience, that the familiar style is of all styles the most difficult to succeed in. To make verse speak the language of prose, without being prosaic, to marshal the words of it in such an order as they might naturally take in falling from the lips of an extemporary speaker, yet without meanness, harmoniously, elegantly, and without seeming to displace a syllable … is one of the most arduous tasks a poet can undertake. (17th January 1782)

This is precisely what he has achieved and it could not be better put.

It is delightful to learn how little newspapers have changed over the centuries. In Cowper's papers, he tells us that

> Cataracts of declamation thunder here,
> There forests of no-meaning spread the page
> In which all comprehension wanders lost.
>
> (IV.73-5)

And that there are advertisements for wigs and false teeth, and cosmetics "for the brows of faded age". *Plus ça change* …

Reading the newspapers allowed him to survey the world in safety and in comfort, just as his love of travel books, especially those of Captain Cook, allowed him to go along with the great explorers, but to get home again unscathed.

He may have closed the shutters to keep out the cold, but there were things about winter that he warmed to nevertheless:

> I crown thee King of intimate delights,
> Fireside enjoyments, home-born happiness,
> And all the comforts that the lowly roof
> Of undisturb'd retirement, and the hours
> Of long uninterrupted evening, know.
>
> (IV.139-43)

In contrast to the idleness in which people waste their evenings in the city – going to the theatre and playing cards – he celebrates evenings such as they spent in Olney, and does so in a long personification which is somewhat reminiscent of William Collins' 'Ode to Evening'; Collins having been the one exception to his conclusion – formed after reading all of Johnson's *Lives* – that "Poets are a very worthless, wicked sort of people" (10th March 1784).

He might at this point have gone off into one of his more excitable diatribes against the city. It would seem that he did think of doing so, but changed his mind:

> But truce with censure. Roving as I rove
> Where shall I find an end, or how proceed?
>
> (IV.232-3)

Indeed, one of the attractions of this part of Book IV is that we are not preached at, but talked to, and here we find Cowper briefly and endearingly, in a very Wordsworthian moment, talking to himself before presenting us with a picture of himself sitting in front of the fire. It is again in the simplicity of this quiet domestic moment that he achieves greatness.

He looks into the flames and imagines he sees

> houses, tow'rs,
> Trees, churches, and strange visages express'd
> In the red cinders, while with poring eye
> I gaz'd, myself creating what I saw.
> (IV.287-90)

We have all done this and it is a comfort to know that we are not alone in sometimes managing to think about absolutely nothing at all (IV.281-5). He had once confessed the same to Newton:

> The description of your meditations at least suits mine; perhaps I can go a step beyond you upon the same ground, and assert with the strictest truth, that I not only do not think with connexion, but that I frequently do not think at all. (9th October 1784)

Then, as his gaze slides down from the hot coals to the bars of the grate, an old superstition flits into his mind, one which Coleridge found so irresistible that he stole it to use in 'Frost at Midnight':

> Nor less amused have I quiescent watch'd
> The sooty films that play upon the bars,
> Pendulous, and foreboding in the view
> Of superstition prophesying still
> Though still deceiv'd, some stranger's near approach.
> (IV.291-5)

Thomson's 'Winter' was one of the most famous descriptive poems of the century, but Cowper excels him, having the better ear:

> Fast falls the fleecy show'r. The downy flakes
> Descending and with never-ceasing lapse
> Softly alighting upon all below,
> Assimilate all objects.
> (IV.326-9)

We not only see the snowfall, but hear that special silence in all those gentle consonants. Cowper also displays a more genuine understanding and concern for those who have to work in such weather, and vividly pictures for us the carter battling along against a blizzard, his eyes screwed up, his "pucker'd cheeks", and having to hold his hat on with his one free hand. The detail is nicely observed, and this time the deliberately clumsy sound of the verse re-enacts the difficulty the carter has in getting his wagon to move at all:

> The wain goes heavily, impeded sore
> By congregated loads adhering close
> To the clogg'd wheels.
> (IV.343-5)

Cowper was well aware of the hardships suffered by the local people and gives an account of one particular family, "Poor, yet industrious", who have hardly enough to keep themselves warm and fed – a brush-wood fire and one loaf to feed them – but are nevertheless too proud to go begging to the parish and suffer the "insolent rebuffs of knaves in office" (411-12). He was not only a close observer of poverty, he did what he could to alleviate it, and he promises aid to this family. Such aid came regularly to Olney from Robert Smith, later Lord Carrington, a banker and MP for Nottingham, who, insisting on anonymity, sent £40 or £50 each winter for Cowper and Mrs Unwin to distribute to the deserving and god-fearing poor. In a letter to Smith he promises that although there are many devout in Olney "none shall touch it, but such as are miserably poor, yet at the same time industrious and honest" (13th November 1782).

In the same letter he admits to Smith that there are some in Olney "so profane, so drunken, dissolute and in every respect worthless, that to make them partakers in this bounty, would be to abuse it". He had no time for such individuals whose poverty was "self-inflicted woe / Th'effect of laziness and sottish waste" (IV.430-1). The very thought of them is enough, sadly, to send him off into one of his more extreme right-wing rages. Such people never work. They won't work. They live by stealing from those who do. And they don't steal for their families' sake. No, they "neglected pine at home", as the money all goes on drink. Unlike Goldsmith, Cowper has nothing good to say of village inns; they are "styes / That law has licens'd".

Briefly he reminds himself that censure, especially in verse, is a vain pursuit, but he has started and finds it hard to stop. Life was so much better once. Virgil sang of scenes of Arcadian innocence and virtue, and even if, as he acknowledges, it was no more than a dream, at least it was not impossible to dream it. In his own day, he says, even simple country lasses try to dress themselves up in the height of fashion. Time was – and how oddly familiar this sounds – when people could go out and leave their doors unlocked (IV.559) and could walk about in safety. Now, he tells us, criminals go scot-free, because the magistrates are either too scared to convict them or have been bribed.

At first he lays the blame for all this on the new materialism, greed and luxury, but then says it is all due to an increase in the standing army, as when young men come home again it is

> To swear, to game, to drink, to show at home
> By lewdness, idleness, and sabbath-breach,
> The great proficiency he made abroad,
> T'astonish and to grieve his gazing friends.
> (IV.651-4)

All continuity has been lost, as well as logic. We are now told that whenever men form groups, either as soldiers or as merchants, they become "A loathsome body" (IV.674). This is why he has always preferred to live in the country. His earliest poems, he says, were rural, and he has never lost his love of Virgil, Milton and "ingenious Cowley".

Love of rural life is born in us, he claims, and city dwellers always long to return to the country, which is why suburban villas have gardens, and even in the centres of town we see so many window-boxes.

The conversational tone has been left behind and rural life is celebrated in a tone we thought we had heard the last of:

> Hail therefore patroness of health and ease
> And contemplation, heart-consoling joys
> And harmless pleasures in the throng'd abode
> Of multitudes unknown, hail rural life!
> (IV.780-3)

But the closing lines do have a quiet dignity to them as he wishes for himself

> an unambitious mind, content
> In the low vale of life, that early felt
> A wish for ease and leisure, and 'ere long
> Found here that leisure and that ease I wish'd.
> (IV.798-801)

Book V contains some of Cowper's finest verse and some of his worst. The country was still in the grip of winter when he began it, but when there were blue skies the low sun cast long shadows, even from the blades of frozen grass. On one such morning when he went out for a walk the shadow of his legs was so long that approaching a whitewashed cottage they seemed to "walk along the plaister'd wall / Prepost'rous sight! the legs without the man" (19-20). At this period of his life he could still laugh at himself.

Winter seems to have brought out his best verse as he recognised himself in a letter to Joseph Hill: " ... the Season of the Year which generally pinches off the flowers of poetry, unfolds mine such as they are, and crowns me with a winter garland" (9th May 1781). What is rather puzzling, though, is that while some of his descriptions are so splendidly vivid and precise, they can be followed by instances of stock poetic diction. The woodman goes off to work and his dog goes with him, but this is not just any dog; this is so evidently one particular dog which Cowper knows well:

> Shaggy and lean and shrewd, with pointed ears
> And tail cropp'd short, half lurcher and half cur
> His dog attends him.
> (V.44-6)

And when he runs ahead into the snow, we see him as he

> with many a frisk
> Wide-scampering, snatches up the drifted snow
> With iv'ry teeth, or ploughs it with his snout;
> Then shakes his powder'd coat, and barks for joy.
> (V.47-50)

It is so right; we want to exclaim, "Yes, that's exactly what dogs do!" But moments later, when the woodman taps his pipe, Cowper cannot bring himself to name anything quite so plebeian, and we are told that he stops now and then

> T'adjust the fragrant charge of a short tube
> That fumes beneath his nose.
> (V.54-5)

The effect is ridiculous. Not quite as ridiculous, but just as jumbled, is his portrayal of hens flying down for the grain that is scattered for them:

Now from the roost or from the neighb'ring pale,
Where diligent to catch the first faint gleam
Of smiling day, they gossip'd side by side,
Come trooping at the housewife's well-known call
The feather'd tribes domestic. Half on wing
And half on foot, they brush the fleecy flood
Conscious, and fearful of too deep a plunge.
                                                    (IV.58-64)

Again there seems to be no doubt that this is something which Cowper has *seen* for himself. He has seen that hens fear sinking into the snow and spread their wings out as they run through it. It is another exact observation, but instead of simply calling them *hens*, they are "The feather'd tribes domestic", and instead of snow, they are contending with a "fleecy flood", and it all takes place one "smiling day". "Smiling" was one of Thomson's favourites adjectives, especially for the benevolence of nature. Poetic diction of this kind was stale, and it is hard to tell why Cowper chose to fall back on it. Nothing is gained by it, and this may be one of those times when, one suspects, he simply wrote too quickly. The six books of *The Task* amount to close on 5,000 lines, and yet he completed it, as he told Newton (30th November 1784) in just over a year, which left him little enough time for any considered self-criticism.

Unevenness would seem to be inevitable, and happily he is soon back to some of his best lines with a series of images describing the "forms so various" made as the spray thrown up by a water-wheel freezes along the banks of the mill-race, and the turrets and columns he sees in his imagination allow him to add a long digression about the ice palace built by the Russian Empress Anna Ivanovna in St Petersburg in 1740. Estimates vary as to its size, but it was evidently a massive structure made entirely from blocks of ice cut from the frozen River Neva. Not only was the building of ice, so were its contents: tables, chairs, curtains and beds, even the pillows on the beds and two pairs of slippers all made of ice. Cowper was able to draw a moral from it on the nature of monarchy: that it was only a scene of "evanescent glory" (IV.167). He could have taken his moralising a good deal further, though, had he explained that the empress had had the ice palace built as an instrument of the most exquisite torture. One of her courtiers had angered her by marrying a Roman Catholic. On the woman's death which came suspiciously soon after the marriage, Anna Ivanovna forced the man to marry an ugly peasant and made them spend their "wedding night" naked on the ice-bed. Somehow, and no doubt to her sorrow, they survived.

But even if Cowper had known the full story, and it is likely that he did, having read it in *The Gentleman's Magazine*, he would have been loth to have included it: *nakedness* and *beds* were not words he would have liked to see even in close proximity.

He follows this by turning his attention to the follies of great princes, one of which is that to them war is simply a game, a game, however, which has been innate in man ever since Cain slew Abel. Murder, Cowper continues, is how the first kings seized and maintained their power, but he is quick to exempt George III from his criticisms. This was a constitutional monarch's rule, unlike that tyrannical absolute monarchy which prevailed in France, opposition to which was a favourite theme among eighteenth-century poets. So was liberty, which now occupies Cowper for more than 200 lines. He might have learned of the poetic perils involved in this if he had given more thought to James Thomson. His *Liberty: A Poem in Five Parts* trundled on for over 3,000 lines. Johnson, who admired Thomson's *Seasons* left his readers in no doubt about what he thought of *Liberty*: " ... when it first appeared, I tried to read and soon desisted. I never tried again."[9] Cowper's lines are no better, and our hearts are not raised when he starts into that "liberty of heart, deriv'd from heav'n / Bought with HIS blood" (545-6).

Keats was right about poetry that has a palpable design on us, and these lines certainly have. They are Cowper at his dullest. It is possible to rush over a digest of these subjects in this way, but to read them is another matter: so much intellectualisation and so little genuine emotion. The ideas are commonplace (in his lines on the Bastille, a prisoner befriends a spider), and so is the language, which is banal and devoid of imagery or anything that might be considered a 'poetic effect'. Coleridge summed up such verse when he wrote:

> ... whatever lines can be translated into other words of the same language, without diminution of their significance, either in sense, or association, or in any worthy feeling, are so far vicious in their diction.[10]

Cowper wrote to Unwin:

> What there is of a religious cast in the volume, I have thrown towards the end of it, for two reasons – first , that I might not revolt the reader at his entrance – and, secondly, that my best impressions might be made last." (10th October 1784)

He was right to do so, but only on one score. Yet we have to recognise and remember that it was his moralising which made him the favourite poet not only of Jane Austen, but, for many years, of most of the British nation.

Book V is eventually saved by Cowper returning to, or at least coming closer to, a personal statement in which his emotions and his faith are both involved. In Book I he had celebrated the power of nature to lift our spirits, citing a prisoner released from his dungeon and an invalid rising from his sickbed, and observing that "The spleen is seldom felt where Flora reigns" (I.455). He then confessed to being puzzled by those who preferred landscape paintings to landscapes themselves, but in Book V there is a very significant change:

> Man views it, and admires, but rests content
> With what he views. The landscape has his praise,
> But not its author.
> (V.791-3)

Cowper himself is not content here with recorded observations such as a graphic artist might produce. There is an inwardness, and a degree of subjectivity to his perceptions, and a new emphasis on the presence of the divine. The important point, however, is that it is not a case of nature leading man to a greater awareness of God – the physico-theologians had put forward that view – but of the grace of God giving man a greater appreciation of nature:

> Acquaint thyself with God if thou would'st taste
> His works. Admitted once to his embrace,
> Thou shalt perceive that thou wast blind before;
> Thine eye shall be instructed, and thine heart
> Made pure, shall relish with divine delight
> Till then unfelt, what hands divine have wrought.
> (V. 779-84)

His mind goes back, I would suggest, to 1763, to that moment during his holiday near Southampton, when the dread of his impending public examination was suddenly lifted in a moment of enlightenment, a moment in which his whole perception of the landscape before him was changed.

It is a moment such as that which is behind his lines on spiritual freedom:

Then we are free. Then liberty like day
Breaks on the soul, and by a flash from heav'n
Fires all the faculties with glorious joy.
A voice is heard that mortal ears hear not
'Till thou hast touch'd them; 'tis the voice of song
A loud Hosanna sent from all thy works,
Which he that hears it with a shout repeats,
And adds his rapture to the gen'ral praise.
In that blest moment Nature, throwing wide
Her veil opaque, discloses with a smile
The author of her beauties.
(V.883-93)

This, we recognise, is a moment of significance not only in Cowper's own religious thinking: it heralds a change in the direction of English poetry. A door had been closed on the Augustan world of James Thomson, even though no one, not Cowper himself, could then have foreseen or guessed what lay this side of it.

In a rather Proustian moment at the start of Book VI, 'The Winter Walk at Noon', the sound of church bells takes him back, as he says it always does, to memories of his childhood. We would all, he continues, like to go back to do things differently, to recognise, for instance, that a father's sternness was really a show of love. Mothers, interestingly, in view of the poem on his mother's picture, receive no more than a passing afterthought.

The past does not hold him for long. There had been another heavy snowfall in April that year, but the blue skies which followed it tempted him out to take again the same path to Emberton which he had taken in Book I (154-361). No one else is about, and the walking is easy under the oaks and elms. Like Wordsworth, his walks led to meditation, allowing him to "settle in soft musings as I tread" (VI.69). But he is always conscious of his surroundings and alert to what is going on around him. "No noise is here, or none that hinders thought" (VI.75). But there is a robin, and the picture he gives us of it has a detail and precision which make it unforgettable:

The red-breast warbles still, but is content
With slender notes and more than half suppress'd,
Pleas'd with his solitude, and flitting light
From spray to spray, where'er he rests he shakes
From many a twig the pendant drops of ice,
That tinkle in the wither'd leaves below.
(VI.77-82)

Equally pleased with his own solitude, Cowper feels the calm of the outside world matched by the world within him, and a quiet meditation follows in which he distinguishes between knowledge and wisdom. It is a matter of the head and the heart:

> Knowledge and wisdom, far from being one,
> Have oft times no connexion. Knowledge dwells
> In heads replete with thoughts of other men,
> Wisdom in minds attentive to their own.
>   (VI.88-91)

It was over a decade later that Wordsworth was saying the same thing in 'The Tables Turned', but his "vernal wood" pales before Cowper's images of spring:

>   trees, and rivulets whose rapid course
> Defies the check of winter, haunts of deer,
> And sheep-walks populous with bleating lambs,
> And lanes in which the primrose 'ere her time
> Peeps through the moss that clothes the hawthorn root,
> Deceive no student.
>   (VI.109-14)

We are all too often blind to the glories of God's created world, he says, and then demonstrates his knowledge as a gardener by listing and detailing the flowers of a dozen different plants. It was a list which so impressed Jane Austen that, when planning her garden in Southampton, she wrote to her sister: "I could not do without a Syringa, for the sake of Cowper's line. We talk also of a laburnam [sic]."[11]

These plants will all soon be in bloom. It is "Nature's progress":

>   when she lectures man
> In heav'nly truth; evincing as she makes
> The grand transition that there lives and works
> A soul in all things and that soul is God.
>   (VI.182-5)

From earlier in the century deists had been arguing for the existence of an absentee God, one who created and set the world in motion but then let it continue without him. Cowper strongly rejected any such idea, yet his rejection does sound oddly deist in itself:

> Nature is but a name for an effect
> Whose cause is God.
>   (VI.223-4)

He was a firm believer, but no theologian. However, on one point he was adamant:

> His presence who made all so fair, perceived,
> Makes all still fairer.
>   (VI.252-3)

But instead of staying with this idea, he returns to his attack on the ways in which city dwellers waste their time: chess, billiards, shopping and auctions. Having no first-hand experience of such things – certainly not during the previous twenty years – his comments, even when couched in mock-heroic terms, are too generalised to be of much interest, and it is with some relief that we find him soon going back to his country walks, where he is such a familiar figure that the squirrel is the only creature disturbed by his presence, and Cowper, in a series of vivid and brilliantly staccato lines, catches his antics to perfection:

> The squirrel, flippant, pert, and full of play,
> He sees me, and at once, swift as a bird
> Ascends the neighb'ring beech; there whisks his brush
> And perks his ears, and stamps and scolds aloud,
>   (VI.315-18)

Cowper had a great fondness for animals, so much so that Orchard Side must at times have been almost overrun by his pets. God, he recalls, had given man dominion over the animals, but in prelapsarian Eden we lived together in harmony until "sin marr'd all." This affected even the animals, some becoming fearful, some fierce. Man, in his ferocity, then began to hunt them. There is real passion in Cowper's opposition to hunting here, and to the maltreatment of domestic and farm animals. God will punish such crimes, he feels sure. Sometimes, he claims, animals themselves take their revenge. To support this he retells (another of Thomson's favourite ploys) a Cornish tale of a young atheist who, determined to show how little he feared death, tried to make his horse jump off the edge of a cliff. The beast refused, even though whipped and spurred till it bled, but later threw his rider down to his death.

Again Cowper seems to have lost all sense of purpose, and after this improbable story he returns to lecturing his readers on the evils of hunting and the virtues, such as fidelity, humans can learn from animals. It is even harder to detect any logic in what follows: an attack on the proposal to perform Handel's *Messiah* in Westminster Abbey, praise for Garrick, a piece on the fickleness of the mob's attitude to politicians, and then, coming back to animals again:

> And I am recompensed, and deem the toils
> Of poetry not lost, if verse of mine
> May stand between an animal and woe,
> And teach one tyrant pity for his drudge.
>
> (VI.725-8)

From here, perhaps with the end of his poem in sight, he considers the end of the world itself, acknowledging that he is "too poor in skill" to write of it, but declaring it to be a theme he cannot fail at least to attempt.

Drawing heavily on the Psalms, what he foresees is a land of plenty, of sempiternal spring, a land where, as predicted by Isaiah, the wolf shall dwell with the lamb, where all is "harmony and love" and the new Jerusalem is built. The change in tone is remarkable. What he gives us is a splendid paean of praise reminding us at times of the exultation of Smart's 'Jubilate Agno'. Following that is what he calls in the 'Argument', "An Invocation and an Invitation of him who shall bring it to pass". Such things are still to come, but meanwhile he celebrates the happiness of the man who lives in peace and away from the gaudy world. It is his own way of life he extols, and the verse changes again as he admits, in a quieter tone, that such a life may appear to be useless and to achieve nothing, but nevertheless he makes a proud claim:

> His sphere though humble, if that humble sphere
> Shine with his fair example, and though small
> His influence, if that influence all be spent
> In soothing sorrow and in quenching strife,
> In aiding helpless indigence, in works
> From which at least a grateful few derive
> Some taste of comfort in a world of woe,
> Then let the supercilious great confess
> He serves his country, recompenses well
> The state beneath the shadow of whose vine
> He sits secure, and in the scale of life
> Holds no ignoble, though a slighted place.
>
> (VI.960-71)

It was a claim that he could justly make and, far from being slighted, he was soon recognised as the most popular and influential poet of his day.

Sadly, when a few lines later he considers his own demise and hopes for a peaceful end and a gentle transition "to a safe retreat / Beneath the turf that I have often trod", we cannot help regretting that this was not to be.

There are many reasons why *The Task* should have become such a success, a significant one being that the volume also included 'John Gilpin', which by that time had become the most popular ballad in the country. People would have been delighted to know at last who had written it and would no doubt have been all the readier to listen to a moralist who could also make them laugh. Furthermore it was a type of poem with which they were familiar, or so it seemed at first. It would have reminded them of Thomson's *The Seasons* which since its first appearance had been going through edition after edition. Like *The Seasons*, it combined description and reflection, included narrative digressions and was essentially of a didactic and devotional nature. But it was not the same. The tone was very different. It was not as verbose as Thomson, and the descriptions contained less of the sublime. It began with a joke and it was perhaps this which allowed it to continue in a far more relaxed and conversational manner. Readers were conscious of being addressed by a particular individual, one of their own kind who told them about things that they knew but perhaps did not sufficiently appreciate. And he told them about himself, where he lived, where he walked and what he saw.

But it is unwise to lay too much stress on the biographical element. It has been suggested that "*The Task* cannot be enjoyed unless we have a good understanding of Cowper's life," and that "If we are to find a unifying principle in the work, we must explore the mind that produced it."[12] This is not true. Its first readers would have known next to nothing of Cowper's life, yet clearly enjoyed the poem, and we can know nothing of the mind which produced it, only the mind which it reveals to us.

To find a unifying principle in the poem has long been an unsolved problem. It is tempting to go along with Bill Hutchings' cheeky suggestion that "A brief summary of the poem's subject matter will be enough to show how easy is the charge that it is simply a rag-bag of the thoughts of a highly individual but slightly cranky countryman."[13]

Cowper's most authoritative biographer, James King, finds a very positive line of thought: "He assumed that his great task would be to write a poem about a corrupt individual – himself – who wanders back into the garden and finds salvation. Such thoughts preoccupied him and he saw *The Task* as a continuation of *Paradise Lost*."[14] It would indeed be wonderful if any of this were so, but there is no evidence that such ideas ever entered Cowper's head.

Norman Nicholson, a man who knew how poets think, took a more sensible approach, saying: "*The Task* is not a philosophical poem, not a reflective, not even an autobiographical poem. It is discursive, a conversation recorded, a correspondence preserved."[15] This allows for the digressions, and Bill Hutchings is right when he says: "The randomness is one of the finest achievements of the conversational method."[16] Nicholson also suggests that the moralising passages were essential if Cowper were to be comfortable in his mind.

In his correspondence with William Unwin, Cowper said that his chief aim in the poem was "to discountenance the modern enthusiasm after a London life" (10th October 1784), but there is also a positive side to this, in that as the moral values seem to be failing in the public world, so he is able to highlight those values which prevail in the world in which he has chosen to live.

In purely material terms, however, the public world seems to have taken advantage of Cowper's naivety. His publisher, Joseph Johnson, agreed to publish *The Task* at "his own risk", but he knew what he was doing and according to Henry Crabb Robinson, went on to make a profit of £10,000, a vast sum of money in those days.[17]

The reviewers were more generous. *The Critical Review* observed that it was a volume "superior to any that has lately fallen into our hands", and *The European Magazine* thought it "possessed more originality of thought, more genuine satire and solid argument, than falls to the share of most of our modern Juvenals".[18] But of far greater importance was the poem's lasting influence. Its autobiographical element, expressed in such clear, straightforward language, established a precedent which Coleridge and Wordsworth were quick to recognise and to follow. In the first chapter of *Biographia Literaria* Coleridge called Cowper "the best modern poet, the first who combined natural thoughts with natural diction".

But the time leading up to publication of *The Task* was not all sweetness and light by any means. Just as he had upset William Unwin by not telling him about his forthcoming publication in 1781 until the last moment, so this time Cowper upset Newton and even seemed to gloat about it when he told Unwin:

> I wrote to Mr. Newton by the last Post to tell him that I was
> gone to the Press again. He will be surprised and perhaps not
> pleased. But I think he cannot complain, for he keeps his
> own Authorly secrets without participating them with me.
> (1st November 1784)

One can well imagine that Newton was not at all pleased. Indeed in a later
letter Cowper, seeming to think that right was on his side, told Unwin that
"His [letter] was fretful and peevish, and mine if not chargeable with exactly
the same qualities, was however, dry and unsavoury enough" (18th
December 1784). By the end of the month, though, Cowper was on the
defensive, assuring Newton: "I have admitted into my description no images
but what are scriptural", whereas we know he had told Unwin in the previous
October that his images were all from nature. Again it seems that Cowper's
view of things depended on who he was writing to. It was not until April
1785 that he was able to tell Unwin:

> I am very much pleased with the following sentence in Mr
> Newton's last. 'I am perfectly satisfied with the propriety of
> your proceedings as to the publication.' Now therefore we
> are friends again. Now he once more enquires after the work,
> which, 'till he had disimburden'd himself of this
> acknowledgement, neither he nor I, in any of our letters to
> each other, ever mentioned. (30th April 1785)

It is not a sentence which would strike many of us as being *friendly*, but
Cowper's ego was satisfied, and that was what mattered. Again it is a situation
which does not reflect well on him, and there are times, this being one, when
it might be wished that his published correspondence were rather less
complete.

12

The Letters

'Tis grace has brought me safe this far

There was no love lost between Cowper and Mrs Unwin's daughter, Susanna. She believed, with some reason, that he was living off her mother's money, but, rather surprisingly, her husband, the Rev. Matthew Powley, vicar of Dewsbury, near Leeds, did not share her ill-feeling. He sought Cowper's opinion on whether he should publish a refutation of a sermon preached by a visiting cleric in his own church, which had upset him, and in the kindliest of letters, Cowper advised against it (24th June 1782). On another occasion (12th May 1788), when the Powleys were visiting Olney, Cowper took him on a walk, "to show him the prettiest place in the country". But it is a letter Cowper wrote to him in 1793 which stops us in our tracks. They had evidently been discussing some nice theological point, but as several months had since elapsed, Cowper could no longer remember exactly what it was, as he had not kept Matthew's letter, and he explains why:

> I keep no letters, except such as are ... what is commonly called business ... In the destruction of all other epistles I consult the good of my friends; for I count it a point of delicacy not to leave behind me, when I die, such bundles of their communications as I otherwise should, for the inspection of I know not whom; and as I deal with theirs, for the very same reason, I most heartily wish them all to deal with mine. In fact, there seems to be no more reason for perpetuating or preserving what passes the pen in the course of a common correspondence, than what passes the lips in everyday conversation. A thousand folios ... are frequently treasured till death, for no use whatever either to ourselves or others. They then, perhaps, go to the grocer's ... or what is fifty times worse, they find their way to the press; a misfortune which never, at least seldom, fails to happen, if

> the deceased has been so unfortunate as to leave behind him
> a friend more affectionate to his memory than discreet in his
> choice of means to honour it.

Did he mean it? It is hard to be absolutely sure, but what is certain is that Powley did not take the hint. He kept the letters Cowper sent him, as did many of the other close friends and relatives – William Unwin, John Newton, Joseph Hill, Lady Hesketh and others Cowper corresponded with. As a result, within a few years of his death, the letters began to be published. Initially, William Hayley's *The Life and Posthumous Writings of William Cowper, Esq.* (1804) included nearly 500, and then, as edition followed edition, the number grew until now, in the five-volume Oxford collection edited by King and Ryskamp, we have over 1,300.

While the eighteenth century is recognised as the golden age of personal letter-writing, letter-writing can also be seen as having had a direct bearing on the course of English literature itself, leading to the growth and popularity of the novel. Samuel Richardson was no more than a reasonably successful London printer when in 1739 some friends suggested to him that a good commercial proposition might be the printing of a small volume of exemplary letters on subjects which could be of use to people who perhaps would have difficulty in composing them for themselves. Richardson took up the idea, but one such letter, purporting to be from a young girl in service asking for her father's advice when threatened by her master's unwelcome advances, gave him the idea for *Pamela, or Virtue Rewarded* (1740), an epistolary novel which, while not the first of its kind, was so successful that it has come to be regarded as having established the genre. What's more, it can also be seen as having given birth to the picaresque novel in England, as Henry Fielding's merciless parody of it, *Shamela*, led directly to his own "comic epic in prose", the brilliant *Joseph Andrews*. And fiction was not alone in adopting the form. Never out of print since its first appearance in 1789, Gilbert White's *Natural History of Selborne* also consists famously of a series of letters to his friends.

As a literary genre *sui generis* the way had first been opened by Alexander Pope, who deviously arranged for some of his missives to be returned to him so that he could rewrite them before publication. In doing so he had established the letter as an art form, which was soon to be graced by the names of Walpole, Gray, Shenstone and Johnson. It is a distinguished list and one in which William Cowper himself occupies a distinguished place. George Saintsbury even suggested that it was "the highest place among English letter-writers", and Blake's view was that the letters were "Perhaps, or rather Certainly, the very best letters that were ever published".[1]

Nothing Cowper wrote was ever the work of a moment casually scribbled down, and letter-writing was something he gave serious thought to; indeed there are several letters almost entirely devoted to expressing his views on the writing of letters. He told his cousin, Lady Hesketh: "When I read your letters I hear you talk, and I love talking letters dearly" (24th April 1786). He often pretends that his own letters are very casual, telling William Unwin: "When a great penury of matter has seemed to threaten me with an utter impossibility in hatching a letter, that nothing is necessary but to put pen to paper and go on" (5th January 1782). And again: "A Letter may be written upon any thing or Nothing, just as any thing or Nothing happens to Occur" (6th August 1780). But there is a great deal of artifice in this pretence, as we see from the quite extraordinary opening to another of his "casual" letters to Unwin:

> As two Men sit Silent after having exhausted all their Topics of Conversation, One says, It is very fine Weather, and the other says, Yes. One Blows his Nose, and the Other rubs his Eyebrow, (by the way this is very much in Homer's manner). Such seems to be the case between you and me. After a Silence of some Days, I wrote you a long Something that I suppose was nothing to the Purpose, because it has not afforded you Materials for an Answer. Nevertheless, as it often happens as in the Case above stated, One of the distressed Parties being deeply sensible of the aukwardness [sic] of a dumb Duette, breaks the Silence again and resolves to Speak though he have nothing to Say, so it fares with me. (27th July 1780)

Cowper was a writer and so would hardly have been unaware of just how good his letters were, and when he learned that Unwin regarded them as "Entertaining and Clever", there follows an immediate and very telling comparison with those of Pope. Cowper says he hopes that Unwin's praise will not make him vain, as

> Now this foolish Vanity would have spoiled me quite, and would have made me as disgusting a Letter-Writer as Pope, who seems to have thought that unless a Sentence was well turned, and every Period pointed with some Conceit, it was not worth the Carriage. Accordingly he is to me, except in

very few Instances, the most disagreeable Maker of Epistles
that I ever met with. (8th June 1780)

Clearly, Cowper was taking his letter-writing very seriously and had a high opinion of his own efforts, though he might have been surprised, and more than a little upset, to learn that Lord David Cecil thought that "the poems are not so good as the letters ... the letters are the best things he ever wrote."[2]

Letter-writing having become a literary genre in the eighteenth century, there is a detectable tendency in some writers to follow rules and conventions such as Robert Dodsley formulated in his treatise *The Preceptor*:

> Letter-writing rejects all pomp of Words, and is most agreeable when most familiar ... A Letter should wear an honest, chearful Countenance, like one who truly esteems, and is glad to see his Friend; and not look like a Fop admiring his own Dress and seemingly pleased with nothing but himself.[3]

While such a description does fit many of Cowper's letters, his overall output is far more varied. Very sensibly, he varies his tone to suit the recipient, as he explained to John Newton:

> You may think perhaps that I deal more liberally with *Him* [Unwin] in the way of poetical export than I do with You & I believe you have reason. The Truth is This – If I walked the Streets with a Fiddle under my Arm, I should never think of performing before the Window of a Privy Counsellor or a Chief Justice, but should rather make free with ears more likely to be open to such Amusement. (31st July 80)

It is at moments such as this that we wish we had both sides to the correspondence.

For the most part, as we have seen, the letters he wrote when he was first released from St Albans in 1765 read more like religious tracts and wearied their recipients into silence, but by 1780, and after Newton had left Olney for London, there are flourishes of wit and letters which are comic from start to finish. Writing to Mrs Newton, he recounts the chaos caused by a runaway horse belonging to "the Gingerbread Baker and his Gingerbread Wife", and ends up by copying out his ballad 'The Doves' for her (5th June 1790). We encounter images so bright we know they come from Cowper the poet.

Describing his diminutive uncle, Ashley Cowper, to Mrs Newton, he tells her of his big white hat with a yellow lining, adding, " … had he lined his Hat with pink instead of yellow, [he] might have been gathered by a natural mistake for a Mushroom and sent off in a basket" (6th August 1781). And after Unwin had suggested that Margate was more lively than Ramsgate, Cowper replied, "So is a Cheshire Cheese full of mites more lively than a Sound one, but that very Liveliness only proves its Rottenness" (July 1779).

That the presence of the poet is evident in the letters is not surprising, but what does surprise us is Cowper's narrative skill. Referring to Olney, he had once assured William Unwin that "No place contributes less to the catalogue of incidents, or is more scantily supplied with anecdotes worth notice" (3rd January 1784), but if anything of note did happen, he was quick to record it, and when the parliamentary candidate, mistakenly thinking that Cowper had a vote, paid him a visit in March 1784, his account of it to Newton catches the confusion and comedy of it all in a way that is not far short of Dickensian:

> Mr. Grenville squeezed me by the hand again, kissed the Ladies, and withdrew. He kissed likewise the Maid in the kitchen, and seemed upon the whole a most loving, kissing, kind-hearted gentleman. He is very young, genteel and handsome. He has a pair of very good eyes in his head, which not being sufficient it would seem for the many nice and difficult purposes of a Senator, he had a third also which he wore suspended by a ribband from his Button-hole. The boys halloo'd, the dogs bark'd, puss scamper'd, the heroe with his long train of obsequious followers withdrew, we made ourselves very merry with the adventure, and in a short time settled into our former tranquillity. (29th March 1784)

For more serious political events one would have to go to the correspondence of Horace Walpole or Lady Mary Wortley Montagu, but for the details of everyday life no one excels Cowper. There is the

> Old Woman at the Bridge End whose Name I forget. She had £400 left her 2 or 3 years ago, and having been given to Drunkenness before, upon this Accession of Wealth, became doubly addicted to it … Her last Words were, give me some more Stuff for I am dying. (14th March 1771)

There is so much comedy in these letters. We are told of the fire in Olney one night when George Griggs entrusted 18 guineas to a "woman who in his hurry he mistook for his wife" but whom he never saw again (3rd January 1783). And of the lion-tamer at a visiting fair who put his head into the beast's mouth and Cowper's advice "to discontinue the practice unless he had a head to spare" (18th July 1778).

His window at Orchard Side looked out onto the market place and there was not much that Cowper missed. He rarely missed his drunken neighbour Geary Ball:

> Mr Perry, whose daughter he married, often visits him, but declares that of all the Insensibles he ever saw, poor Geary is the most completely stupid. So long as he was able to crawl into the street, his journey was to the Royal Oak and home again. And so punctual were we both, I in cleaning my teeth at my window and he in drinking his dram at the same time, that I seldom failed to observe him. But both his legs are now blistered, and refuse to assist him in poisoning himself any longer. (19th February 1785)

Three months later poor Geary was dead.

In another Dickensian piece he tells Newton, who loved receiving the gossip, of the public "flogging" of a young man found guilty of stealing some ironwork:

> Being convicted he was order'd to be whipt, which operation he underwent at the Cart's tail from the Stone house to the High Arch and back again. He seem'd to show great fortitude but it was all an imposition upon the public. The Beedle who peform'd it had filled his left hand with red Ocre, through which after every stroke he drew the lash of his whip, leaving the appearance of a wound upon the skin, but in reality not hurting him at all. This being perceived by Mr Constable Henshcomb who followed the beedle, he applied his cane without any such management or precaution to the shoulders of the too mercifull Executioner. The scene immediately became more interesting, the Beedle could by no means be prevailed upon to strike hard, which provoked the Constable to strike harder, and this double-flogging continued, 'till a Lass of Silver End, pitying the pitifull Beedle

thus suffering under the hands of the pitiless Constable, joined the procession, and placing herself immediately behind the latter, seized him by his capillary Club and pulling him backward by the same, slapt his face with a most Amazonian fury. This Concatenation of events has taken up more of my paper than I intended it should, but I could not forbear to inform you how the Beedle thresh'd the thief, the Constable the Beedle, and the Lady the Constable, and how the thief was the only person concern'd who suffer'd nothing. (17th November 1783)

As well as this gift for prose narrative we encounter descriptions of the natural world which are quite the equal of those of Gilbert White. In a letter to his friend the poet James Hurdis he wrote:

Mrs. Unwin and I, crossing a brook, saw from the footbridge somewhat at the bottom of the water, which had the appearance of a flower. Observing it attentively, we found that it consisted of a circular assemblage of Minnows; their heads all met in a centre, and their tails diverging at equal distances, and being elevated above their heads, gave them the appearance of a flower half blown. One was longer than the rest, and as often as a straggler came in sight, he quitted his place to pursue him, and having driven him away, he returned to it again, no other Minnow offering to take it in his absence. This we saw him do several times. The object that had attached them all, was a dead Minnow, which they seemed to be devouring. (23rd February 1793)

As so often in Cowper's poems, it is the small detail which is most telling.

On a more serious level there are many instances of Cowper explaining his own practice as a poet and expressing his views on the work of others. He claimed he never read any English poetry, telling Joseph Hill:

English Poetry I never touch being pretty much addicted to the writing of it, and knowing that much intercourse with those gentlemen, betrays us unavoidably into a habit of imitation, which I hate and despise most cordially. (23rd November 1783)

But we know that he had read Milton of course, and Pope and Thomson, and Prior and Churchill too, and there are also passing references to Gray (25th October 1765), Goldsmith, "a favourite of mine" (17th November 1785), Shenstone (11th December 1786) and Robert Burns, whose poems he regarded as a "very extraordinary production", calling him "the only Poet these Kingdoms have produced in the lower rank of life, since Shakespeare" (24th July 1787).

And, of course, there is the autobiographical element. The letters enable us to follow Cowper's life on an almost day-to-day basis. That first volume, which Hayley and Lady Hesketh compiled in 1804, was closely edited and censored in order to protect his reputation, but intimate details which he confided to his closest friends are now open for our inspection, and this in itself presents a problem. While short on external events, Cowper's was a life of more than usual inner turmoil and drama with moments of tragic intensity. As we read, we begin to feel, and quite possibly wrongly, that we understand him, that we know what it was like to be a suicidal manic depressive, and this inevitably has attracted the sympathetic but speculative biographer, with the poems sometimes seeming in danger of being sidelined.

Writing in 1928, with what was available to him at that time, Hugh l'Anson Fausset could write that Cowper's letters "offer us an unconditional intimacy with one of the most amiable and cultivated of men".[4] We know much more now, and our views are no longer what he meant by "unconditional". Indeed, perhaps we know too much, and far more than Cowper would have wanted. We have seen how he could write one thing to one person and something quite different to another. We know that he pretended not to know that it was Theadora, whom he had jilted, who was sending him money and gifts, including the famous desk. We know how insensitive he was about the death of Joseph Hill's mother; how pompous and self-defensive he was in writing to William Unwin about his falling-out with Lady Austen; how sarcastic he was to Unwin about his sister, Susanna. We remember his unctuous letter to Lord Thurlow when he sent him a copy of his poems and how rattled his vanity continued to be when he received no reply. There are also dozens of letters – rarely included in the selections – in which he is asking for money, or for things to be bought for him: books, material, a new hat, a new coat, new buckles, even a toothbrush. The term 'freeloader' comes to mind. Time and again he is acknowledging the receipt of oysters, salmon, lobsters, shrimps, even a coconut, but there is no mention of payment for them. He never paid for his own letters, relying on franks sent to him. He seems to have regarded it as his right to be so looked after and was quick to complain if he was not. He even once confessed to William

Unwin that he was "very fond of availing myself of another man's Pocket, when I can do it creditably to myself & without injury to Him" (6th April 1780).

The longest and the most unpleasant letter he ever wrote, however, was to Lady Hesketh in January 1786, shortly after she had renewed their friendship. He wants to tell her all about himself. In an earlier letter he had hinted at his "anguish of mind", but she had failed to take the hint and ask him what he meant, but that did not stop him. "Because you *do not* ask, and because your reason for not asking consists of a delicacy and tenderness peculiar to yourself, for that very cause I will tell you." He then goes on to narrate at length and in detail the story of his mental breakdown of 1773. It is maudlin and oleaginously self-centred. "Methinks I hear you ask, – your affection for me will, I know, make you wish to do so, – Is it removed? I reply, in great measure, but not quite." He appears to wallow in it. Having told her this story, he goes on to give her a very one-sided account of his relationship with Lady Austen. He makes out that really her presence in Olney was a great nuisance and her insistence on seeing him every day kept him from his work, and that he was glad when her ill-health took her off to Bath. There is no mention of his fascination with her or of their "courtship" and how it angered Mrs Unwin. Finally, and again at length, he tells her of a fulsome review he has had in *The Gentleman's Magazine*, but adding: "I do not concern myself much you may suppose about such matters" (16th January 1786).

A week later he tells Lady Hesketh that "Anonymous" has written again, worried about the likely reception of his translation of Homer, bestowing an annuity of £50 a year on him, enclosing two £10 notes and sending him a beautiful tortoise-shell snuff-box with the painting on it done by Romney of his three pet hares. Throughout the letter he repeatedly refers to the donor as *he*, so keeping up the graceless charade that he did not know that it was in fact her sister Theadora.

In the preface to the first volume of their collected edition of the letters, James King and Charles Ryskamp wrote: "Cowper, more than any other, reveals himself utterly in his letters; yet no one is less of an egoist."[5] It is hard to know how they can have reached such a conclusion. The letters give us a fascinating and invaluable insight into Cowper's life, and into the life of the times, but they abound in self-pity, and, worse, have too little to say about Mary Unwin, who pitied and cared for him for close on 30 years.

13

Wider Concerns

Thro' many dangers, toils and snares

Admittedly, the accusations levelled against Cowper at the close of the previous chapter may not be entirely fair, but they were aimed at denting that image of him as a benign but rather pathetic little figure who, after drinking his cup of tea and romping about on the Turkey carpet with his pet hares, toddles out into the garden to look at his cucumbers, before coming back in to help Mrs Unwin wind her wool. Even one of his editors, John Bailey, wrote: "He lived in a dull and obscure country village among old maids and dissenting clergymen and knew nothing of the commanding minds of his day," an assertion which is wrong on every count.[1] Olney was not an obscure village but a lively market town. Mrs Unwin, Lady Austen and Lady Hesketh were not old maids and John Newton was not a Dissenting minister. Cowper had lived in London until his early thirties, was a voracious reader, kept himself well informed and had strong views about what was going on in the world.

Hazlitt also delivered a damning verdict: "There is an effeminacy about him which shrinks from and repels sympathy,"[2] whereas Cowper himself found effeminacy repellent, and it is not unusual in his work to come across lines such as:

> Fops at all corners lady-like in mien,
> Civitted fellows, smelt 'ere they are seen.
> ('Tirocinium', 829-30)

Effeminacy should never be confused with sensitivity. In this respect Cowper was perhaps unlike the majority of the men of his class and time, and it could be argued that he was ahead of his time in the sensitivity of his attitude towards the poor, to African slaves, to animals and to the desecration of the countryside.

Cowper was not of course alone in these humanitarian concerns. The century's growing social conscience is evident simply in the number of hospitals which were built, and not only for the sick: there were maternity hospitals, foundling hospitals and also St. Luke's, that rather more humane alternative to Bedlam. And we must not forget the private establishments such as Dr Cotton's in St Albans.

Evangelicals like Dr Cotton were behind many of these schemes for social improvement, but there was a problem for them in that Evangelicalism was radically opposed to the doctrine of justification by works. This had been a feature of a number of the *Olney Hymns*:

> Works of man, when made his plan,
> Never shall accepted be;
>> ('Not of Works', Hymn 64, ll. 5-6)

But there was a divine commission to aid the poor, and Cowper knew what poverty meant. He lived alongside the poor of Silver End and saw at first hand what they suffered, but to make matters worse, the removal of a tariff on Irish goods was devastating to the lace-makers of Olney. He asked Joseph Hill to try to influence the Lord Chancellor (see the letter of 8th July 1780 quoted on p. 70). An increase in the candle tax in 1784 made their situation even worse:

> I wish he [the minister] could visit the miserable huts of our lace-makers at Olney, and see them working in the Winter months by the light of a farthing candle from four in the afternoon till midnight. I wish he had laid his tax upon the ten thousand lamps that illuminate the Pantheon, upon the flambeaux that wait upon ten thousand chariots and Sedans in an Evening, and upon the Wax-candles that give light to ten thousand card tables. (3rd July 1784)

His concern for them is vividly and tenderly expressed in Book IV of *The Task* in the picture of a poor mother putting the welfare of her family before her own:

> The frugal housewife trembles when she lights
> Her scanty stock of brush-wood, blazing clear
> But dying soon, like all terrestrial joys.
> The few small embers left she nurses well,
> And while her infant race with outspread hands

And crowded knees sit cow'ring o'er the sparks,
Retires, content to quake, so they be warm'd.
                                              (IV.380-6)

But she, it is stressed, is one of the industrious poor, and Cowper was no sentimentalist. He had no time for those who did not work:

But poverty with most who whimper forth
Their long complaints, is self inflicted woe,
Th'effect of laziness or sottish waste.
                                              (IV.429-31)

He was no romantic in this respect either. Gypsies were "a vagabond race", thieves who ate dogs and vermin, and as for those who stole and drank away their ill-gotten gains while neglecting their own families, Cowper advocates the death penalty:

Oh for a law to noose the villain's neck
Who starves his own.
                                              (IV.461-2)

He can also shock us with quite appalling class distinction, looking at the peasants as though they belonged to another species:

The poor, inur'd to drudgery and distress,
Act without aim, think little and feel less.
                                              ('Hope', 7-8)

Yet in contrast with the rich and powerful, the poor he saw – as in the Sermon on the Mount – as blessed. In 'Truth' he pictures for us a simple lace-maker, a "cottager – Pillow and bobbins all her little store", and contrasts her innocent faith with that of intellectuals like Voltaire.

For all the ambiguities of his attitude to the poor, and with what little resources he had of his own, Cowper did what he could. Through his social position he was able to establish contact with wealthy Evangelicals like Robert Smith who wanted to do good but in keeping with their beliefs wanted anonymity to avoid any suggestion of ostentation. And in keeping with his own beliefs, Cowper always ensured that help went to the deserving poor:

> The profane are so profane, so drunken, dissolute and in
> every respect worthless, that to make them partakers of his
> bounty, would be to abuse it. We promise however that none
> shall touch it, but such as are miserably poor, yet at the same
> time industrious and honest. (18th November 1782)

The gratitude of the deserving poor is touchingly described in a letter to
William Unwin:

> When a poor woman and an honest one whom we know
> well, carried home two pair of Blankets, a pair for herself and
> husband, and a pair for her six children, as soon as the
> children saw them they jump'd out of their straw, caught
> them in their arms, kissed them, bless'd them, and danced
> for joy. An Old Woman, a very old one, the first night that
> found herself so comfortably cover'd, could not sleep a wink,
> being kept awake by the contrary Emotions of Transport on
> the one hand, and the fear of not being thankful enough on
> the other. (31st December 1785)

Such depths of poverty are hard for us to understand today.

A decade earlier, Christopher Smart, an Anglican, had had no problem
with charity and good deeds; one of his 'Hymns for the Amusement of
Children' beginning:

> I just came by the prison-door,
> I gave a penny to the poor:
> Papa did this good act approve,
> And poor mamma cried out for love.

And a decade later we find Blake in such 'Songs of Experience', as 'Holy
Thursday' championing a movement in which Cowper had played his own
small part.

He played a much larger part in the movement to abolish slavery, and
this was recognised by Thomas Clarkson in his authoritative *History of the
Abolition of the Slave Trade* (1808), in which he wrote: " ... a great coadjutor
he was when we consider what value was put upon his sentiments, and the
extraordinary circulation of his works."[3]

Having lived in his company for so long, it is likely that Cowper knew
even more about the horrors of the trade than was recorded in Newton's

influential *Authentic Narrative*, but changing the attitudes of the public in general, and of the business community in particular was a slow and difficult process. The accepted belief was that the British economy could not survive without the plantations in the West Indies and that the plantations could not survive without slaves. Even George Whitefield found biblical justification for slavery. It had become a simple matter of fact, as is clear from James Grainger's poem *The Sugar-Cane* (1764), a "West-India georgic" as he called it. After detailed horticultural advice, gained at first hand, he turns to the labour question in Book IV and explains, for the benefit of buyers, which Africans are best suited to which type of work, but advises planters never to buy old ones, no matter where they come from.

> But, Planters, from what coast so'er they sail,
> Buy not the old: they ever sullen prove,
> With heart-felt anguish, they lament their home;
> They will not, cannot work; they never learn
> Thy native language, they are prone to ails
> And oft by suicide their being end.
>
> (IV.66-71)

What a waste of money it would be if they committed suicide after you'd bought them.

But voices – even poetic voices – were slowly beginning to be heard against the trade. In his 'Elegy XX' William Shenstone gives us a slave's lament:

> For them we drain the mine's embowell'd gold;
> Where rove the brutal nations' wild desires?
> Our limbs are purchased, and our life is sold.
>
> (61-4)

Another influential campaigner was Henry Thornton, the son of John Thornton, the wealthy merchant who regularly sent donations of money to Olney to help the poor, and it was Henry's wife who in March 1788 approached Cowper through Newton to ask if he would write some ballads "to be sung about the streets on the subject". Lady Hesketh had already suggested the idea to him, but as he had heard that Hannah More was soon to publish her long poem 'Slavery', he decided against it. He had, as he told his cousin, already expressed his views in his own poem 'Charity' (ll. 157-243): "I have already borne my testimony in favour of our Black Brethren, and that I was one of the earliest, if not the first of those who have in the present day, expressed their detestation of the diabolical traffic in question" (16th February 1788).

There is no doubting the strength of Cowper's detestation. It even shook his faith. In the same week he wrote at length to Newton on a question "which I cannot help asking, although conscious that it ought to be suppressed". The question was: what part of the divine plan is it that Africans should suffer such torments in this world and yet, being pagan, have no hope of happiness in the next? He even feels that his own lot is not dissimilar, adding: "Then I feel – I will not tell you what – and yet I must. A wish that I never had been. A wonder that I am. And an ardent but hopeless desire not to be." With his history of attempted suicide, this must have alarmed Newton, but the mood soon passes, and a moment later he is thanking his friend for "most excellent fish (Hollybuts and Lobster)".

What changed Cowper's mind was the debt he felt he owed to the Thorntons and he lost no time in writing 'The Negro's Complaint' and 'Sweet Meat has Sour Sauce'. By the end of March he was able to tell Samuel Rose: "If you hear Ballads sung in the Streets on the subject of the hardships suffer'd by the poor Negroes in the islands, they are probably mine" (29th March 1788).

'Sweet Meat has Sour Sauce' purports to be sung by a slave-trader at some time in the future when his trade has been abolished, and the subtitle is 'The Slave-Trader in the Dumps'. Like any other trader put out of business he is going to have to sell the tools of his trade, a "curious assortment of dainty regales", and while listing them for potential buyers he reveals the barbarity of what he has been doing:

> Here's padlocks and bolts, and screws for the thumbs,
> That squeeze them so lovingly till the blood comes;
> They sweeten the temper like comfits or plums,
>> Which nobody can deny, deny,
>> Which nobody can deny.
>
> When a negro his head from his victuals withdraws,
> And clenches his teeth and thrusts out his paws,
> Here's a notable engine to open his jaws,
>> Which nobody, &c.
>> (17-24)

But the Committee for the Abolition of the Slave Trade decided not to use it, and it was not printed until Southey's edition of 1835. The irony works, but the Committee probably thought its overall tone too jaunty and comical for their needs. Cowper himself thought it "somewhat ludicrous" (27th March 1788), and it is doubtful if they would have wanted anyone speaking up for the trade, even ironically.

For us, the most interesting feature is stanza 8 which calls to mind so vividly the notorious illustrated deck-plan which Clarkson included in his 1808 *History*:

> 'Twould do your heart good to see 'em below
> Lie flat on their backs all the way as we go,
> Like sprats on a gridiron, scores in a row,
>> Which nobody, &c.
>> (25-7)

The Committee were happy to make full use of 'The Negro's Complaint' which, when put to music, Clarkson tells us, found its way into the streets of the metropolis, with several thousand copies being sent out around the country.

The disappointment we feel may be because we no longer have any experience of such ballads or their political effect. They were not meant to be read, but to be heard by people who could not read, and Cowper, with experience of *Olney Hymns* behind him, knew what he was doing. 'The Negro's Complaint' has the qualities it needs: simple language, straightforward syntax and a strictly regular metre. Its message is also perfectly clear. The final two stanzas read:

> By our blood in Afric wasted
>> 'Ere our necks received the chain,
> By the mis'ries that we tasted
>> Crossing in your barks the main,
> By our suff'rings since ye brought us
>> To the man-degrading mart,
> All sustain'd with patience taught us
>> Only by a broken heart –

Deem our nation Brutes no longer
　'Till some reason ye shall find
Worthier of regard and stronger
　Than the Colour of our Kind.
Slaves of Gold! Whose sordid dealings
　Tarnish all your boasted pow'rs
Prove that *You* have Human feelings
　'Ere you proudly question *Ours*.

It is a public poem written to demand for a public occasion, but while it is a solid presentation of radical ideals, Vincent Newey is right when he says there is no depth to it. The 'dramatic' mode is simply a convenient way of proclaiming a series of self-evident truths. In Blake's 'Little Boy Lost', by contrast, there is a dramatic reversal of roles making the Black Boy the superior and protector of the White Boy: "I'll shade him from the heat till he can bear / To lean in joy upon our Father's knee." Looking at these two poems we see the difference between a versifier and a poet. As Newey puts it,

> Blake, in an audacious fiction that credits a Negro child with a range of basic emotions and drives (love, sympathy, belief, insecurity, aspiration) offers an aggressive challenge to human complacency and an astute study in the fundamental kinship, and artificial distinctions between men.[4]

Rather more successful is Cowper's ballad 'The Morning Dream'. A morning dream being one which is sure to come true, its sprightly tone is in keeping with the optimism of its message. The singer, sailing westward, finds a woman on board, but this is no ordinary woman. She is Liberty, and on landing she defeats the foul fiend Oppression. It concludes:

> That Britannia, renoun'd o'er the waves,
> For the hatred she ever has shown
> To the black-sceptred rulers of Slaves –
> Resolves to have *none of her own*.

As the abolitionist movement gathered momentum, so did the bitterness between the opposing parties. Cowper, much to his credit, had evidently attracted attention to himself, and so attracted criticism. In 1792 he was told that there were rumours spreading that he had had a change of heart about slavery. Someone had noticed that his name was not included in a petition to Parliament which had been got up by the people of Olney, and he had to point out that he was no longer living there. Another rumour was that he still allowed himself the use of sugar and rum. This he seems to have regarded as political correctness run mad, and he replied to it with an epigram printed in *The Mercury* on 12th May 1792:

> To purify their wine some people bleed
> A *lamb* into the barrel, and succeed;
> No nostrum, planters say, is half so good
> To make fine sugar, as a negro's blood.
> Now *lambs* and *negroes* both are harmless things,
> And thence perhaps this wond'rous virtue springs,
> 'Tis in the blood of innocence alone –
> Good cause why planters never try *their own*.

They are lines which still shock us. Nothing else Cowper ever wrote was as bitter or as savage as this. We can see his anger, and we are glad to see it.

One anomaly in this humanitarian side to Cowper's nature appears in a letter he wrote to his cousin Lady Hesketh on 21st March 1788, which begins by saying that he has written two anti-slavery ballads; but in the very next paragraph we find him supporting capital punishment. A house-breaker, he tells her, has been sentenced to hang and he has been asked to draw up a petition for his reprieve, but he was

> averse to the employment for two reasons. First, because I knew the man to have been an offender for many years, and the fittest that could be to be made an example of, which was nowhere more wanted than at Olney. And secondly, because his case afforded not a single plea for mercy, or anything which at all resembled one.

The man was duly hanged. So many offences carried the death penalty in those days that it would perhaps be expecting too much of Cowper to be so far ahead of his time, but his tone is distressingly blunt.

There is considerably more compassion evident in his attitude to animals, especially in his opposition to hunting. He was not ahead of his time in this of course. As early as 1713, in his *Guardian* essay (number 61), Pope had argued: "We should find it hard to vindicate the destroying of anything that has life, merely out of wantonness." James Thomson had painted a memorably lachrymose picture of the stag at bay:

The big round tears run down his dappled face;
He groans in anguish, while the growling pack,
Blood-happy, hang at his fair jutting chest
And mark his beauteous chequered sides with gore.

('Autumn' 454-7)

But kindness to domestic animals was by no means commonplace. Admittedly attitudes had changed since Cicero's suggestion that a pig's life was only a means of keeping the pork fresh, but in his reworking of the Decalogue in 'A Song to David', Christopher Smart was on new ground when he turned the negatives of Judaic Law into positives which asked farmers to

Be good to him that pulls thy plough;
Due food and care, due rest, allow
For her that yields thee milk.

(251-3)

In those famous lines celebrating Jeoffry in his 'Jubilate Agno', Smart had shown what a cat-lover he was, but Cowper went further. Lady Hesketh recorded that

he had at one time five rabbits, three hares, two guinea pigs, a magpie, a jay, and a starling; besides two goldfinches, two canary birds, and two dogs. It is amazing how the three hares can find room to gambol and frolic (as they certainly do) in his small parlour; and I forgot to enumerate a squirrel which he had at the same time, and which used to play with the hares continually.[5]

After the death of Puss, his favourite hare, there were three dogs: Mungo, Marquis and Beau. Beau featured in two light-hearted poems: one rebuking him for killing a young bird and a second 'Beau's Reply' which concludes:

If killing birds be such a crime
(Which I can hardly see)
What think you, Sir, of killing Time
With verse address'd to me?

But when it came to the question of hunting, especially hunting with dogs, Cowper found nothing to smile about. In Book III of *The Task* he called it a

> Detested sport,
> That owes its pleasures to another's pain,
> That feeds upon the sobs and dying shrieks
> Of harmless nature.
> (326-9)

In a long letter to his cousin (3rd March 1788) (it is so artfully written and so skilfully structured that one might rather call it a narrative), he describes being witness to a kill. The poor dead beast had been dragged out of a privy, and the ironies he employs are such that his condemnation is all the more forceful than any straight denunciation: the huntsmen are a *cavalcade*, pursuing an *honourable* cause and the finale is a *ceremony*. But then the pretence is dropped and we are not spared the sickening details:

> The Huntsman remounted. He cut off a foot and threw it to the hounds. One of them swallow'd it whole like a Bolus. He then once more alighted, and drawing down the fox [he had hung it from the branch of an elm tree] by its hinder legs, desired the people who were by this time rather numerous to open a lane for him to the right and left. He was instantly obey'd, when throwing the fox to the distance of some yards, and screaming like a fiend as he is – Tear him in pieces – at least six times repeatedly, he consign'd him over absolutely to the pack, who in a few minutes devour'd him completely.

All this took place in the grounds of the Throckmortons.

14

The Move to Weston

And grace will lead me home

The Throckmortons, a recusant family of some social distinction, had been associated with the Buckinghamshire village of Weston since the middle of the fifteenth century. Partly Elizabethan and partly Queen Anne, Weston Hall, their elegant family home, was little more than a mile south-west of Olney. Sadly, it was demolished in 1827, but in Cowper's day it stood in its own parkland of some 75 acres. The grounds closest to the Hall, having been designed by Capability Brown, had fine views over the River Ouse, and among its celebrated features were a Gothic temple, a splendid avenue of lime trees and a hexagonal Alcove open on three sides, which may still be seen today.

Cowper and Mrs Unwin had once been given a key to the estate, a fact acknowledged, no doubt to the Throckmortons' pleasure, in Book I of *The Task*:

> The folded gates would bar my progress now,
> But that the Lord of this inclos'd demesne
> Communicative of the good he owns,
> Admits me to a share.
> (330-3)

It was one of their favourite walks, but they had little social contact with the Throckmortons until May 1784, when, as he told William Unwin, he received an invitation "in the civilest terms" to join them in witnessing the launching of a balloon in their grounds.

The Throckmortons, he explained rather defensively to Newton, had "lately received many gross affronts from the people of this place, on account of their religion. We thought it, therefore, the more necessary to treat them with respect" (10th May 1784). Hydrogen balloons had become an exciting novelty which had caught Cowper's imagination, and so off they went. Cowper himself, like most Evangelicals, was strongly averse to anything to do with the Roman Catholic Church, but he was no bigot and recognised the Throckmortons for what they were, telling Unwin, "They are papists, but much more amiable than many protestants" (20th May 1784). The balloon launch was a failure, but John Throckmorton and his wife Maria singled Cowper and Mrs Unwin out for special attention, asking them in to drink chocolate, giving them a key to their private gardens and an invitation to dine with them, which Cowper felt he had to decline, explaining to Unwin that the house at Orchard Side was not fit to return such a favour. But in time the relationship between them grew closer and he not only dined with them but even joined them when their chaplain was present. Eventually he was writing letters to Mrs Throckmorton addressing her as "My Dear Mrs Frog", rather an uncouth epithet for the great-granddaughter of Lord Petre, the Baron in Pope's *Rape of the Lock*. But he was far more courteous in his flattering little poem 'The Poet's New Year Gift to Mrs Throckmorton' and in the better-known elegy on the death of her bullfinch.

While this new friendship was growing, so an old one happily resurfaced. There had been no contact between Cowper and his cousin, Lady Hesketh, for eighteen years. The last letters they had exchanged were in 1767 when his Evangelical fervour was at its height and proved to be too much for her. But then the success of *The Task* and 'John Gilpin' roused her curiosity. Who was this now-famous cousin? Her first letter – to judge from Cowper's reply – must have consisted largely of questions, which he answered at length over the following weeks and months. Witty and opinionated, Lady Hesketh was also affectionate and generous, and was very soon bestowing money and gifts on him, a generosity to which he responded with a coyness so mawkish as to be embarrassing:

> You have placed me in a situation new to me, and in which
> I feel somewhat puzzled to know how I ought to behave. At
> the same time that I would not grieve you by putting a check
> on you bounty … (17th November 1785)

But perhaps her greatest gift was to awaken the letter-writer in him and to bring him so much joy – a joy he could scarcely retain when she declared her intention of paying an extended visit. Where she and her servants were to stay occasioned much concern. Orchard Side, despite Cowper's assertions to the contrary, was too small, and after many exchanges of letters it was settled that she should live in the vicarage. He had looked forward to it so much that when the day came, and Lady Hesketh got down from her coach, he was overwhelmed. He confessed to William Unwin:

> ... her first appearance was too much for me; my spirits, instead of being greatly raised, as I had inadvertently supposed they would be, broke down with me under the pressure of too much joy, and left me flat, or rather melancholy throughout the day, to a degree that was mortifying to myself, and alarming to her. (3rd July 1786)

But he got over it, and they were soon riding about in her coach, paying visits and enjoying themselves to such an extent that word reached Newton in London that the inhabitants of Orchard Side were leading a dissipated life, and he wrote to Mrs Unwin in terms to which Cowper, standing up for himself against Newton for once, replied with equal gusto and not a little indignation.

Theadora, we can feel sure, was eager to learn from her sister what this Mrs Unwin was like, the woman with whom the man she loved had been living for so many years, and Harriot's account of her was very positive and full of admiration for the care she had shown him:

> Amidst all the little puritanical words which fall from her *de tems en tems*, she seems to have by nature a great fund of gaiety – great indeed must it have been, not to have been totally overcome by the close confinement in which she has lived, and the anxiety she must have undergone for one whom she certainly loves as well as one human being can love another. I will not say she idolises him, because that she would think wrong, but she certainly seems to possess the truest regard and affection for this excellent creature, and, as I before said, has, in the most literal sense of those words, no will or shadow of inclination but what is *his* ... There is something truly affectionate and sincere in her manner. No one can express more heartily than she does, her joy to have me at Olney; and as this must be for his sake, it is an additional proof of her regard and esteem for him.[1]

It was a portrait of Mary Unwin which cannot have been altogether what Theadora was hoping to hear, but it was one which, as will be seen, was to change dramatically.

Cowper and Mrs Unwin had been living at Orchard Side for eighteen years, and he always gave the impression of being very happy there. *Snug* and *nook* were the words he often used, especially when describing his greenhouse, which in the summer, after the cucumbers had been harvested, he turned into a writing den, carpeting the floor and hanging rugs on the walls to keep it cool. He described it to Joseph Hill:

> I write in a nook that I call my Bouderie; It is a Summer house not much bigger than a Sedan chair, the door of which opens into the garden which is now crowded with pinks, roses, and honey-suckles, and the window into my neighbour's orchard … Having lined it with garden-mats and furnished it with a table and two chairs, here I write in summer-time … secure from all noise, and a refuge from all intrusion. (29th June 1785)

"It is the place of all the world I love most," he had told Newton, adding that "the very stones in the garden wall" were his "intimate acquaintance" and that he would "miss almost the minutest object and be disagreeably affected by its removal" (27th July 1783). Yet, writing in 1803, not so very long after Cowper left there, the writers of *Cowper Illustrated* described Olney as "by no means a desirable spot; lying in a bottom, it is subject to frequent fogs and damps, which are extremely pernicious, and occasion anguish and rheumatic disorders."[2] But then in 1786, having lived in Orchard Side for so long and seemingly so contentedly, Cowper recalled that when William Unwin had first seen it, he thought it looked like a prison and was saddened at the thought of his mother having to live there. Perhaps it was due to the influence of the more sophisticated Lady Hesketh, but Cowper was now leaning more and more towards Unwin's view, even going so far as to say:

> It not only had the aspect of a place built for purposes of Incarceration, but has actually served that purpose through a long, long period, and we have been the prisoners. (3rd July 1786)

The Throckmortons had suggested a few years earlier that he might care to move into Weston Lodge, one of their properties in the village, but at the time Cowper thought that it was too grand, that he did not have the right sort of furniture and could not afford to buy any, but Lady Hesketh not only persuaded him to move to Weston, but she bought the furniture.

It was in November 1786 that Cowper and Mrs Unwin took possession of their new home, and what a change it was. Among the thatched cottages on the main street of Weston Underwood it stood out grandly, as it does in Storer and Greig's print in *Cowper Illustrated*. Stone-built in the seventeenth century and with a tiled roof, it has three sash windows either side of the front door, seven on the floor above and three dormers in the roof. Storer writes of it having "a handsome and extensive front, ornamented by vines and jasmines, which entwine their spreading branches and overhang the windows in verdant wreaths".[3] In the front there was a prospect into an orchard and at the rear a kitchen garden and a shrubbery.

It should have been a paradise for them, but it is recognised now that moving house can be one of the most traumatic experiences in anyone's life. The move itself must have been a great upheaval, added to which Lady Hesketh had left them to go back to London; but then, and with nothing to prepare them for such a thing, and after only two weeks in their new home, they learned that William Unwin had died. Travelling with the philanthropist Henry Thornton, he was suddenly taken ill at Winchester and within days he had died of typhus. It is repeatedly claimed that in his letters about Unwin's death Cowper is *restrained* and *reticent*, yet he told Newton that he felt a "heartache that I remember not to have felt before" (16th December 1786). Unwin had been like a younger brother to him, but whatever the heartache he felt, it can have been nothing compared with Mrs Unwin's anguish. She had lost her only son, and that itself might have been a problem for Cowper. How could he comfort her? Had she been his wife, he would have known how, but she was not. She was his companion and she needed the comfort he could not give her, and he was probably conscious of that.

The winter months often brought on Cowper's fits of depression. This time the combination of events proved to be too much, and poor Mrs Unwin had that to cope with that too. As he admitted to his cousin, "She gives me all her time and all her attention and forgets that there is another object in the world" (14th January 1787). And that only two weeks after her son's death. One might say that the forgetting was entirely Cowper's. When he tried to hang himself, it was Mrs Unwin who cut him down.

There followed a six-month gap in Cowper's correspondence, until July 1787 when he began writing to Samuel Rose. Twenty years old at that time and a graduate of the University of Glasgow, Rose had been asked by his professors to call on Cowper and pay their compliments to him when he came down to England to take up his studies at Lincoln's Inn. He seems to have reminded Cowper of William Unwin, whom he had met at that age, and Rose quickly proved to be an invaluable replacement for him, being a regular correspondent, and prompting some of the poet's finest letters.

As the days grew longer and warmer, so Cowper's letters grew more and more cheerful, and he renewed his close friendship with the Throckmortons to the extent that his help was there when sorrow struck them: he composed an amusing yet moving little epitaph on the death of their spaniel Fop:

> Though once a Puppy, and though Fop by name,
> Here moulders one whose bones some honour claim,
> No sycophant, although of Spaniel-race,
> And though no hound, a martyr to the chase.
> Ye squirrels, rabbits, leverets rejoice,
> Your haunts no longer echo to his voice,
> This record of his fate exulting view,
> He dies worn-out with vain pursuit of you.
> > Yes – the indignant shade of Fop replies –
> > And worn with vain pursuits Man also dies.

They were lines which pleased Mr Throckmorton so much that he had them engraved on the base of an ornamental urn in the grounds of Weston Hall.

Cowper was always proficient when called upon to write to order. In November of that year a Mr Cox, clerk of All Saints in Northampton, called on him to ask if he would be so kind as to furnish him with some verses which it was customary to attach to the Bill of Mortality he published at Christmas. Cowper was not very enthusiastic and suggested a Northampton versifier also by the name of Cox, but was told that he was "a Gentleman of so much reading that the people of our town cannot understand him" (27th November 1787). This did amuse Cowper, and when he found that the clerk had walked all the way from Northampton to ask him, he agreed. It had been an eventful week for visitors. He told Lady Hesketh that a beggar had called at the Hall and had been given a bowl of vermicelli soup but gave it back saying that although he was poor he couldn't eat broth with maggots in it.

Cowper obliged All Saints for six out of the next seven years and did not skimp the task, never writing fewer than nine stanzas and always pretending that they were the work of the clerk. They are, considering the circumstances, remarkably efficient poems, simply worded and preaching the simple message of man's mortality with typically Evangelical admonitions. In the verses for 1788 he suggests that if he could truly predict a person's impending doom,

> Time, then, would seem more precious than the joys
> In which he sports away the Treasure now;
> And Pray'r more seasonable than the Noise
> Of Drunkards, or the Music-drawing Bow.

They do tend, inevitably, to be somewhat gloomy, but are not without stanzas of a quality one has to admire:

> Sad Waste! for which no After-Thrift atones:
> The Grave admits no Cure of Guilt or Sin.
> Dew-Drops may deck the Turf that hides the Bones,
> But Tears of godly Grief ne'er flow within.

And he could look upon his verses with some pride, boasting to Lady Hesketh, "A fig for poets who write Epitaphs upon Individuals: I have written *one* that serves *200* persons" (27th November 1787).

There is another of his epitaphs which calls for special attention and that is 'On the Death of Mrs Throckmorton's Bullfinch'. He had told Samuel Rose in November 1788 that

> Weston has not been without its tragedies since you left us.
> Mrs. Frog's piping Bull-finch has been eaten by a rat, and the
> villain left nothing but poor Bully's beak behind him. It will
> be a wonder if this event does not at some convenient time
> employ my versifying passion.

And indeed he lost no time in versifying it.

The poem's title and its verse form, the 'romance-six', immediately call to mind Thomas Gray's 'Ode on the Death of a Favourite Cat Drowned in a Tub of Gold Fishes'. It too is a mock-heroic in which a relatively trivial event is described in elevated language and overdecorated with classical allusions. Gray's exaggerations are, as in Pope's *The Rape of the Lock,* meant to satirise the foibles of 'polite society', and he ends his poem with a clear moral statement:

> From hence, ye beauties, undeceived,
> Know, one false step is ne'er retrieved,
>   And be with caution bold.
> Not all that tempts your wandering eyes
> And heedless hearts is lawful prize;
>   Nor all that glisters gold.

Cowper's poem, it has to be said, pales rather in comparison with that of Gray. The language is certainly elevated: the River Rhine is given its classical name *Rhenus*, and the bird's breast is the colour "With which Aurora decks the skies", but it does not seem to be satirising anything. William Norris Free believes that "It attacks Mrs Throckmorton's sentimentalism,"[4] a suggestion which would have upset Cowper, who would have had no wish whatsoever to distress his friend and, as we saw in the epitaph on his hare, he knew for himself how painful the demise of a pet can be.

The tone of the opening stanzas is gentle and sympathetic. Nymphs are asked to join Maria in her weeping for the assassination of poor Bully. We notice though that before Bully's gorgeous colours are depicted for us, it is the sound of his voice which is stressed:

> And though by nature mute
> Or only with a whistle blest,
> Well-taught, he all the sounds express'd
> Of flagellet or flute.

The significance of this will become apparent later.

Mrs Throckmorton had, we are told, done everything she could to protect the bird and to ensure its comfort. No cats were allowed anywhere in the house and the lattice of his cage was not made of wire, which might have hurt his feathers, but of peeled willow wands. This, sadly, contributed to Bully's downfall, as the rat had no difficulty in chewing through them. Had there even been a cat in the house it might have seen the creature off. No human concern or intervention, it seems, can stand in the way of fate. There is a delightful touch of almost Gothic horror as the villain comes creeping in:

> Night veil'd the pole. All seem'd secure
> When led by Instinct sharp and sure,
>   Subsistence to provide,
> A Beast forth-sallied on the scout,
> Long-back'd, long-tail'd, with whisker'd snout,
>   And badger-colour'd hide.

It is a light-hearted horror, however, and Cowper tells us that what ratty sniffed in the study was

> Better than all the books he found,
> Food chiefly for the mind.

But the tone of the stanza which follows is sharply different. The language suddenly has a shocking directness:

> Just then, by adverse Fate impress'd
> A Dream disturb'd poor Bully's rest;
>   In sleep he seem'd to view
> A Rat, fast-clinging to his cage,
> And screaming at the sad presage,
>   Awoke and found it true.

In view of the extent and depth of Cowper's knowledge of Milton, that last line cannot be other then a conscious echo of Adam's dream in Book VIII of *Paradise Lost*, which Keats famously condensed to "he woke and found it true." But this is the reverse of Adam's dream, for unlike Adam, who woke to find the beauty of Eve and of Paradise, Bully woke to find that his nightmare was the actuality.

Cowper had written at length about dreams to Lady Hesketh early in 1787, shortly before his breakdown. Referring to views expressed by Elizabeth Carter in *The Rambler*, no. 44, he declared:

> She has had no extraordinary ones, and therefore accounts them only the ordinary operations of the Fancy. Mine are of a texture that will not suffer me to ascribe them to so inadequate a cause, or to any cause but the operation of an exterior agency … As to my own peculiar experience in the dreaming way I have only this to observe. I have not believed that I shall perish because in my dreams I have been told it, but because I have had hardly any but terrible dreams for 13 years, I therefore have spent the greater part of that time most unhappily. They have either tinged my mind with melancholy or filled it with terror, and the effect has been unavoidable. (14th-16th January 1787)

He had, we remember, been told in a dream that he would perish. This nightmare he here projects onto the bullfinch, seemingly aware of his own living nightmare which was to follow. He too is a doomed creature, vulnerable and alone, and facing a future from which no human power can protect him.

There is after this an attempt to rebalance the poem, but it will not go back to the gently ludicrous tone with which it began. The rat had left nothing behind but the bird's beak, but it was a gruesome fact that need not have been included in a mock-heroic. Rather than leave it out Cowper devotes an entire stanza to it, wishing that, if the rat had swallowed that too, it might have choked him:

> He left it – but he should have ta'en.
> That beak, whence issued many a strain
>   Of such mellifluous tone
> Might have repaid him well I wote,
> For silencing so sweet a throat,
>   Fast-stuck within his own.

Again we notice the stress on the bird as singer, and the poem ends with an image of Maria mourning as the Muses mourned the death of Orpheus, whose head was swept down the River Hebrus. There is no *necessity* for this image, but in it the head of a bird has now become specifically that of a bard:

> Maria weeps, the Muses mourn –
> So when, by Bacchanalians torn
>   On Thracian Hebrus' side
> The tree-enchanter Orpheus fell,
> His head alone remain'd to tell
>   The cruel death he died.

As his own fears had come to the surface, it seems that he saw, as Vincent Newey put it, "in poor Bully's fate a mirror-image of his own foreseen destruction".[5] Donald Davie's observation that the poem is a "masterpiece of barely controlled hysteria" may not be the exaggeration it at first seems.[6]

Mrs Throckmorton was, we can feel sure, saddened by the death of her bullfinch, but her husband, as we know for certain, had earlier been furious with his bailiff. Leaving Weston for the winter, he had told the man to cut the tops of the flowering shrubs which lined a delightful serpentine walk in the gardens. The Dunce, Cowper told Lady Hesketh, "misapprehending the order, cut down and faggotted up the whole grove, leaving neither tree, bush, nor twig; nothing but stumps as high as my ankle" (8th May 1786). GBH, it seems, was considered to be quite in order if the fellow was one of your servants, and Cowper added that he could have excused Mr Throckmorton if he had "cudgell'd the man".

This was the shrubbery about which Cowper had written a poem many years earlier, to which the subtitle "Written in a Time of Affliction" was added when it was first published in the 1782 collection. The time of affliction was probably 1773/4 when he was recovering from his period of suicidal despair and had given up attending church, being convinced of his own damnation.

It is a poem which very clearly conjures up for us a feeling of desperate, empty melancholy: the sadness of despair and the despair of sadness. It is there in just three words: "fixt, unalterable care":

> But fixt unalterable care
> > Foregoes not what she feels within,
> Shows the same sadness ev'ry where,
> > And slights the season and the scene.
>
> For all that pleas'd in wood or lawn,
> > While peace possess'd these silent bow'rs,
> Her animating smile withdrawn,
> > Has lost its beauties and its pow'rs.

They are lines which recall a couplet from Coleridge's 'Dejection':

> I may not hope from outward Forms to win
> The Passion and the Life, whose Fountains are within!

But Cowper's cause of melancholy is very different and is evident from what is missing from the poem: any mention of God. In 'Retirement' he gave his view that for any man who has lost favour with God

> No gardens interspers'd with flow'ry beds,
> Nor gales that catch the scent of blooming groves,
> And waft it to the mourner as he roves,
> Can call up life into his faded eye.
> (336-9)

That is exactly what has befallen him here. The landscape has not changed but his response to it has. The last stanza is very sad:

Me fruitful scenes and prospects waste,
　　Alike admonish not to roam,
These tell me of enjoyments past,
　　And those of sorrows yet to come.

To recover his spirits, as he was later to insist in Book V of *The Task*, it was necessary to

Acquaint thyself with God if thou would'st taste
His works. Admitted once to his embrace,
Thou shalt perceive that thou wast blind before.
　　　　　　　　　　　　　　　　(V.779-81)

Hope did, to some extent, re-enter Cowper's life, and there were years when, as he wrote in Book I of *The Task*,

Not rural sights alone, but rural sounds
Exhilarate the spirit, and restore
The tone of languid Nature.
　　　　　　　　　　(181-3)

But it was not to last, and at the end of his life all joy had gone: in 1798, when Lady Hesketh described some delightful scenes, he replied:

the wretch who can derive no gratification from a view of
nature even under the disadvantage of her most ordinary
dress, will have no eyes to admire her in any. In one day, in
one moment I should rather have said, she became a
universal blank to me. (29th July 1798)

Just as Cowper could identify with Mrs Throckmorton's distress over the death of poor Bully, so he could fully understand her husband's feelings about the destruction of his shrubbery. He himself had been greatly distressed when, taking Lady Austen to one of his favourite places in the neighbouring parish of Lavendon, he found that the poplar trees there had all been cut down. He told Lady Hesketh in May 1786 that it was a place

I used to account a little paradise; but the poplars have been
felled, and the scene has suffered so much by the loss, that
though still in point of prospect beautiful, it has not charm
sufficient to attract me now. (1st May 1786)

His poem 'The Poplar-Field', published in *The Gentleman's Magazine* in
December 1784, begins by telling us bluntly that the trees are no more –
"The Poplars are fell'd" – but then Cowper recreates the scene for us as it
was, so that we can share in his feelings and appreciate what it was like once
and, sadly, how little of it left now:

> The Poplars are fell'd, farewell to the shade
> And the whispering sound of the cool colonnade,
> The winds play no longer and sing in the leaves,
> Nor Ouse on his bosom their image receives.

It is not only the poet who is affected by such change; the birds are too, and
we are given a sound picture as well as a visual one:

> The black-bird has fled to another retreat
> Where the hazels afford him a screen from the heat,
> And the scene where his melody charm'd me before,
> Resounds with his sweet-flowing ditty no more.

He is clearly moved by what has happened, and we are left wondering why
the poplars were felled and then just left lying on the ground, but we could
not claim that Cowper is a proto-eco-poet, as it is largely himself he is
writing about:

> Twelve years have elapsed since I last took a view
> Of my favourite field and the bank where they grew,
> And now in the grass behold they are laid,
> And the tree is my seat that once lent me a shade.

One might ask why, if it is a favourite field, it is twelve years since he was last
there, but a kindlier question would be whether the repetition of the word
'shade' from the first line has an intended double meaning, as he goes on to
compare the fate of the trees with the likely brevity of his own existence and
the brevity of even our moments of enjoyment:

My fugitive years are all hasting away,
And I must e'er long lie as lowly as they,
With a turf on my breast and a stone at my head
Ere another such grove shall arise in its stead.

'Tis a sight to engage me if any thing can
To muse on the perishing pleasures of Man;
Though his life be a dream, his enjoyments, I see,
Have a Being less durable even than he.

Professor Free approves of the opening stanza, but unkindly goes on to say: "The singsong of the rest of the poem seems appropriate to its clichés, platitudes and trite sentimentalities."[7] He might not have been so harsh had he been aware that it was a lyric, a poem meant to be put to music and sung. He might then have appreciated the gently wistful note those repeated anapaests bring about. It was one of four pieces all written to favourite tunes of Lady Austen, and the ebb and flow of the rhythm is not only attractive, but singularly appropriate for verses which move so skilfully between past and present, and the sentiments are such as we can all share, being only too conscious that the truths of mortality are far from being platitudes.

Cowper had a great love of trees. In the first book of *The Task* he tells us that

No tree in all the grove but has its charms,
Though each its hue peculiar.
(I.307-8)

And in the twelve lines which follow we have a series of brief but telling observations on nine different trees: the "wannish grey" of the willow, the "deeper green" of the elm, and "deeper still, / Lord of the woods, the long-surviving oak".

One oak he was particularly fond of was known as the Yardley Oak. He would take his friends and visitors to see it and as he confessed to his cousin, "I tell them all that it is a thousand years old, verily believing it to be so, though I do not know it" (15th September 1788).

Accurate portrayals of natural scenery are to be found throughout Cowper's work, but he was never attracted to the grand, or to the fashionable 'sublime'. He preferred "nature in her cultivated trim" (*The Task*, III.357), something which he could represent for us in close detail. As he had told William Unwin, his descriptions were all from nature, none of them second-hand, and his delineations of the heart were from his own experience. It was this first-hand observation, as we have seen, which impressed Coleridge.

Cowper was in his sixties when he wrote 'Yardley Oak', and not in the best of health, so it is nor surprising that the passing of time is one of its main themes. The opening two paragraphs have a rather sombre tone. Hollow-trunked, this single tree is now the sole survivor of a group of oaks which had stood there when he was born. Nevertheless, Cowper admits that were it not downright "Idolatry", he could be tempted to kneel and reverence it, seeing that "our forefather Druids" had worshipped in "thickest shades of oak". But they had been pagans, and had done so long before Christ. He would have no such excuse.

He then thinks back to when the Yardley Oak was no more than an acorn. Playfully, and appropriately, he calls it a "bawble", "a cup and ball which babes might play with", but this playfulness is combined with blank verse so Miltonic that the effect might be termed a mock-georgic ending with a spectacular bathos:

> Thou wast a bawble once; a cup and ball
> Which babes might play with; and the thievish jay
> Seeking her food, with ease might have purloined
> The auburn nut that held thee, swallowing down
> Thy yet close-folded latitude of boughs
> And all thine embryo vastness at a gulp.
>
> (17-22)

But fate had decreed otherwise: rain fell and softened the ground and a "skipping deer" trod on it, so planting it firmly down into the soil. At least, that is how Cowper imagines it, and he challenges anyone to argue with him. The following year "with vegetative force instinct" it sprouts, and being a dicotyledon (as Cowper knows), it first appears as simply two leaves, which gives him a tenuous excuse to squeeze in a reference to "the Fabled Twins", Castor and Pollux. The lines which follow need to be read aloud to savour the exaggeration and one more clump of bathos:

> A leaf succeeded, and another leaf,
> And all the elements thy puny growth
> Fost'ring propitious, thou becam'st a twig.
>
> (37-9)

Another classical reference – this time to Dodona, the sacred grove of oaks in ancient Greece where Zeus spoke through an oracle – has Cowper wishing that his tree could speak. Not that he would look for prophecies; the future is "best unknown", he felt. Rather he would want to learn about the past. And as he now compares the oak tree's past, "thy spreading boughs", with what it has become, "a cave for owls to roost in", we sense that Cowper, in old age, is beginning to identify with it. What is also notable is that if we make due allowance for the Latinate diction, what he is describing is, as he claimed, truly an actual tree:

> Of girth enormous, with moss-cushion'd root
> Upheav'd above the soil, and sides imboss'd
> With prominent wens globose.
> (64-6)

One of the attractions of *The Task* is that we can never be sure where Cowper's line of thought will take him next. His digressions are those of the most companionable of raconteurs, and this is so even on the much smaller scale of 'Yardley Oak'. It is change and the destructive power of time his mind now turns to:

> Change is the diet on which all subsist
> Created changeable, and Change at last
> Destroys them.
> (72-4)

Enduring whatever changes the weather brought, "Calm and alternate storm, moisture and drought" the oak, "seeming most durable", has stood in its place for centuries, and Cowper gives us an amusingly vivid picture of it when it was no more than a sapling, " … when settling on thy leaf, a fly / Could shake thee to the root". In later times even tempests could not do so. At the height of its maturity it had the good fortune to escape being chopped down for timber, and Cowper accepts this as an opportunity to think back to the earlier years of the century when whole forests fell to satisfy the demands of the Royal Navy: 60 acres of mature oak, it has been estimated, went into the building of one 74-gun warship. But returning to his theme, he shows that Time has achieved what the axe did not. The oak's centre has rotted and now is simply a "scoop'd rind", which he pictures for us as "An huge throat calling to the clouds for drink", an image of old age which has a desperate sadness to it.

There is a growing feeling at this point in the poem that Cowper is beginning to identify more and more with this oak:

> Thou, like myself, hast stage by stage attain'd
> Life's wintry bourn …
> (144-5)

His tempests have been spiritual and emotional and, though he has managed to hold on, it seems he is now beginning to have a sense of his own frailty, but he is no more ready to release his hold on life than is the tree:

> Yet Life still lingers in thee, and puts forth
> Proof not contemptible of what she can,
> Even where Death predominates.
> (130-2)

And, because the tree is mute, he decides to speak on its behalf:

> I will perform
> Myself the oracle, and will discourse
> In mine own ear such matter as I may.
> (140-2)

The "discourse" which follows is, however, brief and strangely uneven. Our life is no more than a span, he says, quoting first Jacob's assertion in Genesis 47:9 "Few and evil have the days of the years of my life been," and then from Book VI of his own translation of the *Iliad*, when Glaucus declares:

> Short-lived as foliage is the race of man,
> The wind shakes down the leaves, the budding grove
> Soon teems with others, and in spring they grow,
> So pass mankind.

But this gloomy outlook is not followed up. Instead, Cowper suddenly presents us with a bizarre view of Adam, born, so he explains, with an immediate understanding of all things and so spared the drudgery of a formal education. He was never a teenager, "excused the penalties of dull Minority". And he never went to school:

> No tutor charg'd his hand
> With the thought-tracing quill, or task'd his mind
> With problems.
> (180-2)

It is hard to see the relevance of this, and as the poem has only three further (unrelated) lines to go, it cannot seriously be regarded as an ending. And yet William Hayley, his first biographer, wrote of the manuscript: "I never saw any of his compositions more carefully, or more judiciously corrected."[9] We know that Cowper had been contemplating a long poem on the four ages of man and it is possible that these curious lines on Adam may have been an initial foray in that direction, but he went no further. Instead, the poem concludes with a device much favoured by eighteenth-century poets: personification. Rarely has there been an example of personification quite as vivid as Cowper's portrayal of History:

> History, not wanted yet,
> Lean'd on her elbow, watching Time, whose course
> Eventual should supply her with a theme.
> (182-4)

Paradoxically the poem seems to be unfinished, yet it ends with these powerfully graphic closing lines.

'Yardley Oak' was not published during Cowper's lifetime. Hayley found the manuscript among his papers and included it in the first edition of his biography. It was an instant success. Wordsworth had Sara Hutchinson copy it into his commonplace book, and if we sometimes forget just how popular Cowper was in his day, we are given a reminder by Edward Ferrars, insisting in *Sense and Sensibility* that Marianne would be likely to buy up every copy of Cowper that ever was "to prevent them falling into unworthy hands; and she would have every book that tells her how to admire an old twisted tree."

15

Homer and the Closing Years

And mortal life shall cease

Cowper was not only a popular poet; he was also a public poet in a way which is hard for us to conceive today. He wrote scores of occasional poems on such topics as 'The Burning of Lord Mansfield's Library', 'The Promotion of Edward Thurlow to the Lord High Chancellorship of England', 'The Queen's Nocturnal Visit to London'. and 'The Benefit Received by His Majesty from Sea-Bathing'. Some were circulated privately while others were published in journals like *The Gentlemen's Magazine*, *The Times* and the *Whitehall Evening-Post*, almost every one of them showing that high level of technical ability in rhythm and rhyme which seems to come as second nature to even the most minor of eighteenth-century versifiers.

But while they were public poems, they were never political. Not that Cowper was uninterested in politics. As we have seen, he was a keen reader of the newspapers and told Joseph Hill in 1782:

> Suppose not however that I am perfectly an unconcerned
> Spectator, or that I take no interest at all in the affairs of my
> country. Far from it – I read the News – I see that things go
> wrong in every quarter. I meet now and then with an account
> of some disaster that seems to be the indisputable progeny of
> treachery, cowardice, or a spirit of faction. (31st January
> 1782)

The loss of the American colonies incensed him, but such events never featured in his verse. His concerns were always of a more domestic nature. 'Annus Memorabilis 1789' is a title which, in retrospect, might tempt us to hope for something about the French Revolution. He was certainly appalled by it later, telling William Hayley:

> I will tell you what the French have done. They have made
> me weep for a King of France, which I never thought to do,
> and they have made me sick of the very name of liberty,
> which I never thought to be. (29th January 1793)

But the subtitle of his 1789 poem is 'A Poem Written in Commemoration of His Majesty's Happy Recovery'. It is George III's recovery from mental breakdown that Cowper is celebrating, and one cannot but suspect that there is some degree of fellow-feeling there. He knew for himself what the King had been through, and the understanding he shows for the Queen must have struck a chord with Mrs Unwin:

> Then Peace and Joy again possess'd
> Our Queen's long agitated breast,
> Such Joy and Peace as can be known
> By suff'rers like herself alone,
> Who losing, or supposing lost
> The Good on earth they valued most,
> For that dear sorrow's sake forego
> All hope of Happiness below,
> Then, suddenly regain the prize
> And flash thanksgiving to the skies.
> (46-55)

If it is accepted that there is a certain degree of autobiography in this poem, then there is, as we have come to expect, a corresponding degree of vanity also.

Although the *Collected Poems* shows that Cowper composed a substantial quantity of such occasional poems, they were not enough to keep his own despair at bay. For this he needed, as he said so often, something like *The Task*, which would keep him really busy, and no sooner was that poem finished than he quickly found another task for himself – translating Homer. Once again, however, it was not a task of his *own* making. In 1782, at the height of his friendship with Lady Austen, when he was reading Pope's Homer translation to her, repeatedly complaining of his wayward digressions, and it was she who suggested that as he felt so strongly about it, he should produce his own version.

Writing in 1880, Professor Goldwin Smith hit upon a delightful and telling image to convey to his readers what he saw as the hazards and complexities of the undertaking. "The translation of Homer into verse", he wrote, "is the Polar Expedition of literature, always failing, yet still desperately renewed."[1]

Cowper took his time in risking such a slippery venture for himself, but his opposition to Pope surfaces again and again in his letters over the years. To Newton he insisted that "the sublime of Homer in the hands of Pope becomes bloated and tumid, and his description tawdry" (10th December 1785).

Writing in *The Gentleman's Magazine* in 1785 under the name of Alethes (the truthful one) he pulled many of his criticisms together. He began, wisely, by granting Pope's greatness as a poet, but going on to make the point that he "did not build his glory upon the basis of translation". Pope was "a most excellent rhymist", but that was where the trouble lay. To keep to the rhyme resulted in "an almost unavoidable necessity to depart from the meaning of the original". It is a valid objection, but Cowper goes farther: " … instead of Homer in the graceful habit of his age and nation, we have Homer in a straight waistcoat." His characters, he says, all sound alike, "stately, pompous and stiff", and a few lines later he accuses Pope of being "often turgid, often tame, often careless".

Cowper began translating in November 1784, but it was over a year before he confessed as much to John Newton, fearing that he would disapprove of so much time spent on a pagan work. He defended himself by claiming that he had begun it just to give himself something to do, but then:

> I will nevertheless say that I have not enter'd on this work, unconnected as it must appear with the interest of the Cause of God, without the direction of his Providence, nor altogether unassisted by him in the performance of it. (18th February 1786)

That was what he told Newton, disclaiming any ambition for fame, yet to his cousin it was quite a different story. Only a few months earlier he had told her:

> My Dear, if I can produce a Translation of the Old Bard that the Literati shall prefer to Pope's, which I have the assurance to hope that I may, it will do me more honour than any thing that I have performed hitherto. (17th November 1785)

He explained to her that it was his aim to translate at least forty lines a day, and he set out full of optimism. Even though he was fully aware that he had forty thousand lines ahead of him, he found it "a most agreeable amusement" (3rd December 1785). But inevitably the labour began to pall. By May 1790 he was telling Joseph Hill: "I am still at the old sport; Homer all the Morning and Homer all the Evening." He was even complaining to Newton that there were times when he was by no means sure about God's part in the scheme: "Why it pleased God that I should be hunted into such a business, of such enormous length and labour, by miseries for which he did not see good to afford me any other remedy, I know not" (13th January 1787).

It could be argued that a poet should translate only work to which he is attracted emotionally or imaginatively. For Cowper the attraction was largely intellectual. It provided him with a challenge, and much of the motive could be put down to vanity: he wanted to outdo Pope. But living as he did in such quiet and civilised retirement, he could not be expected to relish the barbarism, butchery and carnage celebrated with such gusto in the *Iliad*. He made his dislike of the bloodshed very plain to Walter Bagot:

> Is it possible for a man to be calm who for 3 weeks past has been perpetually occupied in slaughter. Letting out one man's bowels, smiting another through the gullet, transfixing the liver of another, and lodging an arrow in the buttock of a fourth? … I had need discard all humanity. It is woeful work, and were the best poet in the world to give us at this day such a List of Killed and wounded, he would not escape universal censure, to the praise of a more enlighten'd age, be it spoken. I have waded through much blood, and through much more I must wade before I shall have finish'd. (3rd January 1787)

But he would see the project through to the end. He was no longer simply a gentleman who wrote verses; he saw himself – and referred to himself – as an author. He had agreed a contract, and his letters at that time are full of concerns about his subscribers, his royalties and the critics. He frequently sent copy to friends and family members for their opinions, but was not always happy when he received them. But the comments of one of his advisers, Henry Fuseli, were always welcome. He told Bagot on another occasion:

> ... foreigner as he is, he has an exquisite taste in English
> Verse. The man is all fire, an Enthusiast in the highest degree
> on the subject of Homer, and has given me more than once
> a jog when I have been inclined to Nap with my author. (31st
> August 1786)

Fuseli, a Swiss painter and essayist of some distinction in his day, proved to be a relentless critic, insisting on the closest accuracy and driving Cowper to achieve it. But he was also at times rather irascible and eventually tired of what he had been asked to do, writing to a friend:

> I heartily wish with you that Cowper had trusted to his own
> legs, instead of a pair of stilts to lift him to fame, and this I
> wish as much for my own sake as well as for his; for I am
> deadly sick of revising his foul linen.[2]

Nevertheless, Fuseli had a high opinion of Cowper's ability as a poet and when the translation eventually appeared in print he wrote a long and favourable notice of it in *The Analytical Review*.

Cowper never met Fuseli, nor did they ever exchange letters; all communication went through his publisher Joseph Johnson, but Cowper was quick to acknowledge his help, paying him the warmest of tributes in his preface, calling him "the best critic in HOMER I have ever met with, the learned and ingenious Mr. FUSELI".

Cowper's preface rehearses many of his objections to Pope's version. Concentrating on the differences in their verse forms, he insists from the outset that it is impossible to translate any ancient poet into rhyme. Pope, he argues, did so because he was so used to rhyming couplets that he was incapable of doing anything else. Again he says that the search for a rhyme will inevitably mean adding, omitting or changing something, whereas in his own translation "I have omitted nothing; I have invented nothing."

The truth of this is soon evident if we consider part of the well-known Sarpedon speech to Glaucus from Book XII of the *Iliad*, first in A. T. Murray's prose translation in the Loeb Classical Library, then Cowper's version and lastly Pope's:

> Ah, friend, if once escaped from this battle we were
> for ever to be ageless, and immortal, neither should
> I fight myself among the foremost, nor should I send
> thee into battle where men win glory; but now – for

in any case fates of death beset us, fates past counting,
which no mortal may escape or avoid – now let us go
forward, whether we shall give glory to another, or
another to us.

Oh, Glaucus, if escaping safe the death
That threats us here, we also could escape
Old age, and to ourselves secure a life
Immortal, I would neither in the van
Myself expose, nor would encourage thee
To tempt the perils of the glorious field,
But since a thousand messengers of fate
Pursue us close, and man is born to die –
E'en let us on, the prize of glory yield,
If yield we must, or wrest it from the foe.

Cou'd all our Care elude the greedy Grave,
Which claims no less the Fearful than the Brave,
For lust of Fame I shou'd not vainly dare
In fighting Fields, nor urge thy soul to War.
But since, alas, ignoble Age must come,
Disease, and Death's inexorable Doom;
The Life which others pay, let us bestow,
And give to Fame what we to Nature owe;
Brave, tho' we fall, and honour'd, if we live;
Or let us Glory gain, or Glory give!

There is no doubt about it: Pope stands guilty as charged. He has added and decorated throughout. But how brilliantly. The alliteration gives such sparkle to the lines. The balance and antithesis add such pace. "And give to Fame what we to Nature owe": it is so compact and so exciting to read. It sounds, as of course it should, as though it demands to be declaimed. Cowper's lines give us the facts, but in lines which have just those faults of which he accused Pope: they are turgid and tame.

It is true that Pope's lines always sound like Pope, but that may be why we enjoy them so. In contrast, it is not certain that Cowper's lines sound like Cowper, and that is part of the problem. In favouring blank verse over rhyme, he could hardly be expected not to cite the example of his hero John Milton, "whose genius had angelic wings", he told us in *The Task* (III.255). In the preface he is adamant that

> Having mentioned Milton, I cannot but add an observation
> on the similitude of his manner to that of HOMER. It is
> such, that no person, familiar with both, can read either,
> without being reminded of the other.

But is this true? In looking for a classicist capable of judging the accuracy of
Cowper's translation and also of evaluating it as poetry, we are fortunate in
having Matthew Arnold's authoritative essay 'On Translating Homer', in
which he not only rejects Cowper's claim, but gives it as a reason for the
work's total failure as a translation: "But between Cowper and Homer there
is interposed the mist of Cowper's elaborate Miltonic manner, entirely alien
to the flowing rapidity of Homer." And he goes on to repudiate another of
Cowper's claims:

> It is in vain that Cowper insists on his fidelity: "my chief boast
> is that I have adhered closely to my original … the matter
> found in me, whether the reader like it or not, is found also
> in Homer; and the matter not found in me, how much
> soever the reader may admire it, is found only in Mr Pope."
> To suppose that it is fidelity to an original to give its matter,
> unless you at the same time give its manner; or, rather, to
> suppose that you can really give its matter at all, unless you
> can give its manner, is just the mistake of our pre-Raphaelite
> school of painters, who do not understand that the peculiar
> effect of nature resides in the whole and not in the parts.[3]

It is a damning criticism, and after reading it, perhaps the best one can do
for Cowper's Homer is to go along with Norman Nicholson and say: "Yet
the work is by no means unreadable."[4]

Being better suited to his temperament, there are sections of his *Odyssey*
which are more successful, but even in Book VII, where one might expect the
description of Alcinous' palace and garden to have brought out the best in
Cowper, we find the Miltonics thundering through:

> Mastiffs, in gold and silver, lined the approach
> On either side, with art celestial framed
> By Vulcan, guardians of Alcinous' gate
> For ever, unobnoxious to decay.

And this from a man who felt that it might be said of him "that my diction is often plain and unelevated".

After six years of writing and rewriting, Cowper's Homer was at last published on 1st July 1791. As he was a respected literary figure at this time, the work attracted a good deal of critical attention in all the leading journals, but the tone was respectful rather than enthusiastic. The majority of reviewers, themselves classicists to a man, noting Cowper's repeated assertions of the accuracy of his translation, were happy to demonstrate their own erudition with line-by-line comparisons and exegesis, and rarely to Cowper's advantage. The general feeling was that he had failed because of the essential impossibility of trying to combine exactness and inspiration. His frequent distortions of syntax were remarked upon, and *The Critical Review* hit home by stating that he had simply exchanged the extravagances of Pope for those of Milton. Often there was the implication that he could have spent his time more profitably by writing more of his own poetry. It was not, we sense, what his readers wanted, and later critics were no kinder. Goldwin Smith concludes: "Pope delights school-boys; Cowper delights nobody,"[5] and Gilbert Thomas judges: "Homer is grand and lively; Cowper's Homer is grand and dull."[6] But subscriptions are collected before publication, and it has been estimated that Cowper made over £1,000 from the project – a very considerable sum in 1791.

His fame was such at this time that when Thomas Warton died in 1790, Cowper was the strongest candidate for the post of Poet Laureate, and it would probably have been his for the asking, but when he learned that his cousin was thinking of canvassing at court on his behalf he was horrified and, wisely, asked her not to:

> … heaven guard my brows from the wreath you mention, whatever wreath beside may hereafter adorn them. It would be a leaden extinguisher clapp'd on all the fire of my genius, and I should never more produce a line worth reading. (28th May 1790)

The post went instead to Sir Henry James Pye, of whom, though he held it for the next 23 years, almost nothing is now remembered other than that, as MP for Berkshire, he was a faithful supporter of Pitt the Younger. Indeed that is probably why he was appointed, even though he was perhaps England's worst poet to be made Laureate with the possible exception of Alfred Austin.

Having lived in such quiet retirement for so long, Cowper must have found the early years of the 1790s positively tumultuous: so many new people; so many new places. The first of the new people was John Johnson, a cousin by marriage from the Donne side of the family. Cowper had had no contact with any of these relations for almost 30 years, but was attracted to "Norfolk Johnny", as he was soon affectionately calling him, from the moment they first met, and it was as a result of this meeting that his aunt, Mrs Bodham, sent him the portrait of his mother. Cowper described Johnny to her as "so harmless, cheerful, gentle and good-temper'd that I am so entirely at my ease with him" (9th September 1790), but at that time neither could have guessed that within a very few years the young man would become his cousin's full-time carer.

It was probably Cowper's established reputation which gave his publisher, Joseph Johnson (not a relation) the idea of a new project: putting his name to a grandiose edition of Milton with notes and commentaries together with translations of the Latin and Italian poems. Cowper had, as we know, the highest admiration for Milton, and had been greatly angered by Dr Johnson's criticisms of him, but such things as notes and commentaries were quite outside his range of experience, and he was far away from any academic library. It was an attractive idea, but he was not sure that it was a good one, and he turned for advice to Samuel Teedon.

Teedon had settled in Olney in 1775 at the suggestion of John Newton, and became the village schoolmaster. He had a smattering of Latin and Greek, but Cowper at first could not stand the man. In 1785 he described him to Joseph Hill:

> He is the most obsequious, the most formal, the most pedantic of all creatures. So civil that it would be cruel to affront him, and so troublesome that it is impossible to bear him … he never says that my garden is gay, but that the flowery tribe are finely variegated and extremely fragrant. The weather with him is never fine, but genial, never cold and uncomfortable, but rigorous and frowning. (29th June 1785)

But slowly Cowper learned to tolerate him and eventually warmed to him. They had one thing in common, and that was their conviction: Teedon's of his salvation and Cowper of his own damnation. Strangely, Cowper began to look upon Teedon as his spiritual adviser, and between 1791 and 1794 they exchanged dozens of letters – Cowper for the most part bewailing his misery.

And so, uncertain about the wisdom of editing Milton, it was to the "semi-educated, self-opinionated, unctuous, and irrepressible"[7] Teedon that Cowper turned. Teedon referred the matter to God and was assured that it was the will of God that Cowper should undertake the work. Sadly, Teedon may have misheard. Cowper translated the Latin and Italian poems, but he made little progress with the notes, and by the end of 1792 he was referring to the book as a mountain on his shoulders which made everything else impracticable. In the end whole project was quietly shelved.

And yet, in one respect, the effort had a major influence on the rest of Cowper's life as it introduced him to William Hayley, who became not only one of his closest friends but his first biographer. Hayley has increasingly come to be seen as someone it is safe to mock. Why this is so is not immediately obvious. He was not so regarded then and certainly not by Cowper. Hayley was commissioned by the publishers Boydell and Nicholl to write a biography of Milton, and a newspaper, aware that Cowper was working on an edition, tried to make out that they were in competition, antagonists even. Neither man was temperamentally suited to the kind of Popeian literary warfare that the press presumably hoped would follow. Hayley was in fact horrified by the suggestion and quickly wrote to Cowper enclosing a sonnet in which he called him the true inheritor of Milton's genius. Cowper liked that and was soon addressing him as "My Dear Friend" and telling him that "I feel a disposition of heart towards you, that I never felt for one whom I had never seen, and that shall prove itself, I trust, in the event a propitious omen." It was indeed propitious, and within weeks it was agreed that Hayley should pay a visit.

He arrived on 15th May 1792, and within less than a week Cowper ended a letter to John Johnson:

> Mr Hayley is here on a visit, one of the most amiable of men. We have formed a friendship that I trust will last for life, and render us an edifying example to all future poets. (20th May 1792)

Interestingly, only three years after this was written Wordsworth met Coleridge.

The meeting between Cowper and Hayley, though less productive of poetry, nevertheless proved to be momentous for these two men. Cowper was happy to find a new walking companion. Mrs Unwin had been in poor health ever since January 1789, when she slipped on an icy path and had a heavy fall, injuring her hip. She was 65 and it affected her badly. It was several weeks before she was able to get about the house unaided. Even in the following November she was still not fully recovered, and Cowper told John Newton: "She has almost constant headaches, almost a constant pain in her side which nobody understands, and her lameness, within the last half year, is very little amended" (22nd November 1789). Added to this, in December 1791 she had a mild stroke. It affected her speech and vision – she saw things upside down for a day or two – but she made a good recovery, and by February she was walking in the garden again. But it was while Cowper and Hayley were out walking together in May that she suffered a more serious attack and was paralysed down her right side. Cowper was distraught and helpless, but Hayley immediately took command of the situation. Fortunately he was a poet with a practical interest in science. At home in Eartham in Sussex he had one of the new electric-shock machines which were beginning to be used in the treatment of various ailments, and he discovered that there was one such machine in Weston owned by the happily named Mr Socket. The machine – which is still to be seen in the Olney Museum – consisted of a large glass cylinder which was rotated against a leather pad, thus producing static electricity. The machine was borrowed; Mrs Unwin was connected to it and within three weeks she was talking coherently again and able to walk unaided from room to room.

The emotional shock her illness had on Cowper is evident from a letter he wrote to Samuel Rose after the first attack:

> She has been my faithful and affectionate nurse for many
> years, and consequently has a claim on all my attentions. She
> has them, and will have them as long as she wants them,
> which will probably be, at the best, for a considerable time to
> come. (21st December 1791)

And of course it happened at the very worst time of year, when he himself was so often disposed to melancholy.

We are tempted to say that it is high time he gave some thought to that poor woman. He was, however, at least aware of his failings, confessing to Newton once that "The unhappy, I believe, are always selfish" (16th October 1785). The shock of realising that he had come close to losing Mrs Unwin made him even more aware of this, as can be seen from his poem 'To Mary'.

It is a love poem written by an old gentleman in his sixties to an old lady nearing her seventies, and, what's more, an old lady who has had a stroke and is perhaps not fully in her right mind. How is it then that it is not embarrassing? The answer is: because it is honest and true. In its depiction of old age it avoids absolutely nothing. Each of its 14 triplets is followed by the refrain "My Mary!" How is it not cloyingly sentimental? Because of its sheer simplicity, a simplicity enhanced by the quiet of the repeated m's. There is tenderness in the words too. We are slightly taken aback by the use of her first name as throughout his correspondence she has been Mrs Unwin, a somewhat shadowy figure adding her good wishes now and then. Now she is flesh and blood. And she is *his* Mary, and the wonderment and delight in that single fact is there, I believe, in the exclamation mark.

At last he recognises what she has done for him over the years, but he goes beyond that and now recognises the distressing consequences of it all: what the cares and disturbances of *his* life have done to *her*. In this it is both a brutal and a courageously honest poem.

The poem was written in 1792, almost 20 years to the day since Cowper himself had been stricken by a fit of suicidal despair and it is with this sombre fact that it begins:

> The twentieth year is well-nigh past,
> Since first our sky was overcast,
> Ah would that this might be the last
> > My Mary!

He is not holding out any great hopes for her recovery. She is growing daily weaker and he acknowledges at the outset that it is the care she has devoted to his distress which has brought her to this:

> Thy spirits have a fainter flow,
> I see thee daily weaker grow –
> 'Twas my distress which brought thee low
> > My Mary!

The precise domestic detail is what gives this poem its force. Lady Hesketh had once observed – perhaps rather patronisingly – of Mrs Unwin:

> Her constant employment is knitting stockings, which she does with the finest needles I ever saw, and very nice they are (the stockings I mean). Our cousin has not for many years worn any other than those of her manufacture. She knits silk, cotton, and worsted. She sits knitting one side of the table in her spectacles, and he on the other reading to her.[8]

Cowper regrets that she can no longer do this, adding the telling point that the needles – rather like both of them – now rust:

> Thy needles once a shining store
> For my sake restless heretofore,
> Now rust disused, and shine no more
> > My Mary!

Observing that her once auburn locks are now turned to silver is not unexpected in this context, but Cowper is also prepared to admit that when she speaks it is not always possible to understand her:

> Thy indistinct expressions seem
> Like language utter'd in a dream,
> Yet me they charm, whate'er the theme
> > My Mary!

These are statements of fact, presented without sentiment and not demanding of our sympathy. They still manage, he explains, to communicate with each other and the most moving part of the poem is the picture he gives us of holding her hands in his and her slight response as he gently presses them:

> Partakers of the sad decline,
> Thy hands their little force resign,
> Yet gently prest press gently mine
> > My Mary!

Though an expression of love, it is a painful poem. and ends with Cowper's painful realisation that her awareness of his grief only adds to her sorrow, such is her selflessness. Recalling the poem's beginning, he grants that if, as 20 years before, he were again to succumb to melancholy and despair, it would be the end of her:

> But ah by constant heed I know
> How oft the sadness that I show
> Transforms thy smiles to looks of woe
> > My Mary!

And should my future lot be cast
With much resemblance of the past,
Thy worn-out heart will break at last
    My Mary!

He is confessing, it seems, to his own guilty inadequacy here, his inability to change. It is an astonishing poem, quite unlike anything he had written before and highly accomplished in its stark simplicity.

But change there was and, surprisingly, it was in Mrs Unwin's state of health; within a matter of weeks she was walking again. The electric-shock machine seems to have worked wonders, but an even greater wonder was that before Hayley departed he persuaded Cowper to leave Weston and visit him in Eartham. Others had given Cowper such invitations in the past, but they were always turned down as out of the question. Early in his correspondence with Hayley, he reacted in the same way: "But how should I who have not journey'd 20 miles from home these 20 years, how should I possibly reach your country?" (24rd March 1792).

One can only marvel at the persuasive powers of William Hayley. His house at Eartham near Chichester was not 20, but 120 miles away and it would take three days to get there. Yet, on 1st August, in a coach drawn by four horses, off they went: Cowper. Mrs Unwin, Johnny Johnson, the servants Sam and Nanny Roberts, and Cowper's spaniel, Beau. Three days, squashed together in a coach on eighteenth-century roads, would have been taxing enough if they had been young, fit and well, but they arrived safely, and reporting back to Samuel Teedon after a few days' rest, Cowper assured him that they had met no terrors on the way, adding: "I indeed myself was a little daunted by the tremendous height of the Sussex hills in comparison with which all that I have seen elsewhere are dwarfs" (5th August 1792). It must have been the most adventurous undertaking of his whole life.

Hayley's estate delighted him, embellished as it was with a grotto, imitation Gothic towers and shaded alleyways to walk in. "Almost a paradise" was how he described it, and Mrs Unwin was more cheerful than she had been for months.

The visit must also have been intellectually stimulating for him, as among Hayley's other guests were the novelist and poet Charlotte Smith, the poet James Hurdis, who was soon to become Oxford Professor of Poetry, and the artist George Romney, who drew the famous pastel study of Cowper while they were together at Eartham.

But, for all this, the old fears never fully left him, and in the week before he departed we find him telling Samuel Teedon: "I know myself to be an object of the enemy's particular and peculiar malice, for reasons best known to God" (3rd September 1792). And he was missing his own home at Weston:

> The Genius of that place suits me better; it has an air of snug concealment in which a disposition like mine feels itself peculiarly gratified; whereas here I see from ev'ry window woods like forests and hills like mountains, a wildness in short that rather increases my melancholy, and which, were it not for the agreeables that I find within doors, would soon convince me that mere change of place can avail me little.
> (9th September 1792)

In this he seems to have been more right than he realised, and their return to Weston did little to raise his spirits. When he took up work again on the Milton project his reading of *Paradise Lost* only convinced him that his own fate was akin to that of Lucifer: doomed for all eternity. His nightmares returned:

> Dreamed that in a state of the most insupportable misery I looked through the window of a strange room being all alone, and saw preparations making for my execution. That it was about four days distant, and then I was destined to suffer everlasting martyrdom in the fire. (17th November 1792)

When Hayley paid a brief visit in November 1793 he found Mrs Unwin teetering towards dementia and realised that if something were not done for Cowper very soon there would be no hope for him. It was then, when he was casting around for some way of helping, that there occurred one of the oddest of literary coincidences.

Among the people he discussed the matter with was the Rev. Thomas Carwardine and into their hands – it is not known how – came a document which they thought might help, as it was "a fair specimen of the nature of poetic insanity".[9] That document proved to be Christopher Smart's 'Jubilate Agno'. What they made of it we can have no idea, but it remained in the hands of the Carwardine family until its significance was recognised by W.F. Stead who published it in 1939. That Hayley later became the friend and patron of William Blake reveals him as a totally unexpected link between the three great "mad" poets of the eighteenth century.

Hayley made one final practical suggestion: that they should collaborate on extending a sequence which Cowper had already begun but abandoned. It was to be called 'The Four Ages of Man', and he held out the possibility of illustrations by Flaxman and Romney, but after adding a few unremarkable lines Cowper lost interest.

When Lady Hesketh arrived to take charge of the situation in November 1793 she found things were already out of control, and then in January Cowper fell into a depth of depression from which he would never fully recover. Johnny Johnson's description of him is distressingly graphic:

> The dear soul hardly ever speaks, but sits by the hour together with his eyes on the ground in the deepest silence, which he never interrupts except when he breaks out into the most distressing speeches that can be conceived.[10]

She sought the aid of Dr Francis Willis, the doctor who had attended George III and was regarded as the leading expert in such cases. He recommended medication, which Cowper would not take, and suggested that a separation from Mrs Unwin would help. In this Lady Hesketh was in full agreement. She seems to have thought that Mrs Unwin was the cause of the trouble. After yet another stroke she had become senile, irascible and demanding, and Cowper would hide himself in his bedroom in order not to hear her. Lady Hesketh was convinced that "the sooner it pleased God to remove the old woman from his side the better it would be on all accounts,"[11] but Mrs Unwin would not hear of being separated from him. Lady Hesketh had met her match and could do no more.

It is difficult to be sure how Lady Hesketh and Mrs Unwin regarded each other. We do know that Mrs Unwin had eventually come to object strongly to the presence of Lady Austen in Orchard Side and seems to have been responsible for the final severance of that relationship. She was always very possessive about Cowper, and it would not be surprising if she also felt jealous of Lady Hesketh. On the other side one may detect a note of slightly amused condescension in Lady Hesketh's account of how Mrs Unwin would sit knitting all the time. It is, we are made to feel, something she herself would never do. Did she look down on her? Calling her "the old woman" would suggest so, and Samuel Greatheed, we remember, said she "entertained no small contempt and aversion for her; and frequently indulged her unequalled turn of satire at Mrs U's expense." Cowper's letters to Lady Hesketh sometimes close with an expression of Mrs Unwin's "kind regards", but rarely more. We do, however, have one direct communication between them. It is a postscript Mrs Unwin added in her own hand to Cowper's letter of 22nd March 1790:

> You cannot imagine how much your Ladyship would oblige
> your unworthy servant if you would be so good as to let me
> know in what point I differ from you. All at present I can say
> is, that I will readily Sacrifice my own opinion, unless I can
> give you a Substantial reason for adhering to it.

The whole tone of what she writes – especially addressing her as "your Ladyship" – suggests a high degree of pique about something. There is no evidence of any real affection between them. Cowper may have seen the advantages in a *ménage à trois*, but the ladies do not seem to have shared his opinion.

Lady Hesketh stayed with them for almost two years, but then her own health began to suffer. Johnny Johnson was summoned, but he could not linger in Weston. He had a parish to care for, and the decision was made that they should go back with him to Norfolk.

On 28th July they left Weston, and, aware that he would never return, Cowper wrote on the shutter of his bedroom:

> Farewell, dear scenes, for ever closed to me,
> Oh, for what sorrows must I now exchange ye.

But sadder by far were the few hundred words which he wrote in pencil on some blank pages at the beginning of a copy of his own translation of the *Odyssey*. They have been called his 'Spiritual Diary' and have been called "disjointed reflections", but have at times a frightening lucidity. He begins by lamenting that now he is so watched over that he has no chance of being able to end his life, and regrets the missed opportunity he had in 1773. It is for this failure, he still believes, that he is damned. And yet the injustice of it still appals him:

> I who must suffer as none ever did, whatever else I may
> deserve, have not deserved so terrible a doom, and He who
> made me, with such a probable catastrophe in prospect,
> would have shown himself more merciful had he never made
> me at all.

In a startling image he adds:

> I have been a poor Fly entangled in a thousand webs from
> the beginning.

This spiritual diary is so moving as to be almost above and beyond comment, and yet there is in his assessment of himself a degree of self-centredness which has been with him throughout his life: "What sort of Mercy is that which a poor forlorn creature reduced to childish imbecility through infinite distress may forfeit for ever in a moment?" To believe oneself the only damned is as (insanely) vain as to see oneslf as the only chosen. But he was sane enough to know what was happening, concluding:

> I have, I can have no faith in this Norfolk journey, but am
> sure that either I shall never begin it, or shall never reach the
> place. Could ye spare me, what mercy should I account it.

He did reach Norfolk, but it must all have been done in a great hurry and when they set off, in two post-chaises, Johnson had not settled on anywhere for them to live. The rectory in North Tuddenham, he discovered, was vacant and he managed to lodge them there, but only for two weeks. Then they went to Mundesley on the coast, only to be moved again to Dunham Lodge, a rambling and dreary-looking house near Swaffham. There they lived for a year, followed by another brief stay in Mundesley before finally settling in Johnson's house in East Dereham in October 1796.

One might have expected so many upheavals to have caused Cowper the greatest distress, but by this time he seems to have become so divorced from the actualities of life that very little impinged upon him. The presence of visitors was hardly acknowledged, and though Johnson did his best to cheer him by reading to him and taking him for walks along the Norfolk coast to places where in his youth he had spent many happy holidays, the gloom never lifted. Everything he saw reminded him of his own situation:

> At two miles' distance on the coast is a solitary pillar of rock,
> that the crumbling cliff has left at the high water-mark. I
> have visited it twice, and have found it an emblem of myself.
> Torn from my natural connexions, I stand alone and expect
> the storm that shall displace me. (27th August 1795)

Lady Hesketh seems to have tried to lift the gloom with a cheerful letter describing the delights of Clifton where she was now living, but received a negative and self-pitying reply in return. It proved to be one of Cowper's last letters:

> You describe delightful scenes, but you describe them to
> One, who if he ever saw them, could receive no delight from
> them; who has a faint recollection, and so faint as to be
> almost like a forgotten dream, that once he was susceptible
> of pleasure from such causes ... the wretch who can derive
> no gratification from a view of nature even under the
> disadvantage of her most ordinary dress, will have no eyes
> to admire her in any. In one day, in one moment I should
> rather have said, she became an universal blank to me, and
> though from a different cause, yet with an effect as difficult
> to remove, as blindness itself. (13th October 1798)

This failure to respond to anything outside himself even included the death of Mrs Unwin. Her mind had long before given way, and her physical frailty finally overcame her in the afternoon of 17th December 1796. Cowper was fully aware of her condition, and on the day before her death he asked one of their servants, in the oddest wording, "Sally, is there life above stairs?" Johnson took him up to her bedside and recorded in his diary: "He bore the sight better than expected," but then added what seems to show the coldest lack of concern: that they went down "into the study to the customary employment of the Novel". They went on reading their book. But the following evening when he was taken to see her laid out, it was different:

> After looking at her a few seconds, with one hand holding
> back the bead-curtain, he bore himself away in an agony and
> clasping his hands together, he lifted them up with great
> violence, and exclaimed, looking up towards the ceiling of
> the room – *"Oh God – was it for this?"*[12]

She was buried on the evening of the 23rd in St Edmund's Chapel in the church of East Dereham, quietly and by candlelight so as to spare his feelings, but he had in fact made no enquiry whatsoever about her funeral and never named or mentioned her again as long as he lived.

Hayley composed a clumsy, but well-meaning epitaph:

> Trusting in God, with all her heart and mind,
> This woman prov'd magnanimously kind;
> Endur'd affliction's desolating hail,
> And watch'd a poet thro' misfortune's vale.
> Her spotless dust, angelic guards defend!

It is the dust of Unwin, Cowper's friend!
That single title in itself is fame,
For all who read his verse revere her name.

Shut up inside himself Cowper certainly was, but his intellectual capacity was as alive as ever. The elegant structure of the sentences in that last letter to Lady Hesketh is proof enough of that, but he also continued to revise his Homer, translated a few Latin epigrams into English, as well as some more of Vincent Bourne's verse. He even translated some of John Gay's *Fables* into Latin, the most poignant being Fable no. 50, 'The Hare and Many Friends'. Gay's *Fables* had been given to him as a child, and this particular one we know he had recited to his father's guests.[13] It tells the story of a much-loved hare, but one which, when pursued by the hounds, finds its friends – a horse, a bull, a goat, a sheep and a calf – abandoning it one by one to its fate. Gay had seen it as an image of his own predicament, and here, shortly before his death, Cowper – once a lover and protector of hares – seems to see himself likewise forgotten and about to meet a similar end. It is a sad choice for him to have made, but it is pleasing to see that the facility with which he composed Latin verse had not left him. Nothing, however, quite prepares us for the appearance of his last poem in English, one which was to become perhaps the most celebrated and anthologised of all his poems, 'The Castaway'.

The *OED* cites this as the first recorded use of the word to mean 'one cast adrift at sea'. Previous to this it had meant a 'reprobate', but both meanings seem to be in evidence here.

Cowper was an avid reader of travel books, and the narrative element of this poem comes from his reading of Richard Walker's *A Voyage round the World by George Anson* (1748), which records:

> … one of our ablest seaman was canted overboard; we perceived that, notwithstanding the prodigious agitation of the waves, he swam very strong, and it was with the utmost concern that we found ourselves incapable of assisting him; indeed we were the more grieved at his unhappy fate, as we lost sight of him struggling with the waves, and conceived from the manner in which he swam that he might continue sensible, for a considerable time longer, of the horror attending his irretrievable situation.

The more one thinks about the poor man's situation, the more desperate and terrifying it becomes. Cowper thought about it and found, not surprisingly, that it contained a parallel to his own.

Shipwrecks and storms had often featured in his poetry. There had been that fine extended image in his poem 'On the Receipt of my Mother's Picture out of Norfolk', and they are present in his letters too, to the extent that 'The Castaway' may be seen as the culmination they had, almost inevitably, been leading up to.

The first stanza is enough to indicate that this will not be a simple retelling of Richard Walter's narrative:

> Obscurest night involved the sky,
>   Th'Atlantic billows roar'd,
> When such a destin'd wretch as I
>   Wash'd headlong from on board
> Of friends, of hope, of all bereft,
> His floating home for ever left.

"Involved", apart from its Latin root *involvere* ('to roll around, to envelop'), also implies participation in something not quite right, suggesting that the elements are united in an onslaught against him. But who is *he*? Momentarily, it might be taken from line 3 that we are hearing a first-person speaker, but then it becomes apparent that this is a comparison. Nevertheless, our first impression remains, establishing a close connection between the speaker and the castaway. Both are "destin'd", a word with the strongest of Calvinist associations, pointing to the essential helplessness of their joint situation. One might flinch slightly from the periphrasis "floating home", but it is more than simply a ship the seaman has lost. Cowper too has been removed from his home in Weston, has been cast out and now, without Mary, he is bereft. 'Floating' also suggests a lack of security.

In stanza 3 we learn that the seaman was a very strong swimmer:

> Not long beneath the whelming brine
>   Expert to swim, he lay,
> Nor soon he felt his strength decline
>   Or courage die away;
> But waged with Death a lasting strife
> Supported by despair of life.

He did not quickly go under, but struggled on, as Cowper himself had. "Supported by despair of life" seems to entail an odd contradiction, but hints indirectly at the complexities of Cowper's personal struggle.

In order to avoid making the situation too personal, however, he adds, in a controlled and straightforward manner, the vivid detail of the crew throwing overboard whatever they had that might float and which he could cling to:

> Some succour yet they could afford,
>   And, such as storms allow,
> The cask, the coop, the floated cord
>   Delay'd not to bestow;
> But He, they knew, nor ship nor shore.
> Whate'er they gave, should visit more.

The seaman, on his part, understands their plight and realises that they cannot, in such a storm, turn the vessel around to rescue him. But he is naturally not without thought for himself:

> Yet bitter felt it still to die
> Deserted, and his friends so nigh.

Cowper was aware that his friends were doing all they could, but knew too that there was no help for him.

Keeping close to Walker's narrative now, he makes the point that to be able to swim for an hour in such a sea would be a surprising feat, but stresses that such survival – the postponement of death while fully aware every second of its approaching inevitability – is the real and horrific tragedy of the situation.

Stanza 8 represents an exceptional achievement in many ways:

> At length, his transient respite past,
>   His comrades, who before
> Had heard his voice in ev'ry blast,
>   Could catch the sound no more;
> For then, by toil subdued, he drank
> The stifling wave, and then he sank.

"At length" points again to his awful predicament of struggling for life in the face of certain doom: a terror Cowper knew himself only too well. The rather elaborate Latinism of "his transient respite" helps to bring out the brutal simplicity of the final couplet. "Drank" is normally an active verb denoting a voluntary action, but here it is a prelude to death and that slight but telling hesitation in the line-ending before "the stifling wave" enacts his despairing attempt to avoid it. Furthermore, while drinking and water are central to the life-giving sacraments of the Eucharist and Baptism, here they combine to deliver up that death.

There then comes a change of tone as the poet steps back from the scene to address the reader. Anson's sorrow, he says, is enough in itself to immortalise the drowned sailor, and he does not seek to add to it:

> But Mis'ry still delights to trace
> Its semblance in another's case …

and he concludes with a stanza which is sublime in its picture of suffering:

> No voice divine the storm allay'd,
>   No light propitious shone,
> When, snatch'd from all effectual aid,
>   We perish'd, each alone;
> But I, beneath a rougher sea,
> Am whelm'd in deeper than gulphs than he.

The negatives here are so final. With the words "Peace, be still," Christ once allayed the storm which threatened to overwhelm his disciples, but now no voice is heard. In Cowper's hymn 'Light Shining Out of Darkness' God "plants his footsteps in the sea / And rides upon the storm", but here there is no sign of God and no such light shines down.

The fourth line of the stanza suggests that the seaman and Cowper are both already dead and that they died alone, but the closing couplet insists that, despite all that has gone before, their deaths are not comparable; Cowper's exceeds anything known to man. Abandoned by God, he now abandons God.

At this point it seems meaningless to accuse him of self-pity or to argue that any such idea as that of his singular and personal damnation is simple folly. It is what he believed, and if we should manage to make that imaginative leap which enables us, for the briefest of moments, to share this belief, it is to be frighteningly engulphed. Hopkins understood it:

O the mind, mind has mountains; cliffs of fall
Frightful, sheer, no-man-fathomed. Hold them cheap
May who ne'er hung there.

It was a belief Cowper took with him to his death. The night before he died, his nurse offered him some cordial. "What can it signify?" were his last words. He died quietly on the afternoon of April 25th 1800 and was buried in St Edmund's Chapel on 2nd May alongside Mrs Unwin. No member of the Cowper family was present.

Notes

Chapter 1 His Mother's Son
1   Louise B Risk, *A Portrait of William Cowper* (Glen Echo, Md., 2004), p.3.
2   William Free, *William Cowper* (New York, 1970), p.17.
3   James King, *William Cowper: A Biography* (Durham, NC, 1986), p.7.
4   James King and Charles Ryskamp, (eds), *Letters and Prose Writings of William Cowper* (Oxford, 1979-86), V, pp.4-6.
5   Vincent Newey, *Cowper's Poetry* (Liverpool, 1982), p.236.

Chapter 2 School Days
1   King and Ryskamp, *Letters and Prose Writings*, I, p.5.
2   Ibid., I, p.6.
3   Ibid.
4   William B. Ober, *Boswell's Clap* (London, 1988), p.166.
5   Charles Ryskamp, *William Cowper of the Inner Temple Esquire* (Cambridge, 1959), p.23.
6   Ibid.
7   Ibid., p.15.
8   Maurice J. Quinlan, *William Cowper: A Critical Life* (Minneapolis, 1953), pp.6-7.
9   King and Ryskamp, *Letters and Prose Writings*, I, p.7.
10 King, *William Cowper*, p.17.
11 King and Ryskamp, *Letters and Prose Writings*, II, p.302.

Chapter 3 Living and Loving in London
1   King, *William Cowper*, p.17.

2   King and Ryskamp, *Letters and Prose Writings*, I, p.8.
3   F.C. Pottle (ed.), *Boswell's London Journal* (New York, 1950), p.299.
4   Ryskamp, *William Cowper*, p.67.
5   King, *William Cowper*, p.165.
6   King and Ryskamp, *Letters and Prose Writings*, V, p.9.
7   David Cecil, *The Stricken Deer* (London, 1929), p.35; and Caroline Geary, *Cowper and Mary Unwin* (London, 1900), p.13.
8   King and Ryskamp, *Letters and Prose Writings*, I, p.8.
9   Ryskamp, *William Cowper*, p.126.
10 King and Ryskamp, *Letters and Prose Writings*, I, p.9.
11 Ibid.
12 Hugh l'Anson Fausset, *William Cowper* (London, 1928), p.36.
13 King and Ryskamp, *Letters and Prose Writings*, I, p.9.
14 King, *William Cowper*, p.32.
15 Ryskamp, *William Cowper*, p.100.

Chapter 4 The Black Dog
1   King, *William Cowper*, p.24.
2   King and Ryskamp, *Letters and Prose Writings*, I, p.5.
3   D.B. Hindmarsh, 'The Olney Biographers', *Journal of Ecclesiastical History*, 49, no.1 (1998), p.74.
4   King and Ryskamp, *Letters and Prose Writings*, I, p.5.
5   Ibid., I, pp. 7, 8, 10.
6   Ibid., p.15.
7   Ibid., p.17.
8   Ibid., pp.17-18.
9   Ibid., p.18.

10 Ibid., p.19.
11 Ibid.
12 Ibid., p.20.
13 Ibid.
14 Ibid., p.21.
15 Ibid.
16 Ibid., p.23.
17 Ibid.
18 Ibid., p.25.
19 Ibid., p.27.
20 King, *William Cowper*, p.6.
21 King and Ryskamp, *Letters and Prose Writings*, I, p.32.
22 Cecil, *The Stricken Deer*, p.71.
23 King and Ryskamp, *Letters and Prose Writings*, I, p.33.
24 Risk, *A Portrait*, p.38.
25 King, *William Cowper*, p.51.
26 King and Ryskamp, *Letters and Prose Writings*, I, p.34.
27 Ibid., p.38.
28 Ibid.
29 Ibid.
30 Ibid., p.40.
31 Ibid., p.42.
32 Ibid., p.43.
33 Ryskamp, *William Cowper*, p.164.
34 King and Ryskamp, *Letters and Prose Writings*, I, p.43.
35 Gilbert Thomas, *William Cowper and the Eighteenth Century* (London, 1935), p.146.
36 King, *William Cowper*, p.65.
37 Thomas Wright, *The Town of Cowper* (London, 1886), p.253.
38 S.C. Carpenter, *Eighteenth Century Church and People* (London, 1959), pp.200-3.
39 Thomas, *William Cowper*, p.60.
40 Carpenter, *Church and People*, p.197.

Chapter 5 John Newton

1 Josiah Bull, John Newton: *An Autobiography and Narrative* (London, 1868), p.12.
2 John Newton, *An Authentic Narrative* (London, 1805), p.15.
3 Bull, *John Newton*, p.23.
4 Ibid., pp.25-6.
5 Ibid., p.27.

6 Ibid., p.49.
7 Jonathan Aitken, *John Newton* (London, 2007), p.69.
8 Bull, *John Newton*, p.60.
9 Aitken, *John Newton*, p.107.
10 Ibid., pp.106-7.
11 Carpenter, *Church and People*, p.204.
12 King, *William Cowper*, p.68.
13 Aitken, *John Newton*, p.129.
14 Ibid., p.147.
15 Thomas, *William Cowper*, p.207.
16 Aitken, *John Newton*, p.130.
17 Bull, *John Newton*, p.189.
18 Ibid., pp.189-90.
19 Aitken, *John Newton*, p.149.
20 Bull, *John Newton*, p.138.

Chapter 6 *Olney Hymns*

1 M.F. Marshall and J. Todd, *English Congregational Hymns in the Eighteenth Century* (Lexington, Ky., 1982), p.15.
2 F.J. Gillman, *The Evolution of the English Hymn* (London, 1929), p.135.
3 I. Watts, *Works* (Leeds, 1800), I, p.xiv.
4 S. Johnson, *Lives of the English Poets* (Oxford, 1905), III, p.310.
5 Ryskamp, *William Cowper*, p.186.
6 *Olney Hymns*, p.xi.
7 Ibid., p.vii.
8 Ibid.
9 Marshall and Todd, *Congregational Hymns*, p.96.
10 Ibid., p.97.
11 *Olney Hymns*, p.ix.
12 Ibid., p.vi.
13 J.D. Baird and Charles Ryskamp, *The Poems of William Cowper* (Oxford, 1980-5), I, p.xvi.
14 Ibid., p.486.
15 N. Nicholson, *William Cowper* (London, 1951), pp. 63-4.
16 Fausset, *William Cowper*, p.118.
17 Ibid., p.121.
18 King and Ryskamp, *Letters and Prose Writings*, I, p.484.
19 Ibid., p.8.
20 Fausset, *William Cowper,* p.122.
21 Cecil, *The Stricken Deer*, p.45.

Chapter 7 Despair

1 King and Ryskamp, *Letters and Prose Writings*, I, p.51.
2 Ibid., p.51
3 Ibid., p.50.
4 Ibid., p.52.
5 Ibid., p.55.
6. Ibid., p.57.
7 Ibid., p.56.
8 Fausset, *William Cowper*, p.115.
9 King and Ryskamp, *Letters and Prose Writings*, p.49.
10 A. Brink, *Loss and Symbolic Repair* (Hamilton, 1977), p.46.
11 Bull, *John Newton*, pp.184-5.
12 Ibid., p.185.
13 G. Saintsbury, *The Peace of the Augustans* (London, 1948), p.333.
14 Bull, *John Newton*, p.185.

Chapter 8 Some Light Verse

1 Thomas, *William Cowper*, p.251.
2 Aitken, *John Newton*, p.196.
3 King and Ryskamp, p.43.
4 Ibid., p.43,
5 Ibid., p.44.
6 Baird and Ryskamp, *Poems*, II, p.311.

Chapter 9 *Moral Satires*

1 Ryskamp, *William Cowper*, p.158.
2 King, *William Cowper*, p.49.
3 King and Ryskamp, *Letters and Prose Writings*, I, p.31.
4 Baird and Ryskamp, *Poems*, I, p.514.
5 Nicholson, *William Cowper*, p.45.
6 P.L. Carver, *The Life of a Poet: A Biographical Sketch of William Collins* (London, 1967), pp.72-3.
7 J. Keats, *Selected Letters* (New York, 1951), p.108.
8 Bill Hutchings, *The Poetry of William Cowper* (London, 1983), p.48.
9 Newey, *Cowper's Poetry*, p.53.
10 King and Ryskamp, *Letters and Prose Writings*, I, p.31.
11 Baird and Ryskamp, *Poems*, I, p.532.

Chapter 10 Lady Austen

1 Cecil, *The Stricken Deer*, p.185.
2 Thomas, *William Cowper*, p.271.
3 Quinlan, *William Cowper*, p.127.
4 Cecil, *The Stricken Deer*, p.187.
5 James Boswell, *Life of Johnson* (Oxford, 1934), II, p.359.
6 King and Ryskamp, *Letters and Prose Writings*, V, pp.23-4.
7 Ibid. p.37.
8 Hutchings, *Poetry of William Cowper*, p.52.
9 *Paradise Lost*, I.94.
10 Nicholson, *William Cowper*, p.155.
11 W.N. Free, *William Cowper* (New York, 1970), p. 167.
12 King, *William Cowper*, p.136.
13 M. Golden, *William Cowper: In Search of Stability* (New York, 1960), p.60.
14 Newey, *Cowper's Poetry*, p.230.
15 Povey, Kenneth, 'The Banishment of Lady Austen', *RES*, XVI (1939), pp.293-4.
16 Kenneth Povey, 'Cowper and Lady Austen', *RES*, X (1934), p.423.
17 Baird and Ryskamp, *Poems*, II, p.315.
18 Povey, 'The Banishment of Lady Austen', p.400.

Chapter 11 *The Task*

1 King, *William Cowper*, p.143.
2 A. Ashfield and P. de Polla, *The Sublime: A Reader in British Eighteenth-Century Aesthetic Theory* (Cambridge, 1996), p.38.
3 W. Gilpin, *Observations upon Western Parts of England* (London, 1798), p.328.
4 J.S. Storer and John Greig, *Cowper Illustrated* (London, 1804), p.36.
5 M. Priestman, *Cowper's Task* (Cambridge, 1983), p.36.
6 Ibid., p.200.
7 Sir Geoffrey Keynes, 'The Library of William Cowper', *Transactions of the Cambridge Bibliographical Society*, III, no. 1 (1960).
8 H. Blair, *Lectures on Rhetoric and Belles Lettres* (Halifax, 1842), pp.429-30.
9 Johnson, *Lives*, III, p.301.
10 S.T. Coleridge, *Biographiea Literaria* (London, 1817), p.22.
11 J. Sambrook, *William Cowper, The Task and Other Poems* (London, 1994), p.201.

12 Free, *William Cowper*, p.109.
13 Hutchings, *Poetry of William Cowper*,
    p.191.
14 King, *William Cowper*, p.145.
15 Nicholson, *William Cowper*, p. 90.
16 Hutchings, *Poetry of William Cowper*,
    p.197.
17 L. Hartley, *William Cowper,
    Humanitarian* (Chapel Hill, NC, 1938),
    p.7.
18 King, *William Cowper*, p.54.

Chapter 12 The Letters
1 King and Ryskamp, *Letters and Prose
   Writings*, I, pp.v-vi.
2 Cecil, *The Stricken Deer*, p.180.
3 Robert Dodsley, *The Preceptor*, I
   (1755), p.108.
4 Fausset, *William Cowper*, p.170.
5 King and Ryskamp, *Letters and Prose
   Writings*, p.v.

Chapter 13 Wider Concerns
1 John Bailey (ed.), *Poetical Works of
   William Cowper* (London, 1925) p.ix.
2 William Hazlitt, 'On Thomson and
   Cowper', in *Lectures on the English Poets*
   (London, 1964), p.9.
3 Thomas Clarkson, *The History of the
   Abolition of the Slave Trade* (London,
   1808), I, p.108.
4 Newey, *Cowper's Poetry*, pp.237-8.
5 Wright, *The Town of Cowper*, p.121.

Chapter 14 The Move to Weston
1 Geary, *Cowper and Mary Unwin*,
   pp.170-1).
2 J.S. Storer and John Greig, *Cowper
   Illustrated* (London, 1804), p.49.
3 Ibid., p.42.
4 Free, *William Cowper*, p.161.
5 Newey, *Cowper's Poetry*, p.224.
6 Donald Davie, *A Travelling Man*
   (Manchester, 2003), p.153.
7 Free, *William Cowper*, p.156.
8 James Sambrook, *William Cowper, The
   Task* (London, 1994), p.306.

Chapter 15 Homer and the Closing Years
1 Goldwin Smith, *Cowper* (London,
   1895), p.91.
2 King, *William Cowper*, p.217.
3 Matthew Arnold, *Poetry and Criticism*
   (Boston, 1961), p.223.
4 Nicholson, *William Cowper*, p.147.
5 Smith, *Cowper*, p.49.
6 Thomas, *William Cowper*, p.349.
7 Ibid., p.367.
8 James Croft, *The Early Productions of
   William Cowper* (London, 1825), p.183.
9 Christopher Smart, *Rejoice in the
   Lamb*, ed. W. Force Stead (London,
   1939), p.15.
10 Quinlan, *William Cowper*, p.183.
11 King, *William Cowper*, p.168.
12 Ibid., p.273.
13 Ryskamp, *William Cowper*, p.56.

Bibliography

Primary Sources

Baird, John D. and Ryskamp, Charles (eds), *The Poems of William Cowper*, three volumes (Oxford, 1980-5)

Cowper, William, *Olney Hymns*, The Trustees of the Cowper and Newton Museum (Olney, 1979)

Croft, James, *The Early Productions of William Cowper* (London, 1825)

King, James and Ryskamp, Charles (eds), *Letters and Prose Writings of William Cowper*, five volumes (Oxford, 1979-86)

Secondary Sources

Aitken, Jonathan, *John Newton* (London, 2007)

Arnold, Matthew, *Poetry and Criticism*, ed. A. Dwight Culler (Boston, 1961)

Ashfield, Andrew and de Polla, Peter, *The Sublime: A Reader in British Eighteenth-Century Aesthetic Theory* (Cambridge, 1996)

Bailey, John (ed.), *Poetical Works of William Cowper* (London, 1925)

Blair, Hugh, *Lectures on Rhetoric and Belles Lettres* (Halifax, 1842)

Boswell, James, *Life of Johnson* (Oxford, 1934)

Brink, Andrew, *Loss and Symbolic Repair* (Hamilton, 1977)

Bull, Josiah, *John Newton: An Autobiography and Narrative* (London, 1868)

Carpenter, S.C., *Eighteenth Century Church and People* (London, 1959)

Carver, P.L., *The Life of a Poet: A Biographical Sketch of William Collins* (London, 1967)

Cecil, David, *The Stricken Deer* (London, 1929)

Clarkson, Thomas, *The History of the Abolition of the Slave Trade* (London, 1808)

Coleridge, S.T., *Biographia Literaria* (London, 1817)

Curry, Neil, *Christopher Smart* (Tavistock, 2005)

Curry, Neil, *Six Eighteenth-Century Poets* (London, 2011)

Davie, Donald, *Purity of Diction in English Verse* (London, 1952)

Davie, Donald, *The Eighteenth-Century Hymn in England* (Cambridge, 1993)

Davie, Donald, *A Travelling Man* (Manchester, 2003)

Durbridge, Nicola, *Object of the Month* (Olney, 2011)

Ella, George, *William Cowper: The Man of God's Stamp* (Dundas, Ont., 2000)

Fausset, Hugh l'Anson, *William Cowper* (London 1928)

Free, William Norris, *William Cowper* (New York, 1970)

Geary, Caroline, *William Cowper and Mary Unwin* (London, 1900)

Gillman, F.J., *The Evolution of the English Hymn* (London, 1925)

Gilpin, William, *Observations upon Western Parts of England* (1798)

Golden, Morris, *William Cowper: In Search of Stability* (New York, 1960)

Hartley, Lodwick, *William Cowper, Humanitarian* (Chapel Hill, NC, 1938)

Hartley, Lodwick, *The Continuing Revaluation* (Chapel Hill, NC, 1960)

Hayley, William, *The Life and Posthumous Writings of William Cowper, Esquire* (London, 1804)

Hazlitt, William, 'On Thomson and Cowper', *Lectures on the English Poets*, Everyman Library (London, 1964)

Huang, Roderick, *William Cowper: Nature Poet* (London, 1957)

Hutchings, Bill, *The Poetry of William Cowper* (London, 1983)

Johnson, Samuel, *Lives of the English Poets*, ed. C. Birkbeck Hill (Oxford, 1905)

Keats, John, *Selected Letters*, ed. Lionel Trilling (New York, 1951)

King, James, *William Cowper: A Biography* (Durham, NC, 1986)

Malpas, Simon, *William Cowper: The Centenary Letters* (Manchester, 2000)

Marshall, Madeleine Forell and Todd, Janet, *English Congregational Hymns in the Eighteenth Century* (Lexington, Ky., 1982)

Neve, John, *Concordance to the Poetical Works of William Cowper* (New York, 1887)

Newey, Vincent, *Cowper's Poetry* (Liverpool, 1982)

Newton, John, *An Authentic Narrative of Some Remarkable and Interesting Particulars in the Life of …* (London, 1805)

Nicholson, Norman, *William Cowper* (London, 1951)

Nicholson, Norman, *William Cowper* (London, 1960)

Ober, William B., *Boswell's Clap* (London, 1988)

Priestman, Martin, *Cowper's Task* (Cambridge, 1983)

Quinlan, Maurice J., *William Cowper: A Critical Life*
    (Minneapolis, 1953)
Redford, Bruce, *The Converse of the Pen* (Chicago, 1986)
Risk, Louise B., *A Portrait of William Cowper* (Glen Echo, Md., 2004)
Ryskamp, Charles, *William Cowper of the Inner Temple Esquire*
    (Cambridge, 1959)
Saintsbury, George, *The Peace of the Augustans* (London, 1948)
Sambrook, James, *William Cowper, The Task and Other Poems*
    (London, 1994)
Sargeaunt, John, *Annals of Westminster School* (London, 1898)
Smith, Goldwin, *Cowper* (London, 1895)
Smith, K.E., *William Cowper: A Reappraisal* (Olney, 2001)
Spacks, Patricia, *The Poetry of Vision* (Cambridge, Mass., 1967)
Storer, J.S. and Greig, John, *Cowper Illustrated* (London, 1804)
Thomas, Gilbert, *William Cowper and the Eighteenth Century*
    (London, 1935)
Watts, Isaac, *Works* (Leeds, 1800)
Wright, Thomas, *The Town of Cowper* (London, 1886)

Index

SELECTED LITERARY TITLES
from GREENWICH EXCHANGE

W.H. DAVIES
Man and Poet: A Reassessment

Michael Cullup

978-1-906075-88-0 (pbk)
146pp

Even though he was once one of Britain's most popular writers, the reputation of the poet and memoirist W.H. Davies has, in recent decades, gone into decline.

Davies's colourful early life as a hobo and a tramp – captured by his most famous work *The Autobiography of a Super Tramp* – and his apparently 'innocent' poems about nature, tales about the seamier sides of life, his experiences on the road and verse portraits of those characters he met there – has led to the Welsh poet being placed under the cosy heading 'Georgian'.

It has been a tag which does serious disservice to the tone, nature and ambition of Davies's lyrics.

As poet and critic Michael Cullup shows in this brief but insightful exploration of the entirety of Davies's output – the memoirs, the short stories as well as the poems – there was a more complex personality than the one suggested by his public persona. True, he was a figure at home with the Georgian literary world – Edward Thomas and Hilaire Belloc were close friends – yet he was also capable of impressing more avant-garde talents like Ezra Pound and Jacob Epstein.

In this bracing reappraisal Cullup judiciously undermines preconceived notions of Davies the writer to reveal a poetic imagination richer, more insightful, more thoughtful than that for which he is generally given credit.

RAYMOND CHANDLER

Anthony Fowles

978-1-906075-87-3 (pbk)
206pp

The position of Raymond Chandler in the pantheon of American letters has long been subject to much debate.

Naturally imbued with a literary sensibility Chandler helped to revolutionise the crime genre, bringing to it a colourful, hardedged vernacular allied to a modern social commentary.

Through the figure of private eye Philip Marlowe, Chandler created a contemporary knight errant whose not so picturesque adventures trudging the mean streets of Los Angeles helped to vividly define the moral dilemmas of a dark, uncertain post-war world.

And yet … can *The Big Sleep, Farewell, My Lovely* and *The Lady in the Lake* be considered 'literature'?

Author Anthony Fowles – who freely admits to writing half-a-dozen 'sub-Chandlerian' thrillers – brings to the discussion both the detached eye of the professional critic and the sympathetic understanding of the practitioner.

It is a background which allows Fowles to make a balanced, finely-nuanced contribution to the ongoing Chandler debate, refusing to relegate the noir master to the wilderness of 'genre writer' but equally avoiding outlandish claims of literary pre-eminence.

In circumventing the pitfalls and simplicities of 'either/or', Fowles places Chandler's achievements in a fully-realised context, enabling the reader to appreciate more deeply the peculiar strengths and limitations of the prose lyricist of the American mid-century.

SWEETLY SINGS DELANEY

A Study of Shelagh Delaney's Work, 1958-68

John Harding

978-1-906075-83-5 (pbk)
204pp

Shelagh Delaney rose to fame following the instant success in 1958 of her first play *A Taste of Honey*. Lauded as Britain's answer to the controversial French novelist Françoise Sagan, Delaney's work scandalised her home city of Salford but established her as one of the country's most original and exhilarating young playwrights during a period in theatre history when women writers were rare and acceptance hard to achieve.

Delaney has served as an inspiration to countless young artists down the succeeding years. Rock star Morrissey wrote, 'She has always been a part of my life as a perfect example of how to get up and get out and do it.' Novelist Jeanette Winterson claimed, 'She was like a lighthouse – pointing the way and warning about the rocks underneath.'

Sweetly Sings Delaney is the story of her first exciting decade as a writer when she not only produced challenging and dramatic work in prose and on stage but also collaborated with some of the most innovative film and documentary-makers of the decade such as Ken Russell, Tony Richardson, Lindsay Anderson, not to mention actor and fellow Salfordian Albert Finney during his first and only foray as a film director.

JOHN KEATS
Against All Doubtings

Andrew Keanie

978-1-906075-75-0 (pbk)
110pp

Having identified him as a sort of semi-educated little cockney chancer, Keats's contemporary reviewers savaged him in the pages of Britain's most influential magazines. High ambition, unaccompanied by high birth, and radical affiliations and liberal inclinations, made him an object of contempt to those of, or aping the opinions of, the literary Establishment. In the short term, he never stood a chance.

Long after his death, his reputation was eventually brightened by much more enthusiastic – if, as some have since argued, misguided – appreciations for his beautiful and powerful otherworldliness.

Later still, in reaction to Keats-lovers' gushing admiration, a much more worldly Keats has been written up – including some bracing insights that seem to owe something to his first reviewers. As Martin Seymour-Smith has said, 'Many privately regard [Keats] with a condescension that is more smug than they would like to admit.'

This largely text-focused study promotes the best energies of a more Romantic view of a key Romantic figure. Keats was inspired and ill. By the time of his death, his genius and tuberculosis had pressurised him into poetry. The best he had to offer – including searching and scintillating confidences concerning how to live one's life in this world of suffering, 'the Vale of Soul-making' – are more accessible to the reader with a taste for poetry than they are to the consumer of ideologically appropriate journalism or ostentatiously unemotional academic analyses.

SECOND WORLD WAR POETRY IN ENGLISH

John Lucas

978-1-906075-78-1 (pbk)
236pp

John Lucas's book sets out to challenge the widely-held assumption that the poetry of the Second World War is, at best, a poor relation to that produced by its predecessor. He argues that the best poetry that came out of the 1939-45 war, while very different from the work of Owen, Rosenberg, Gurney, and their contemporaries, is in no sense inferior. It also has different matters to consider. War in the air, war at sea, war beyond Europe, the politics of Empire, democratic accountability – these are no subjects to be found in the poetry of the Great War. Nor is sex. Nor did American poets have much to say about that war, whereas the Americans Randall Jarrell, Anthony Hecht and Louis Simpson, are among the greatest English-speaking poets of World War Two. Both Hecht and Simpson write about the Holocaust and its aftermath, as do the English poets, Lotte Kramer and Gerda Mayer. For these reasons among others, English-speaking poetry of the Second World War deserves to be valued as work of unique importance.

A.E. HOUSMAN

Spoken and Unspoken Love

Henry Maas

978-1-906075-71-2 (pbk)
978-1-906075-73-6 (hbk)
61pp

A Shropshire Lad by A.E. Housman is one of the best-loved books of poems in English, but even now its author remains a shadowy figure. He maintained an iron reserve about himself – and with good reason. His emotional life was dominated by an unhappy and unrequited love for an Oxford friend. His passion went into his writing, but he could barely hint at its cause. *Spoken and Unspoken Love* discusses all Housman's poetry, especially the effect of an existence deprived of love, as seen in the posthumous work, where the story becomes clear in personal and deeply moving poems.

ERNEST DOWSON

Poetry and Love in the 1890s

Henry Maas

978-1-906075-51-4 (pbk)
978-1-906075-73-6 (hbk)
48pp

Ernest Dowson is the archetypal poet of the 1890s. His best work comes entirely from the decade, and he died at the end of it.

Steeped in the Latin poets of antiquity and French 19th-century poetry, he developed an individual style which pared down the exuberance of Poe and Swinburne to a classical simplicity marked by meticulous attention to sound and initiating the move to more informal verse, which made his work attractive to the generation of D.H. Lawrence, Pound and Eliot.

His life was archetypal too. Born to respectable wealth and comfort, he was dragged down by family misfortune. His father's business failure and early death, his mother's suicide and his own advancing tuberculosis began the decline. It was hastened by drink and an impossible love for a young girl who never began to understand him.

In the end Dowson, the poet admired by Yeats, Wilde and a host of contemporaries, was reduced to living little better than a tramp in Paris, to die at thirty-two almost a pauper and alcoholic in a London workman's cottage, leaving posterity some of the finest love poetry in English.

BETWEEN TWO WORLDS

A Survey of Writing in Britain, 1900-1914

Hugh Underhill

978-1-906075-55-2 (pbk)
188pp

In 1924 Philip Gibbs, one of the first 'war correspondents' in the modern sense, wrote in his book *Ten Years After: A Reminder*, 'One has to think back to another world in order to see again that year 1914 before the drums of war began to beat. It is a different world now ... ' A certain popular view has persisted of the Edwardian and pre-war Georgian period as a kind of swan-song to a past elegance and grace, and one of pleasure and freedom from anxiety.

The reality, along with, for many, the leisurely pace and settled way of life, was not only one of great intellectual and artistic excitement, but also of unrest, change and controversy. The first section of this survey, 'Britain 1900-1914: Hope, ferment and the abyss', looks at the political, cultural and economic elements of that ferment and the strains evident in British society: the reaction against Victorian attitudes, the pressure for social reform, the campaigns for women's suffrage and Irish Home Rule, the stirrings of Modernism and the move towards social realism in literature and the arts.

Underhill vividly demonstrates how these forces fed into the writing of the period. In the second section of the book, the work of the major authors of the period, Bennett, Wells, Conrad, Forster, Lawrence, Joyce, James, Shaw, Synge, Yeats, Hardy and Edward Thomas, is critically surveyed.

This is followed, in the final section, by a resumé of the work and varying significance of other authors against which those major figures need to be seen.

OTHER TITLES OF INTEREST

STORY
The Heart of the Matter
Maggie Butt (editor)
978-1-871551-93-8 (pbk)   184pp

MATTHEW ARNOLD AND 'THYRSIS'
Patrick Carill Connolly
978-1-871551-61-7 (pbk)   204pp

MILTON'S *PARADISE LOST*
Peter Davies
978-1-906075-47-7 (pbk)   108pp

LIAR! LIAR!
Jack Kerouac – Novelist
R.J. Ellis
978-1-871551-53-2 (pbk)   294pp

JOHN DRYDEN
Anthony Fowles
978-1-871551-58-7 (pbk)   292pp

THE AUTHOR, THE BOOK & THE READER
Robert Giddings
987-1-871551-01-3 (pbk)   240pp

POETRY MASTERCLASS
John Greening
978-1-906075-58-3   142pp

DREAMING OF BABYLON

The Life and Times of Ralph Hodgson

John Harding

978-1-906075-00-2 (pbk)   238pp

WORDSWORTH AND COLERIDGE

Views from the Meticulous to the Sublime

Andrew Keanie

978-1-871551-87-7 (pbk)   206pp

POETRY IN EXILE

A Study of the Poetry of Auden, Brodsky & Szirtes

Michael Murphy

978-1-871551-76-1 (pbk)   270pp

ALEISTER CROWLEY AND THE CULT OF PAN

Paul Newman

978-1-871551-66-2 (pbk)   224pp

IN PURSUIT OF LEWIS CARROLL

Raphael Shaberman

978-1-871551-13-6 (pbk)   146pp

To find out more about these and other titles visit
www.greenex.co.uk